# Claiming Exodus

# Claiming Exodus

## *A Cultural History of Afro-Atlantic Identity, 1774–1903*

Rhondda Robinson Thomas

BAYLOR UNIVERSITY PRESS

Waco, Texas 76798-7363



*Cover design* by Matt Roeser
*Cover image:* © Veer / Image Source Photography

Library of Congress Cataloging-in-Publication Data

Thomas, Rhondda Robinson.
Claiming Exodus : a cultural history of Afro-Atlantic identity, 1774–1903 / Rhondda Robinson Thomas.
211 p. cm.
Includes bibliographical references and index.
ISBN 978-1-60258-531-7 (hardback : alk. paper)
1. American literature—African American authors—History and criticism. 2. Exodus, The, in literature. 3. African Americans in literature. 4. African Americans—Race identity. 5. Bible—In literature. I. Title.
PS153.N5T475 2013
810.9'896073--dc23

2012028965

Printed in the United States of America on acid-free paper with a minimum of 30% post-consumer waste recycled content.

For my beloved parents, Earle B. and Naomi Williams Robinson,
my first teachers

# Contents

# Acknowledgments

Many colleagues, students, and friends have supported my work for *Claiming Exodus*. I acknowledge Gladys D. S. Lewis, my friend in the fray, as well as Carey C. Newman, my thoughtful, enthusiastic editor at Baylor University Press, along with Team Baylor, who were attentive to details at every step of the production process. I am especially grateful for my college friend Mitzi Smith, who connected me with Carey Newman at BUP.

In the earliest stages of the project, John Ernest served as my careful reader, Carla L. Peterson as my dissertation director, Barry Pearson as my folklife and folklore consultant, and Joycelyn Moody as the first publisher of a portion of this monograph in *African American Review*. Then my colleagues at Clemson University, particularly Cameron Bushnell, Erin Goss, Michael LeMahieu, Brian McGrath, Angela Naimou, Barbara Ramirez, Elizabeth Rivlin, and Elisa Sparks, provided valuable feedback on my early drafts and musings about my proposal and manuscript, and cheered each success during the research and writing process. Clemson graduate assistants Fredrika Salley and Antonio Shaw assisted with archival research projects. Students in my African American and American Literature classes at Clemson have read and discussed key texts with me, providing fresh perspectives to the works.

I could not have completed my work without the generous grants from Clemson University's College of Architecture, Arts and Humanities and Department of English. And I acknowledge the exceptional research assistance provided by the staff at the American Antiquarian Society, the Moorland-Spingarn Research Center of Howard University, and the Library of Congress. As my project progressed, my recovery of critical primary texts was also continually eased by fine online resources such as the Library of Congress' Digital Archives, Cornell University's Chronicling America, Florida Memory, the Digital Archive, New York Public Library's Digital Archive, and Google Books, an unparalleled digital repository for pre-twentieth-century publications.

I am also thankful to a host of friends and family who have always buoyed me with their praise and confidence, particularly my brothers, Donald E. Robinson and Carlton D. Robinson, my sister-in-law, Ingrid Robinson, my cousin, Cheryl Kisunzu, and my daddy, Earle B. Robinson. Most of all, I appreciate my husband, William L. Thomas Jr.—thoughtful listener, reliable walking encyclopedia, cherished soul mate.

# List of Illustrations

INTRODUCTION

# From Egypt to Canaan An Afro-Atlantic Journey

*And the LORD said, I have surely seen the affliction of my people which are in Egypt, and have heard their cry by reason of their taskmasters; for I know their sorrows; And I am come down to deliver them out of the hand of the Egyptians, and to bring them up out of that land unto a good land and a large, unto a land flowing with milk and honey.*

—Exodus 3:7-8[1]

*[T]hanks that the voice of the Lord was heard in the North, which said, "Go quickly to the South and let my prison-bound people go free, for I have heard their cries from cotton, corn and rice plantations, saying, how long before thou wilt come to deliver us from this chain?" And the Lord said to them, "Wait, I will send you John Brown who shall be the key to the door of your liberty, and I will harden the heart of Jefferson Davis, your devil, that I may show him and his followers my power; then shall I send you Abraham Lincoln, mine angel, who shall lead you from the land of bondage to the land of liberty." Our fathers all died in "the wilderness," but thank God, the children reached "the promised land."*

—Jacob Stroyer, *Sketches of My Life in the South*

In *Sketches of My Life in the South*, part I (1879), as Jacob Stroyer recalls how he obtained freedom, he recasts the history of African Americans as a type of Exodus experience, asserting that their liberation was effected by divine intervention. Like the enslaved Israelites who pleaded with God for relief from oppression, enslaved African Americans prayed for divine deliverance in Stroyer's Afro-Atlantic Exodus narrative. Instead of anointing an African American Mosaic leader for American slaves, however, Stroyer contends that God sent a white abolitionist and a US president to lead African Americans to the border of their promised land. John Brown initiated their liberation from Jefferson Davis, whose strong commitment to slavery compels Stroyer to characterize the Confederate president as a devil rather than as Pharaoh. President Abraham Lincoln initiated African Americans' wilderness journey through the plague of the Civil War, in which thousands of America's sons died on the battlefields. In both the biblical and black Exodus narratives, however, the majority of people who entered the Promised Land were the children of slaves.

Stroyer's reliance on the biblical story of Exodus exemplifies how Afro-Atlantic people embraced the story of God's emancipation of the Israelites from slavery in Egypt to chart their journey to freedom in the New World. The Exodus narrative, the central cultural metanarrative of the Afro-Atlantic community, resonated because it encouraged Afro-Atlantic peoples to remember the story and reimagine themselves as citizens in their adopted homelands. When the Israelites departed from Egypt, God instructed them to commemorate their miraculous deliverance in an annual celebration called Passover. This feast reminded them that the Lord had passed over their blood-splattered doorposts on the night that he slew the firstborn in every Egyptian household. During the Passover meal, the Jews ate bitter herbs, which symbolized their oppressive Egyptian bondage, unleavened bread, which recalled their hasty exit from Egypt, and roasted lamb, which foreshadowed the sacrifice the Savior would make for their sins. In so doing, they affirmed their faith that God could deliver them from all troubles. Once each year, they paused to remember the event that enabled them to reimagine themselves as a Jewish nation.

The book of Exodus does not refer only to this moment of liberation, however. Although it focuses on the Israelites' emancipation from slavery in Egypt, wandering in the wilderness, and arrival at the border of the Promised Land, the term "exodus" encompasses a broader story. Most scholars locate the beginning of this narrative in the first chapter of Exodus. Yet the author of Exodus bids us to consider a wider historical context for the narrative:

> And all the souls that came out of the loins of Jacob were seventy souls: for Joseph was in Egypt already. . . . And the children of Israel were fruitful, and increased abundantly, and multiplied, and waxed exceeding mighty; and the land was filled with them. Now there arose up a new king over Egypt, which knew not Joseph. (Exod 1:5-8)

The saga began in the biblical book of Genesis when Joseph's brothers, jealous of their father's favoritism toward their younger sibling, sold him into slavery to Ishmaelite traders, their distant relatives. The traders transported Joseph to Egypt, where he labored in the home of Potiphar, captain of Pharaoh's guard. Joseph soon encountered the perils of favor again when he was imprisoned after Potiphar's wife falsely accused him of rape. He regained his freedom after interpreting Pharaoh's dream of a coming famine, and his career culminated in his appointment as prime minister of Egypt. During the famine, Joseph was reunited with his brethren and the entire family settled in Goshen, the most fertile land in Egypt. When the Hebrew populace became numerous, however, a new pharaoh enslaved and oppressed them. God sent Moses to demand immediate emancipation of the Israelites, and then unleashed a series of plagues that forced Pharaoh to liberate his people. As the Israelites fled Pharaoh's army, they escaped when God miraculously parted the Red Sea but allowed the waters to drown the Egyptians. Within forty days, the Israelites reached the border of the Promised Land but returned to the wilderness for forty years of wandering because they did not believe God would peacefully settle them in their new home. The books of Leviticus, Numbers, and Deuteronomy provide additional details about their forty-year journey. After Moses' death, God appointed Joshua to lead the conquest of Canaan. Several verses in the last chapter of Deuteronomy, particularly "And Joshua the son of Nun was full of the spirit of wisdom; for Moses had laid his hands upon him: and the children of Israel hearkened unto him, and did as the LORD commanded Moses" (Deut 34:9), encourage us to consider Joshua's recollections of Israel's settlement in Canaan as the culmination of Exodus.

Afro-Atlantic writers such as Stroyer appropriated the Exodus story to articulate their spiritual journey and advance their sociopolitical struggle. During the colonial period, "[The Bible] quickly came to function as a language-world, the storehouse of rhetorics, images, and stories that, through a complex history of engagements, helped establish African Americans as *a circle of the biblical imaginary.*"[2] The Bible was one of *the books*, a significant text that most Europeans were familiar with in the eighteenth and nineteenth centuries. In the New World, it was also a text that many knew, claimed as their own, and used to define themselves and others. As Afro-Atlantic people became acquainted with *the Book* and understood its importance, authority, and power, the Exodus story captured their attention. They did not see Exodus as a Jewish story; rather, they viewed it as a narrative that depicted God's love for all oppressed populations and his willingness to intervene on their behalf. Afro-Atlantic people did not need a preacher to explain how the story related to their lives. They believed God not only performed miracles, but also gave humans such as Joseph, Moses, and Joshua access to divine power to accomplish his will. The Israelites' experiences in the Exodus narrative reflected their struggles in the New World and revealed a way to shift the direction of their lives from slavery to freedom.

As Afro-Atlantic people embraced the Exodus narrative to retell their life stories, a distinct literary tradition emerged. This study argues that Phillis Wheatley's appropriation of the Exodus story in "Letter to Reverend Samson Occum" (1774) inaugurates the tradition, and W.E.B. Du Bois' analysis of Booker T. Washington as a potential Joshua in *The Souls of Black Folk* (1903) marks the end of its initial phase. The 129-year period between these works began during the American Revolution and ended during the Nadir as the Afro-Atlantic community struggled to select a new national leader after Frederick Douglass' death in 1895.[3] Although many scholars have examined Afro-Atlantic Exodus narratives, none has provided a comprehensive analysis of the early development of these stories. Most critical discussions omit the Joseph and Joshua narratives, which provide the essential bookends of Exodus. Quite simply, without an examination of these two stories, any critique of the topic is incomplete, and perhaps even misleading. While scholars have considered John Marrant's and Harriet Wilson's invocations of the Joseph story in their narratives, they have not yet fully explored it in eighteenth- and nineteenth-century works such as Quobna Ottobah Cugoano's *Thoughts and Sentiments on the Evil and Wicked Traffic of the Slavery and Commerce of the Human Species* (1787), analyzed in chapter 1, or in Sunday School lessons and narratives of upward mobility that are based on Joseph's life story, examined in chapter 5. Studies of black authors' pre-twentieth-century Joshua narratives are nonexistent. Critics have also neglected many lesser-known writers, such as post–Civil War authors who invoke the Joseph story to reconfigure the American dream in their demands for equality as US citizens. A critique of these texts illustrates a greater depth and intricacy of Afro-Atlantic Exodus narratives that cannot be fully accounted for by focusing solely on major writers such as Martin Delany, Frederick Douglass, Henry Highland Garnet, Frances E. W. Harper, Absalom Jones, Maria W. Stewart, and David Walker. Examinations of the pervasiveness of black Exodus stories in the mid-eighteenth, nineteenth, and early twentieth centuries supports the contention that their use was far more complex than scholars have acknowledged. The close readings of Afro-Atlantic Exodus stories presented in *Claiming Exodus*, including fiction, slave narratives, poetry, prayers, essays, newspaper articles, speeches, cartoons, and lyrics, identify and examine a variety of rhetorical strategies the writers rely on in constructing multifaceted Exodus narratives.

By appropriating the Exodus story, Afro-Atlantic people posited themselves as protagonists in a major narrative of the New World filled with communities where the Bible functioned as "the single most important *centering* object for social identity and orientation among European dominants."[4] At pivotal points in US history, including the American Revolution, when George Washington was characterized as Moses, the era of Manifest Destiny, when white Americans viewed the West as the newest extension of their promised land, and the Civil War, when Andrew Johnson anointed himself as black Americans' Moses, white writers repeatedly turned to Exodus to affirm their superior status and claim divine authorization for their causes. When Afro-Atlantic authors appealed to Exodus, however, they *decentered* the narratives by giving different roles to Europeans and new meanings to English and American Exodus experiences. The term "decenter" reflects "ideological critique [which] serves as an important critical tool for *decentering* the reading subject and the subject matter being read. This means first recognizing the privileged identification made between the reader's interest and the narrative and then deliberately shifting that identification to allow for the text to be a text 'for' another reader and reading experience."[5] Through the reading of literary texts, ideological critique challenges binary definitions of oppressed-oppressor and uncovers power structures by exposing authority figures and bringing once marginalized people into view. Instead of simply constructing a Afro-Atlantic/marginal versus Anglo/national Exodus narrative binary, however, *Claiming Exodus* complicates traditional approaches to the study of these texts through its inclusion of a third subset of stories written by white abolitionists. Chapter 1 includes an examination of Samuel Sewall's 1700 *The Selling of Joseph: A Memorial* which introduces the rhetorical strategy that white abolitionists later adopted in appropriating Exodus to demand the abolition of slavery without the assurance of equality for Afro-Atlantic people. These three distinct strands of Exodus stories emphasize the cultural, theological, and ideological tensions that arose as different groups claimed the biblical narrative for both inspiration and affirmation of their competing goals for freedom, equality, and opportunity.

*Claiming Exodus*' examinations of the ways that Afro-Atlantic authors decentered and rewrote Europeans' and white Americans' Exodus narratives investigates the influences of historical, political, and religious events and experiences on the development of their Exodus narrative tradition from the mid-eighteenth to the early twentieth centuries. As Afro-Atlantic people moved from slavery to freedom, their experiences often mirrored the varied events of Exodus, particularly the Israelites' forty-year wilderness journey. In the Bible, however, Exodus is a linear story: slavery in Egypt, sojourn in the wilderness, and settlement in Canaan. New England Puritan writing follows a similar linear pattern: God rescued the Puritans from religious bondage in England, protected them during wilderness wanderings on their transatlantic journey, and then enabled them to establish lasting communities in the New World, their promised land. While most Europeans arrived in the New World with some knowledge of the Exodus narrative, few Africans had heard the biblical story, and many were initially uninterested in the Christianity that missionaries sought to impose on them. After Afro-Atlantic peoples began to embrace an evangelical form of Christianity during the First Great Awakening, they incorporated the Exodus story into their oral traditions, such as the Negro spirituals "Go Down, Moses" and "There's a Great Camp Meeting in the Promised Land." When they recorded their Exodus narratives in writing, however, they continually created and adapted innovative rhetorical strategies to reflect their experiences, advance their causes, and sustain their struggle. In their published Exodus narratives, Afro-Atlantic writers selected specific fragments of the biblical narrative to help them make their points. They relied on fissures—chronological breaks in the Exodus story—to represent their diverse perspectives. Women writers such as Maria W. Stewart, whose works are discussed in chapter 2, were responsible for some of the major fissures. They conflated biblical and secular/republican discourses to demand equality and citizenship. They layered the Exodus figure with another, or a series of other, biblical figures to represent their complex circumstances as outsiders in the Atlantic world. They presented an unstable Canaan that could be located in their native lands, ancestral homes, or elsewhere. Finally, they characterized locations as simultaneously Egypt and Canaan.

Afro-Atlantic Exodus writings raise and attempt to answer a series of questions. Could Afro-Atlantic people have a Joseph experience? Would any slaves receive favor from their captors as Joseph and Moses had from the Egyptians? Who was Pharaoh? Were slave states their only Egypt? Would a Moses figure arise from within the community to lead all slaves to freedom? Could a woman be Moses? What role would women play in their Exodus stories? Could Mosaic laws be used to justify slavery? Would Afro-Atlantic people become undisciplined and disobedient like the liberated Israelites after they were emancipated? Would they have to cross a Red Sea to leave Egypt and a Jordan River to enter Canaan? Where was their promised land? Would they need a Joshua when they reached their Canaan? If they reached their promised land, would they experience freedom and equality? Who would write their Exodus stories? Would writing their Exodus narratives help them accomplish their goals? Their answers to these questions produced narratives of fragmentation, discontinuity, and instability that reflect the ultimate insufficiency of the Exodus story to help Afro-Atlantic peoples *fully* achieve their goals of freedom, equality, and opportunity. As they invoked the Exodus narrative, no Moses appeared to unite slaves and free blacks and demand that British kings and American presidents outlaw slavery and lift slaves from degradation. And no promised land loomed on the horizon where former black peoples and their brethren could permanently enjoy freedom and equality.

In 1879 Jacob Stroyer may have felt he had entered a Massachusetts promised land after enduring the brutality of slavery in a South Carolina Egypt. But the nation had not yet become a promised land for African American citizens. From 1774 to 1903 the Exodus narrative met the varied needs of a community of enslaved and free Afro-Atlantic people who relied on an arsenal of narrative strategies, rhetorical devices, and practical tools to map paths from slavery and oppression to emancipation and equality. The biblical story of Exodus enabled Stroyer and hundreds of other Afro-Atlantic authors and their supporters to express the complexities of their lives in nations that enslaved and oppressed them. They pieced together stories, carefully selecting specific episodes of the Exodus narrative and then augmenting these with episodes of other biblical stories or secular history to share their experiences and delineate their demands. Through diverse invocations of a biblical narrative that embodied their hope for civil liberties and a safe home, Afro-Atlantic authors repeatedly confronted obstacles that blocked the paths to their varied promised lands, believing an Exodus experience would one day be theirs. Although forces from within and without their communities limited the effectiveness of early Afro-Atlantic Exodus narratives, the biblical story empowered Afro-Atlantic people and sustained their struggle even as freedom remained an elusive pursuit well into the twentieth century.

CHAPTER ONE

# Exodus and the Politics of Liberty (1774–1800)

Obj. 2. *The Nigers are brought out of a Pagan Country, into places where the Gospel is Preached.*
Answ. *Evil must not be done, that good may come of it. The extraordinary and comprehensive Benefit accruing to the Church of God, and to Joseph personally, did not rectify his brethrens Sale of him.*

—Samuel Sewall, *The Selling of Joseph, a Memorial*

*[F]or in every human Breast, God has implanted a Principle, which we call Love of Freedom; it is impatient of Oppression, and pants for Deliverance; and by the Leave of our modern Egyptians I will assert, that the same Principle lives in us.*

—Phillis Wheatley, "Letter to Rev. Samson Occum"

*We in this land are, as it were, led out of Egypt by the hand of Moses. And now we are in the wilderness, i.e. in a state of trouble and difficulty, Egyptians pursuing us, to overtake us and reduce us. There is the Red Sea before us, I speak metaphorically, a sea of blood in your prospect before you, perhaps.*

—Nicholas Street, "The American States Acting over the Part of the Children of Israel in the Wilderness"

Approximately three months after American colonists staged the Boston Tea Party, Phillis Wheatley inaugurated the Afro-Atlantic Exodus literary tradition when she penned her most blistering attack against slavery. The twenty-year-old had just completed a successful tour of England, where she had been feted as a celebrated poet. Upon her return to Boston, she obtained her freedom. In her letter to Samson Occum, a Mohegan Indian and ordained Presbyterian minister who advocated for the rights of Native Americans, Wheatley evoked the Exodus story to emphasize the hypocrisy of colonists who demanded liberty while enslaving Africans.[1] In so doing, she challenged a national narrative in which colonists characterized themselves as Israelites breaking free of bondage from an English Pharaoh. Her appropriation of the biblical story established a publishing history for counter-Exodus narrative crafted and controlled by Afro-Atlantic writers who claimed the right to freedom by virtue of their oppression.

During the First Great Awakening, from 1730 to 1780, prominent white Protestant ministers, such as George Whitefield, introduced African Americans to evangelical Christianity and renewed the colonists' vision of themselves as settlers in a promised land. Whitefield encouraged his listeners to imagine themselves as Israelites liberated from "Egyptian bondage, and marching under the conduct of our spiritual Joshua, through the wilderness of this world, to the land of our heavenly Canaan."[2] The Exodus narrative provided language that enabled Afro-Atlantic people to articulate their desire for emancipation and equality in an alien land. However, English colonial writers dramatically shifted the focus of their national Exodus narrative from a story rooted in Christian love and trust in divine power to one motivated by arrogance and self-confidence. The success of the American Revolution inspired colonists to adopt "more active and aggressive virtues" and "celebrate their own achievements as a nation."[3]

Rather than reject Exodus as insufficient to represent their experiences, Afro-Atlantic writers decentered the national Exodus narrative by repeatedly appropriating the biblical story to challenge their marginal status and make themselves visible to oppressors who were intimately familiar with the power of Exodus to effect change. Their intricately crafted hybrid narratives draw on the conventions of popular eighteenth-century literature, including the epistolary form, spiritual autobiography, travel narrative, captivity tale, and adventure story, to represent captivity as transformative. Some stories also feature specific portions of the Exodus narrative augmented with episodes from the experiences of other prominent biblical figures to reveal how Afro-Atlantic people providentially overcame outsider status in oppressive societies. By conflating the Exodus story with political and historical rhetoric, they illustrate the complexity of their lives and convey their hope for acceptance by white Christians, who would ultimately need more than a few compelling narratives to change their perspectives of Afro-Atlantic people.

## The Puritans
### *Religious Persecution Initiates Exodus*

In evoking Exodus Wheatley and other Afro-Atlantic writers adopted a rhetorical strategy that Puritans who traveled to the New World employed when they left England to escape religious persecution. The Puritans undertook their journey into the wilderness to establish a model Christian society in a new promised land. Their embrace of the Exodus story is unremarkable, however, since British Puritans had earlier appropriated the narrative to inspire their citizenry to political action. Oliver Cromwell cited Exodus to justify overthrowing the monarchy during the English Civil War, and John Dryden embraced the story when he encouraged the English to support their king during the Restoration.[4] For their part, New World Puritans believed their journey was providentially ordained, and they trusted God to enable them to build prosperous colonies that offered religious freedom. From the moment they entered the New World, Europeans constructed their identity through the creation of "official stories" to identify themselves as a favored people. These stories "surface in the rhetoric of nationalistic movements and initiatives—legal, political, and literary. . . . Neither static nor monolithic, they change in response to competing narratives of the nation that must be engaged, absorbed, and retold: the fashioning and endless refashioning of 'a people.'"[5]

This "refashioning of a people" through national Exodus stories is reflected in the continual shifting of the narratives from the arrival of the Puritans to the establishment of the republic. John Winthrop, leader of their Massachusetts Bay Colony, wrote one of the first official stories, a sermon titled "A Modell of Christian Charity" (1630), which he composed on the *Arbella* during his transatlantic journey to the New World. In the sermon Winthrop admonishes his passengers to enter into a covenant with God in which they pledge to exhibit love, mercy, and justice in a promised land inhabited by both rich and poor, or face divine destruction. Within thirty years, however, the colonists began to exhibit traits that many writers interpreted as a betrayal of their covenant. In "God's Controversy with New England" (1662), Michael Wigglesworth laments that

> Pride, and Luxurie
> Debate, Deceit, Contention, and Strife,
> False-dealing, Covetousness, Hypocrisie
> (With such like Crimes) amongst them are so rife

that God sent a drought to punish the colonists, the same punishment the Israelites had suffered after they worshipped other gods.[6] Exodus provided American colonists with a means to interpret their environment, understand their experiences, envision their future, and ultimately control the lives of peoples they encountered in and forcefully transported to the New World.

### Samuel Sewall
### *Exodus and Abolition in Colonial America*

At the turn of the eighteenth century, in a bold departure from the Puritan tradition of seeing America as God's New Israel, Puritan judge, merchant, and clergyman Samuel Sewall turned to the Exodus narrative in a vain attempt to avert the colonists' continued reliance on enslaved Africans' labor. Sewall, who had served as a judge in the Salem witch trials and later recanted and expressed public remorse for his participation, was one of the first and few authors to establish the Exodus story as a compelling paradigm for the examination of slavery and the plight of Africans in the colonies.[7] A petition for freedom from an enslaved African named Adam and his wife sparked a battle between Sewall and slavery proponent John Saffin and led to the publication of his antislavery tract *The Selling of Joseph: A Memorial* (1700). Sewall adapted the convention of the traditional Puritan sermon to refute common justifications for slavery, namely the Curse of Ham, the paganism of Africa, and the practices of biblical patriarchs. He characterized Adam, the enslaved African, as a descendant of Adam, the first man God created, and identifies Africans as "our Friends and Kinsfolk" (12). He asserted that the enslaved man named Adam, like the biblical Joseph, had been illegally sold into slavery; therefore, Adam's master was obligated to free him. Though Sewall's tract did not lead to the release of Adam and his wife, the liberation of slaves in Boston, or the abolition of the transatlantic slave trade, it offered a template for antislavery tracts that other abolitionists would adapt in appropriating Exodus to challenge slavery well into the nineteenth century.

### American Colonists
### *Exodus Inspires Revolution*

Other colonists employed the Exodus narrative as an effective rhetorical tool in positing *themselves* as unjustly enslaved Israelites. They claimed they had escaped religious and civil persecution in England, their Egypt, at the hands of King George III, their Pharaoh, to come to America, their promised land. The colonists viewed forced adherence to the tenets of the Church of England and payment of taxes without representation as slavery.

In *Liberty and Property Vindicated, and the St--pm-n Burnt* (1765), Benjamin Church acknowledged his readers' familiarity with the Exodus story and then drew an analogy between the biblical narrative and colonial history to protest King George III's taxation policies in the colonies. Such writers clearly expected God to liberate the colonists from their oppressive bondage to England.

The colonists' success in their war with England inspired new Exodus stories to commemorate their victory. The *Journals of the Continental Congress* for August 20, 1776, include the report that Benjamin Franklin suggested for the US seal a drawing of "Moses (in the Dress of High Priest) standing on the Shore, and extending his Hand over the Sea, thereby causing the same to overwhelm Pharoah who is sitting in an open Chariot, a Crown on his Head and a Sword in his Hand. Rays from a Pillar of Fire in the Clouds reaching to Moses, (expressing) to express that he acts by (the) Command of the Deity" (690). Thomas Jefferson recommended a representation of "Pharoah sitting in an open chariot, a crown on his head and a sword in his hand passing thro' the divided waters of the Red sea in pursuit of the Israelites: rays from a pillar of fire in the cloud, expressive of the divine presence, (reach) and command, reaching to Moses who stands on the shore and, extending his hand over the sea, causes it to over whelm Pharoah" (690). Both men recommended including the motto "Rebellion to Tyrants is Obedience to God" on the seal. Prominent New England preachers Ezra Stiles and Samuel Langdon supported the development of new national Exodus narratives by characterizing the nation as "God's American Israel" and "God's New Israel," boasting that the young republic had become the most prosperous nation in the world, without acknowledging its dependence on a slave economy. As white Americans established their nation as a promised land, they increasingly oppressed free and enslaved Afro-Atlantic people, confining them to an Egypt experience in the new democracy.

## Phillis Wheatley
### *Exodus Re-envisions Revolution for American Slaves*

Eight-year-old Phillis Wheatley arrived in Boston in 1761 on the slave ship *The Phillis*, traumatized by the Middle Passage from Africa to the Americas. She escaped the more brutal forms of colonial slavery when prosperous Bostonian merchant John Wheatley purchased her as a personal slave and companion for his wife, Susanna Wheatley, which ultimately provided her a path to activism. Wheatley received an education that exceeded the training of most New England youths, and published her writings with the assistance of her mistress and her patron, the Countess of Huntingdon. Her transformation from devoted slave to outspoken abolitionist likely crystallized during her visit to England in 1773 to regain her health, meet the countess, and publish her collection of poetry. The trip seemed a natural event for a young woman whose master had given her privileges other slaves rarely received. Once she disembarked in London, however, she could have chosen to stay. The year before, the judgment by Lord Mansfield in *Somerset v. Stewart* forbade masters from forcing their slaves to return to the colonies.[8] Although Wheatley likely knew of the *Somerset* ruling through her association with English abolitionist Granville Sharp, after six weeks in England she returned to Boston at the behest of her ill mistress. Upon her arrival, colonial newspapers briefly acknowledged her exceptional achievements. The *Boston Post-Boy* hailed her as "Phillis, the extraordinary Negro Poetress, Servant of Mr. John Wheatley," and the *Massachusetts Spy* noted the return of the "celebrated young negro poetess, Phillis."[9] In September 1773, her master emancipated her "at the desire of my friends in England," according to a letter she wrote to Colonel David Worcester (147).[10] She informed Worcester that she had visited Lord Dartmouth, Lord Lincoln, Dr. Solander, Granville Sharp, Benjamin Franklin, and Lady Cavendish, and received gifts from her new friends, which "astonishes me on the reflection" (146). Wheatley seemed particularly pleased that freedom had placed her "upon my own footing and whatever I get by [selling *Poems*] is entirely mine, & it is the Chief I have to depend upon" (147). Scholars have argued that by 1774 Wheatley was a celebrity and that colonial and English publications had increased her popularity. From December 1767 to December 1774 at least six colonial newspapers and several English publications printed Wheatley's poetry and letters, notices about her travels, and advertisements for her poetry collection.[11]

Being "on [her] own footing" may have given the celebrated Wheatley the confidence to evoke Exodus in penning her strongest abolitionist statement in "Letter to Reverend Samson Occum" (1774), published within five months of her return to Boston, on the eve of the American Revolution. The letter to Occum appeared in at least ten colonial newspapers, four of which included a note describing it as a "Specimen of her Ingenuity."[12] The impact of her antislavery message was strengthened by the letter being addressed to the respected Reverend Occum, a Native American minister with whom she had begun corresponding when she was twelve years old. Occum openly supported the American Revolution as an opportunity for marginalized races to obtain freedom in America. He was recognized in the colonies as the first Native American to publish works in English, including sermons, hymns, and an autobiography. The Presbyterian Church ordained Occum to serve as a missionary among his people, the Mohegan tribe. When the church needed money to build a school for Native Americans, they asked him to raise funds by going on the lecture circuit in England. Although Occum's tour was successful, church officials did not allocate the money as they had promised. Instead, they built an educational institution that ultimately became Dartmouth College in 1769.[13] This experience disillusioned Occum; nevertheless, he clung to his faith and worked tirelessly among the Mohegans until his death. Although Wheatley and Occum enjoyed the praise of many prominent men and women in America and England, they did not forget the plight of their people. Both used their positions of limited prominence to thrust themselves into the antislavery cause.

In her letter Wheatley draws on the rhetoric of the Exodus narrative and Enlightenment theory to elevate Africans from abject bondsmen to rational, spiritual human beings. In so doing, she shifts the objective of the Revolution from the colonists' emancipation to the physical, religious, and political liberation of all Americans—including Africans. Wheatley exhibits an acute awareness of the opportune moment the American Revolution presents for her to be a savior to her people. She begins by affirming Occum's support of the "vindication of [Africans'] natural rights." Her words echo the Enlightenment discourse associated with the Revolution, such as James Otis' *The Rights of the British Colonists Asserted and Proved* (1764), as well as later texts such as Thomas Paine's *Common Sense* (1776) and Thomas Jefferson's Declaration of Independence (1776). Wheatley immediately asserts that recognition of the "natural rights" of enslaved Africans should be an integral component of American Revolution ideology. She goes on to argue that God will enable Africans to enjoy the same "glorious dispensation of civil and religious liberty" that the colonists were seeking when they refused to remain subject to King George III and the Church of England and formed an independent nation. Wheatley then strengthens her argument by invoking biblical precedence, suggesting that Africans' pleas for liberty are equivalent to ancient Israel's prayers for deliverance from Egyptian slavery. She carefully creates a philosophical, political, and religious matrix for her argument, challenging her readers to view the Africans' plight through the logic of reason, the principles of a democracy, and the teachings of Scripture. Wheatley's conflation of the rhetoric of Revolution, Enlightenment, and Exodus decenters the colonists' claim that America is God's New Israel, for they reached their promised land only to enslave innocent Africans.

Wheatley further challenges the colonists' embrace of Exodus to script their New World experience by casting enslaved Africans in a major role. She declares, "for in every human Breast God has implanted a Principle, which we call Love of Freedom; it is impatient of Oppression, and pants for Deliverance; and by the Leave of our modern Egyptians I will assert, that the same Principle lives in us" (153). By identifying slaveholders, including her former "benevolent" owners the Wheatleys, as "modern Egyptians," Wheatley undermines sentiments regarding humane masters. Situating herself firmly within the enslaved African community, she argues that Africans are the true modern manifestation of Hebrew slaves; they view the American colonies as Egypt and seek liberation as fervently as did the ancient Israelites. Enslaved blacks had already begun expressing their "Love of Freedom" in petitions submitted to the Massachusetts House of Representatives in May 1774 for relief from "a state of Slavery within the bowels of a free and Christian Country" for "we have in common With all other men a naturel [*sic*] right to our freedoms without Being depriv'd of them by our fellow men."[14] Like Wheatley, in identifying themselves as "fellow men" with "naturel rights," they challenged the colonists' exclusive desire for the "pursuit of happiness."

Thus, Wheatley's letter is a plea for the divine deliverance offered by the Exodus narrative. Unlike the colonists who demanded immediate separation from King George III and England, however, Wheatley does not stipulate the means nor set the time for the establishment of an integrated American Canaan. She trusts God to liberate enslaved Africans on his own terms: "God grant Deliverance in his own Way and Time, and get him honour upon all those whose Avarice impels them to countenance and help forward the Calamities of their fellow Creatures" (153). Wheatley believes God will punish American slaveowners in a timely, righteous fashion just as he punished Egyptian slaveholders through a series of plagues and destruction in the Red Sea. Her letter is a warning to those who do not view slavery as evil and a reminder for those who boldly ignore biblically based moral principles. She is keenly aware that "avarice" compels men to enslave Africans and build empires based on slave labor. Instead of lashing out against her former captors, however, Wheatley issues a logical appeal:

> This I desire not for their Hurt, but to convince them of the strange Absurdity of their Conduct whose Words and Actions are so diametrically opposite. How well the Cry for Liberty, and the reverse Disposition for the exercise of oppressive Power over others agree,—I humbly think it does not require the Penetration of a Philosopher to determine." (153)

For Wheatley, it is illogical for American colonists to be as willing to die for liberty as they are determined to keep innocent Africans enslaved. She insists that Americans do not need a philosopher's intellect to help them grasp this basic idea. If two marginalized individuals—a recently emancipated African woman and a Native American preacher—fully understand and eloquently articulate the human desire for freedom, enlightened colonists can certainly comprehend the concept.

## Ottobah Cugoano
### *Exodus Justifies Radical Abolition in England*

At about the same time Phillis Wheatley was emancipated in the American colonies, Quobna Ottobah Cugoano gained his freedom in England and embarked upon a similar route to antislavery activism through favor from a slaveholder. Cugoano's master, Alexander Campbell, Esq., took him from the West Indies to England in 1772, just as the *Somerset* case was resolved, which likely led to Cugoano's self-emancipation. Within a year, at the urging of friends, Cugoano was baptized and adopted the English name John Stuart to guard against being returned to slavery. Being non-European meant running the risk of being taken into slavery, and some Europeans relied on religious difference to identify outsiders.[15] But baptism did not secure civil rights for free Afro-Britons. As Cugoano settled in England, acquired literacy, and eventually found work with the royal artist Richard Cosway, he encountered slavery proponents who invoked biblical discourse to liberate white Christians from sin, and to enslave Africans and oppress free blacks. The continued existence of slavery despite the ruling in the *Somerset* case impelled English activists such as Sharp and William Wilberforce, as well as Afro-Briton abolitionists including Cugoano, William Green, Olaudah Equiano, and Ignatius Sancho, to intensify their antislavery efforts. In 1787 Cugoano published a blistering treatise titled *Thoughts and Sentiments on the Evil and Wicked Traffic of Slavery, and Commerce of Human Species*, in which he calls for the immediate abolition of the slave trade and the emancipation of enslaved Africans. He frames his argument through the Joseph story to situate the fate of Africans within the purview of Providence and to offer his own educational, economic, spiritual, and political success as evidence of the positive good that would result from the abolition of slavery.

Cugoano establishes himself within a Joseph narrative that reveals the complicity of Africans and the English in human trafficking that is decimating his homeland. In the biblical narrative, Joseph's brothers sell him into slavery to the Ishmaelites, his family's distant relatives. Similarly, Cugoano recalls that he was "first kid-napped and betrayed by some of my own complexion" when he was about thirteen years old (16). Africans stole him from his West African home and sold him to European slave traders headed for Grenada. On the slave ship, one of his "countrywomen," who "slept with some of the head men of the ship," divulged the plot devised by Africans to blow up and burn the vessel (15). Cugoano represents African slave traders as Joseph's brothers and European slave traders as Ishmaelites, making both buyers and sellers members of an extended family disrupted and corrupted by a brutal system of slavery. When Joseph's brothers sold him into slavery, they nearly destroyed their family. When Africans became involved in the slave trade, they set in motion a chain of events that led to the conquest of a continent. Africans were torn away to toil for Europeans on West Indian plantations. Through his representation of the impact of slavery on African families, Cugoano encourages his readers to see him as Joseph: a cherished son forcefully removed from a community that is being destroyed, rather than a cursed descendant of Ham divinely destined to a life of servitude.

Cugoano further solidifies his identity as a son rather than a slave by placing the fate of Africans within the realm of Providence rather than under the control of British slavers. Like Joseph, Cugoano received relief from slavery's hardships and eventual emancipation through favor from a benevolent master. However, he characterizes this favor as being orchestrated by God, declaring, "This Lord of Hosts, in his good Providence, and in great mercy to me, made a way for my deliverance from Grenada.—Being in this dreadful captivity and horrible slavery, without any hope of deliverance, for about eight or nine months, beholding the most dreadful scenes of misery and cruelty" (16). Cugoano's deliverance was precipitated by the actions of a new master, Campbell, in taking him to England, where he gained his freedom. Cugoano's quick transition from enslaved African to free black confirms Wheatley's assertion in her "Letter to Reverend Samson Occum" that "in every human breast God has implanted a Principle, which we call Love of Freedom; it is impatient of Oppression, and pants for Deliverance." His improbable escape and elevation affirm his belief that humanity—including Africans—is subject to Providence. He asserts that God's "*providence rules over all, and [He] is the only Potent One that rules in the nations over the children of men. It is unto Him, who is the Prince of the Kings of the earth, that I would give all thanks*" (17; emphasis in original). The British monarchy was heavily invested in the slave trade, granting licenses and establishing companies to ensure its profitability. In placing God as the earth's sovereign, Cugoano argues that even British royals are subject to a divine ruler. He is also convinced that God's Providence extends to Africans, who are covered by God's grace even when they are ignorant of his concern for them. Because he has escaped, Cugoano believes God will emancipate all enslaved Africans.

The spiritual paradigm that Cugoano constructs for world governance enables him to appropriate directly the Joseph story as evidence that God overrules the plans of slavers and restores the natural rights of Africans. He declares, "I may say with Joseph, as he did with respect to the evil intention of his brethren, when they sold him into Egypt, that whatever evil intentions and bad motives those insidious robbers had in carrying me away from my native country and friends, I trust, was what the Lord intended for my good" (17). By embracing the Joseph narrative, Cugoano offers justification for his characterization of slavery as evil, the result of the theft of humans. Nevertheless, he is compelled to forgive his English captors and admit that his enslavement has led to a positive transformation. Cugoano's appropriation of the Joseph narrative gives his pious English readers a familiar lens through which to view African life, revealing how both Africans and Europeans are implicated in the business and practice of slavery. Given their awareness of the Joseph narrative and its later fictional versions in texts such as Daniel Defoe's *The Fortunes and Misfortunes of Moll Flanders* (1722), Samuel Richardson's *Pamela, or, Virtue Rewarded* (1722), and Henry Fielding's *History and Adventures of Joseph Andrews* (1742), Cugoano's readers readily intuited the biblical resonances of such plots. Cugoano's transformation is accomplished through a British education. He writes, "I am highly indebted to many of the good people of England for learning and principles unknown to the people of my native country. But, above all, what have I obtained from the Lord God of Hosts, the God of the Christians! in that divine revelation of the only true God, and the Saviour of men" (17). In singling out "good" Englishmen for praise, Cugoano recognizes the work of British reformers and subtly encourages them to extend these opportunities to other Africans. While he acknowledges the advantages afforded by an English education, he affirms the superiority of Christian teachings. English education produced slavery; biblical instruction offered both spiritual and physical freedom.

Indeed, Cugoano emphasizes both his secular and spiritual education in presenting himself as a well-informed savior for Africans. He writes, "I have endeavoured to improve my mind in reading, and have sought to get all the intelligence I could, in my situation of life, towards the state of my brethren and countrymen in complexion, and of the miserable situation of those who are barbarously sold into captivity, and unlawfully held in slavery" (17). Cugoano, the servant, becomes the master of English political, historical, and religious ideologies, enabling him to produce a tract that forcefully challenges England's rationale for slavery. He characterizes slavery as both a moral and legal issue that requires a religious and political solution. His astute grasp of the biblical and sociological rationales that Englishmen relied on to justify the slave trade undermined arguments that Africans were best suited for servitude and directed the English to see the potential for free Africans to become productive members of their churches and communities.

## Olaudah Equiano
### *Exodus, Abolition, and Christian Consciousness*

Like Cugoano, Olaudah Equiano was kidnapped, sold into slavery, and transported to the "land of bondage"[16] in the West Indies (98). After purchasing his freedom and settling in England, he too became active in the abolition movement. Equiano may have assisted Cugoano in publishing his *Thoughts and Sentiments*, as the two were close associates. He crafts a more complex, yet sympathetic approach to his *Interesting Narrative*, however, by penning a hybrid slave–spiritual–travel–sea adventure–economic success narrative that draws on Exodus to present English readers with a model for an African's journey from freedom to slavery, conversion, emancipation, and integration into British society facilitated by enlightened English subjects.

To help his readers sympathize with the slave trade's devastating impact on his homeland, Equiano presents a parallel between the kinship system in his African community and that of ancient Israel's forefathers. He recalls, "our government was conducted by our chiefs or judges, our wise men and elders; and the head of a family with us enjoyed a similar authority over his household with that which is ascribed to Abraham and other patriarchs" (44). By creating a connection between his Igbo people and God's ancient people of Israel, Equiano develops a new genealogy for Africans that challenges the racial hierarchies of the eighteenth-century Atlantic world.[17] Aware that his readers would question his parallels between African and Jewish history when the complexions of these peoples' descendants were obviously different, he shifts the responsibility for accounting for such differences from Europeans to God, adding, "As to the difference of colour between the Eboan Africans and the modern Jews, I shall not presume to account for it" (44). By intimating that humans lack the ability to understand such mysteries, Equiano challenges Europeans' authority to emphasize difference as justification for oppression. Constructing similarities permits Equiano to assert that his people are God's people and possess the capacity to become a great nation just as God had promised Abraham that Israel would be.

Like Cugoano, Equiano confidently asserts his belief in Africans' eventual liberation by situating his fate within the realm of Providence, which places him beyond the control of European slavers. On the opening page of his *Interesting Narrative*, he declares,

> I believe there are a few events in my life, which have not happened to many; it is true the incidents of it are numerous: and, did I consider myself an European, I might say my sufferings were great: but, when I compare my lot with that of most of my countrymen, I regard myself as a *particular favourite of Heaven,* and acknowledge the mercies of Providence in every occurrence of my life." (31; emphasis in original)

Equiano distinguishes himself from Africans who labored in the West Indies' brutal plantation system by detailing his experiences with several benevolent masters who had favored slaves like Joseph and himself for centuries. He acknowledges the providential appearance of Michael Henry Pascal, an officer in the British Royal Navy who removed him from the confines of a Virginia plantation and introduced him to a seafaring life that took him all over the world. Pascal treated him so well that Equiano says of their relationship, "The kind and unknown hand of the Creator (who in very deed leads the blind in a way they know not) now began to appear, to my comfort" (63). Equiano is careful to attribute the source of his favored status solely to God, thereby destabilizing notions of humane slavers and the beneficial effects of slavery for Africans. He alludes to the prophecy of Isaiah regarding the restoration of Israel in intimating that both slaves and slaveholders are "blind" to their true condition, in need of God to restore their sight and direct them along the path to freedom.[18] Later Equiano recounts the favor of yet another master in the West Indies Robert King, whom he characterizes as a kindhearted man who put him in charge of many business and household matters and allowed him to learn navigation, become a merchant, keep a portion of his pay, and buy his freedom. Equiano shares his friend Cugoano's belief that God has providentially worked in his life even before he knew God existed. In this favored position, Equiano views himself as a valuable member of his community, "almost an Englishman," as he recalls, rather than a commodity (77). Becoming "almost an Englishman" means that Equiano has mastered the English language, acquired rudimentary sailing skills, and pledged allegiance to England by fighting in the Royal Navy. Equiano, the "*particular favourite of heaven*," is not shielded from betrayals that punctuated the life of Joseph and England's slaves, however. One of Equiano's keenest disappointments occurred when instead of giving him his freedom, Pascal sold him to Captain James Doran, who was sailing to the West Indies. Like other pious slaves who lost the benevolence of their masters, Equiano learned that favor from God and man does not guarantee security in the volatile world of the slave trade. Equiano's faithfulness to his master, loyalty to England, and conversion to Christianity do not provide him access to freedom. Although his masters vouched for his "good character," they still sold him as personal property.

Despite these setbacks, Equiano eventually prevailed, and in his narrative he presents himself as uniquely positioned to elevate Africans and educate Englishmen. He differentiates himself from other eighteenth-century Afro-Atlantic writers by appropriating the roles of other biblical persons—Peter, Jacob, Moses, and Elijah—and adapting larger portions of the Exodus narrative to advance abolition in England. In so doing, he constructs the most sophisticated performance by a black writer in the eighteenth-century Atlantic world, recreating himself as an African fully acculturated to the ways of upstanding Englishmen. This radical enactment begins with the *Interesting Narrative*'s frontispiece. As Joseph the Israelite was arrayed in the fine linen and gold of Egyptian royalty and given the name Zaphnath-Paaneah,[19] Equiano wears the refined clothing of an English gentleman and identifies himself as both Olaudah Equiano and Gustavus Vassa, the African. But unlike Joseph, he does not possess the political power to transform his world. Joseph used his authority as an Egyptian official to relocate his free brethren to Egypt's most fertile land. In contrast, Equiano invokes the power of Pentecost to challenge the British to liberate his enslaved brethren. In the frontispiece, Equiano holds a Bible opened to Acts 4:12: "Neither is there salvation in any other; for there is none other name under heaven given among men, whereby we must be saved." The Apostle Peter uttered these words after he and the Apostle John were released from prison immediately following the Holy Spirit's empowering of the early Christian Church on the day of Pentecost. Scholars have suggested that Equiano's focus on this text emphasizes "Christian universalism" and establishes his autobiography as instructive for the British and reflective of his own growth.[20] In identifying with Peter, who had denied his discipleship to Christ before becoming a powerful preacher in the early Christian Church, Equiano offers a reminder that God enables men to accomplish tasks they are unable or unwilling to fulfill themselves. Gazing directly at his audience as a Joseph figure who wields the authority of a modern Peter, he bridges the Old and New Worlds by claiming access to the divine power of Pentecost to confront and convert his people's oppressors and convince them to abolish slavery.

Whereas the paratext of Equiano's *Interesting Narrative* exhibits his transformed self, the book itself details his progression into a patriarchal salvific abolitionist. When Equiano is enslaved, he recalls, "I was called Michael" (63). When he is sold to a new master in Virginia, he reports, "In this place, I was called Jacob" (63). After Equiano is sold and heads out to sea, he writes,

> While I was on board this ship, my captain and my master named me *Gustavus Vasa* [*sic*]. I at that time began to understand him a little, and refused to be called so, and told him as well as I could that I would be called Jacob; but he said I should not, and still called me Gustavus. (64)

After suffering beatings from his new master, Equiano accepts his new name. The conferring of these names reflected the common practice of masters assigning their slaves the identities of revered biblical or historical figures in order to emphasize their godlike authority over their bondsmen and women. Although Michael was a popular English name, its biblical and historical significance as the name of the archangel who defeats Satan, as well as of numerous prominent religious and political figures, suggest that Equiano's owners may have chosen the name to reinforce his subordinate state as a slave. Equiano's recollection of being named Michael and Jacob may have resonated with his Christian readers, for Equiano seeks to overthrow slavery and become a patriarch like Jacob, Joseph's father, the progenitor of a new family in the African Diaspora. He embodies the experiences of the Israelites, who were not only enslaved in Egypt, but ultimately gained their freedom and reached the Promised Land. Equiano's Egypt is the Black Atlantic, however, and his exodus is singular, negotiated through a purchase agreement rather than a miraculous deliverance. Prior to that deliverance, Equiano's master had insisted on changing his name from Jacob to Gustavus Vassa, perhaps to hide Equiano's slave status.[21] Moreover, Equiano's English readers were familiar with the story of Gustavus Vasa, a Swede who had led his people to freedom from the Danish in 1521–23. Equiano's transformation from a slave named Jacob on a Virginia plantation to an enslaved sailor named Gustavus Vassa on an English naval vessel signals the beginning of his integration into English society. His travels as a sailor enable him to become familiar with the English way of life and prepare him for his successful work as an abolitionist.

Yet, as a slave, Equiano cannot be Jacob, the patriarch of a new African community in the Americas, or Gustavus Vassa, a courageous abolitionist. While working in the West Indian "land of bondage" and witnessing the terrible impact of slavery on his brethren, Equiano desires to be like Moses. His sympathy for the enslaved Africans' suffering is evident in his recollection of his acquaintance with a poorly treated Creole in Montserrat. The slave's master and other white men often take his fish without compensating him. Equiano does not console his friend like the revered patriarch Jacob or the beloved son Joseph. Rather, he yearns to be Moses, the militant liberator. He writes, "This artless tale moved me much, and I could not help feeling the just cause Moses had in redressing his brother against the Egyptian. I exhorted the man to look up still to the God on top, since there was no redress below" (110–11). Here Equiano is referencing the incident in which Moses slew an Egyptian taskmaster who was mistreating an enslaved Israelite and then hid the Egyptian's body in the sand.[22] He describes Moses' murder of the overseer as a "just cause," yet he himself refrains from violence in helping his Creole friend.[23] The reality of slave life may have compelled Equiano to control his anger, for slave codes mandated execution for enslaved Africans convicted of murder.[24] Even Moses became a fugitive after Pharaoh learned that his adopted Hebrew grandson had killed the taskmaster. Although Equiano longs to exercise his own agency in liberating a fellow slave, he encourages the enslaved Creole to trust God who decimated Egypt to liberate the Israelites. He thus posits himself as a judicious, faithful Moses at this juncture in his journey. Moses, the pampered prince, needed forty years of training as a shepherd to learn to trust God to deliver his people. Equiano positions himself as a pacifist who eschews the violent overthrow of slavery even after witnessing its oppressive effects in the West Indies, thereby encouraging the English to adopt his rational course of action for the eradication of slavery and the African slave trade.

For Equiano, rationality eventually effects emancipation, which could best be understood as being akin to translation to heaven. When Equiano gains his freedom, he evokes the biblical story of Elijah's fiery chariot ride from earth to heaven to describe his initial response to liberty. He exclaims, "All within my breast was tumult, wildness and delirium! My feet scarcely touched the ground, for they were winged with joy, and, like Elijah, as he rose to Heaven; they 'were with lightning speed as I went on'" (136).[25] Although Equiano offers a vision of himself as overcome with joy, he hovers over the earth instead of being transported to a perfect world. While Elijah's ascension occurred at the end of his prophetic work on earth, Equiano's emancipation inaugurates his new life as a free man in a slave society where he can never experience eternal bliss. His recollection of his emancipation heightens his readers' understanding of the reality of "freedom" for Africans in a slave society, for his audience soon learns that his happiness is short-lived. When he begins earning wages as a free black seaman, Equiano encounters abusive white men and racial discrimination in the maritime industry.

These brushes with bias do not prevent him from acting more like a recently emancipated Israelite overseer than a savior of his people, however.[26] Like the Israelites, who practiced slavery after gaining their freedom and leaving Egypt, Equiano does not immediately seek to abolish involuntary servitude. He accepts his friend British scientist Dr. Charles Irving's invitation to help establish a plantation in Jamaica, expecting to use the venture as a missionary endeavor. Ironically, on the day he acts as Irving's agent in purchasing slaves, he leaves church service, condemns individuals who are buying and selling on the Sabbath, and walks immediately aboard a "Guinea-man" and chooses "all my own countrymen" as bondsmen (205). He characterizes himself as a humane slaver who "always treated [the slaves] with care and affection, and did every thing I could to comfort the poor creatures and render their condition easy" (211).[27] Equiano soon becomes so disgusted by slaveholding culture, however, that he forsakes plantation life and moves to England. His departure sparks a series of tragic events, leaving the property ruined and the enslaved Africans drowned after a boat accident. He encounters several sea captains who beat and deceive him and threaten to return him to slavery. Equiano's decision to become a slaver exemplifies the assertion in the frontispiece of the *Interesting Narrative* that only God can save humanity and create unity in a diverse, integrated community. Equiano needs a providential deliverance from slavery as a bondsman and overseer as much as the English who depend on slaves to build their empire.

After Equiano leaves the West Indies, his life is more analogous to the Joseph narrative during his final transformation from slaver into abolitionist. Like Joseph, Equiano marries a woman from his adopted homeland and works for the salvation of his people. He petitions the queen to raise his brethren "from the condition of brutes, to which they are at present degraded, to the rights and situation of freemen, and admitted to partake of the blessings of your Majesty's happy government" (232). Following the Joseph model, Equiano not only demands the liberation of Africans, he requests that they be integrated into English society. Having risen from the status of slave to free African, Equiano, like Cugoano and Wheatley, offers his life as an example of what his brethren can achieve and what converted Englishmen can accomplish in the new Christian communities they would build throughout the British Empire.

## John Marrant
## *Exodus and Spiritual Transformation*

While enslaved Africans such as Wheatley, Cugoano, and Equiano turned to Exodus and other biblical narratives to augment their demands for liberty, some free black writers embraced the narrative to explore spiritual transformation. In 1785 Methodist missionary John Marrant recounted his spiritual-travel-captivity experience in his *Narrative of the Lord's Wonderful Dealings with John Marrant, a Black*. Marrant constructs a complex tale in which he characterizes himself as a fourteen-year-old Joseph figure whose decision to give up his career as a musician and devote himself to God and evangelism leads to separation from his family. The narrative's intricacy lies in Marrant's coupling of the Joseph story with the familiar biblical narratives of the Hebrew captive Daniel and his friends, the Prodigal Son, and John the Baptist to delineate his transformation from a pleasure seeker to a gospel minister. In so doing, he makes his life story serve as a rebuke to white Americans and Englishmen by revealing God's favor for black Christians, and exemplifies how a common faith can produce reconciliation between the English, white Americans, and Afro-Atlantic peoples.

Marrant's conversion to Christianity sets him on a path that leads to persecution, captivity, and transformation, experiences that aligned his life with those of major biblical figures and provided evidence of God's favor. At home, the young convert experiences persecution from his family and neighbors while attempting to share his faith. When Marrant's community rejects his witness, he initially considers suicide before seeking solace in the wilderness with his Bible and a copy of Dr. Isaac Watts' hymnbook. Marrant's retrospective evocation of a wilderness journey suggests the possibility of transformation; Joseph, Moses, Elijah, John the Baptist, Jesus, and other biblical figures underwent spiritual growth when temporarily separated from their brethren, enjoyed spiritual renewal alone with God, and thus became fit to lead spiritual reforms in their communities. Isolation in the wilderness nurtures Marrant's spiritual growth and strengthens his faith. Wilderness experiences are never void of trials, however. A Native American hunter interrupts Marrant's communion with God, and Marrant decides to join him. Young and inexperienced, Marrant soon finds himself facing more persecution when he enters Cherokee territory without permission. Marrant's imprisonment by Native Americans is similar to the hardships that Israelites such as Joseph, Daniel, and other captives experienced because they were perceived as outsiders who violated laws governing foreign nations.

Indeed, during his captivity, Marrant initially turns to the stories of Daniel, the young Hebrew who was thrown into a lion's den, and the three Hebrew worthies who were cast into a fiery furnace, to convey the providential turn of events that enables him to experience the benevolence of his oppressors. After trespassing into Cherokee territory, Marrant is imprisoned and given a death sentence, a fate he describes as a lion's den and fiery furnace, but his ability to speak his captors' language saves his life. He explains, "I prayed in English a considerable time, and about the middle of my prayer, the LORD impressed a strong desire upon my mind to turn into their language, and pray in their tongue. I did so, and with remarkable liberty, which wonderfully affected the people" (118). Later, Marrant reads from the Bible in the presence of the Cherokee king and prays for the king's sick daughter, who is then miraculously healed. Like King Nebuchadnezzar, who exalted Daniel after the Hebrew exile disobeyed the king's decree against praying to anyone for thirty days, and who promoted the three Hebrew boys after they refused to follow his orders to worship a golden statue, the Cherokee king treats Marrant as a prince, giving him gold jewelry and allowing him to travel freely. In turn, Marrant enacts the role of Daniel and the Hebrew boys who assimilated into their Babylonian community, adopting the Native Americans' dress and learning to speak their language fluently. Europeans who were subjected to Indian captivity rarely experienced such favor.[28] In Afro-Atlantic captivity narratives, however, writers always emphasize how their relationship with God leads to favor with their captors. Here Marrant positions Cherokees as being more responsive to Providence than Europeans who enslave and oppress Africans. He subtly challenges Europeans' authority to control Africans' lives, positing Africans as individuals whose prayers for deliverance from their oppressors are answered, often in miraculous ways.

Spiritual renewal in the wilderness and miraculous deliverance from a death sentence sharpen Marrant's perception of himself as being "lost" both to God and his family, which leads to both reconciliation and restoration. He conflates the Joseph narrative with the parable of the Prodigal Son to confirm his conversion, orchestrate his family reunion, and justify his calling to the ministry. After visiting several Native American communities, Marrant reports, "I now and then found, that my affections to my family and country were not dead; they were sometimes very sensibly felt, and at last strengthened into an invincible desire of returning home" (121). His resolve to return to his homeland had strengthened as he traveled further away from his family, for his conversion to Christianity convinced him to reconcile with them. In recalling his reunion with his family, Marrant illustrates how his "lost" condition shifts their attitude from anger to acceptance of him. A friend he meets on his way home tells him that his family is well, except one "lately lost." He explains,

> After [Marrant] had quitted school, [he] went to Charles-Town to learn some trade; but came home crazy, and rambled in the woods, and was torn in pieces by the wild beasts. . . . I, and his brother, and uncle, and others . . . went three days into the woods in search of him, and found his carcass torn, and brought it home, and buried it, and they are now in mourning for him. (122)[29]

The young man's remembrance of the search for Marrant recalls the portion of the Joseph story in which the young Hebrew's brothers presented his bloodstained coat of many colors to Jacob and, rather than confess their deed, told him a wild beast had devoured Joseph. No deception is involved in Marrant's story, however. His family seems genuinely sorry that their actions led to his death and continue to mourn him. Their sorrow compels Marrant to acknowledge his "lost" condition and admit that, as a Christian, he should have worked through his differences with his family.

Marrant's conflation of the story of Joseph with the parable of the Prodigal Son illustrates how his reconciliation with his family fits him for public ministry. In the biblical narrative, Joseph was unfamiliar to his brothers, who traveled to Egypt to purchase food during a famine. Marrant situates himself as a Joseph who returns home, arriving dressed as a Cherokee who is not recognized by his friends or family because they think he is dead. Marrant weeps over his condition as he begins to understand he has been "lost" both physically and spiritually. His family invites him into their home and answers his questions, but they soon become uncomfortable and ask him to leave. Marrant complicates his Joseph narrative of family reunion with allusions to the parable of the Prodigal Son to present evidence of his full conversion. When his eleven-year-old sister comes home from school, she immediately declares that the black man dressed as a Cherokee is John: "She ran and clasped me round the neck, and, looking me in the face, said, 'Are not you my brother John?' I answered yes, and wept" (122). Like the Prodigal Son, Marrant chooses to leave and return home. In his prodigal narrative, however, a loving sibling rather than a faithful father welcomes him home. His younger sister had not persecuted Marrant during the initial phase of his conversion. She may represent the younger generation that has not been tainted by the oppressive behaviors exhibited against Afro-Atlantic peoples and thus may be more receptive to Marrant's message. He recounts, "I was then made known to all the family, to my friends, and acquaintances, who received me, and were glad, and rejoiced: Thus the dead was brought to life again; thus the lost was found" (122).[30] In the parable of the Prodigal Son, the Prodigal's brother becomes angry when his father makes a feast for the son who had squandered his inheritance on riotous living and arrived home smelling like the pigsty where he had been forced to work. His father responds, "It was meet that we should make merry, and be glad: for this thy brother was dead, and is alive again; and was lost, and is found" (Luke 15:32). Earlier in his *Narrative*, Marrant informs his readers that much like the Prodigal Son during his wilderness wandering, he slept in trees to escape wild animals, ate grass because he had no food, and drank muddy water that wild pigs had left behind. By shifting his position from Joseph to the Prodigal Son, Marrant takes responsibility for his estrangement from his family. His experiences as a "lost" son in the wilderness and his captivity with the Cherokees bring about his conversion and prepare him for the ministry.[31] Although Marrant wins converts during his journey home, as a Christian he cannot devote himself to evangelism until he and his family are reunited and reconciled. The ministry gives him the opportunity to introduce Afro-Atlantic people to Christianity and encourage them to develop piety. Marrant, his converts, and Europeans now had the opportunity to come together and build new communities grounded in their common faith.

## Conclusion

Afro-Atlantic writers entered the biblical language-world and embraced portions of the Joseph story and other biblical narratives to explore the relationship among piety, politics, and freedom for people of African descent in the eighteenth-century Atlantic world. With an emphasis on betrayal by brethren, captivity in a foreign land, favor from God and benevolent masters, reconciliation with family, and transformation from marginalized other to valued member of a new community, Joseph's story and other biblical narratives provided a familiar language-world in which Afro-Atlantic writers could articulate their experiences and challenge the belief that Africans were cursed to lives of perpetual slavery. But their experiences in communities controlled by European dominants complicated their embrace of biblical narratives to represent their experiences, often leading them to double portions of the Exodus story with episodes from the lives of revered biblical figures such as Abraham, David, Peter, and the Prodigal Son. By positing themselves as Afro-Atlantic biblical figures, black writers challenged European colonists to consider possibilities of new communities of believers and citizens who experienced favor from man and God. Despite the presence of familiar biblical narratives in these stories, however, Afro-Atlantic people did not achieve their goals for equality and freedom in eighteenth-century England or America. Individually, they experienced a measure of favor and liberty, but most of their brethren continued to languish in slavery. Nearly all lived long enough to see that freedom did not lead to equality in a world where race was increasingly becoming the determining factor through which people of European descent differentiated themselves from Africans and justified the perpetual enslavement and oppression of Afro-Atlantic peoples.

CHAPTER TWO

# Exodus as the Blueprint for Building Free Black Communities (1800–1840)

*I shall need, too, the favor of that Being in whose hands we are, who led our fathers, as Israel of old, from their native land and planted them in a country flowing with all the necessaries and comforts of life.*

—Thomas Jefferson, Second Inaugural Address

*The ears of Jehovah have been constantly open to them: He has heard the prayers that have ascended from the hearts of his people; and he has, as in the case of his ancient and chosen people the Jews, come down to deliver our suffering country-men from the hands of their oppressors.*

—Absalom Jones, *A Thanksgiving Sermon*

*As in their religious belief they have a tradition which has been handed down from time almost immemorial, that all the Ethiopian nations, in short that all africans descended from Jethro, the priest of Midean.*

—Boyrereau Brinch, *The Blind African Slave, or, Memoirs of Boyrereau Brinch, Nicknamed Jeffrey Brace*

*The book of Exodus furnishes many conclusive evidences of the direct sanction of slavery.*

—William Drayton, *The South Vindicated from the Treason and Fanaticism of Northern Abolitionists*

In the first decade of the nineteenth century, England and America's divergent approaches to slavery caused a significant shift in the development of Afro-Atlantic Exodus narratives. Abolitionists gained a major victory when both countries outlawed the transatlantic slave trade. Each nation developed different philosophies regarding its continued involvement with slavery, however. The United States further entrenched itself as a slave society through a profitable domestic slave trade, while England began to consider how to improve the condition of slaves in the West Indies and legislate for their gradual emancipation. As it expanded territorially, the United States maintained an equal number of free and slave states, reflecting the country's contentious division over slavery. In contrast, in 1833 Parliament abolished slavery throughout the British Empire.

As England's antislavery movement flourished and emancipation day drew near, Afro-British writers' literary production diminished. By 1800, many of the late eighteenth-century Afro-British authors who invoked the Exodus narrative in their writings had died or disappeared from public record. Other black writers in England published a variety of texts, most notably John Jea's *The Life, History, and Unparalleled Sufferings of John Jea, the African Preacher, Compiled and Written by Himself* (1815), Robert Wedderburn's *The Axe Laid to the Root* (1817) and *The Horrors of Slavery* (1824), and Mary Prince's *History of Mary Prince, a West Indian Slave, Related by Herself* (1831). Two of these writers appropriated the Exodus narrative in their work: Jea to encourage release from the slavery of sin and Wedderburn to demand the slaying of English slaveholders in Jamaica similar to God's destruction of the Israelites' Egyptian oppressors. British abolitionists continued to circulate stories in antislavery newspapers about enslaved Africans laboring in the West Indies, but they rarely contributed to the Afro-Atlantic Exodus tradition that Equiano, Cugoano, Marrant, and Wheatley had introduced.

The Second Great Awakening, a religious revival that swept the United States from the late eighteenth to the mid-nineteenth century, reintroduced free and enslaved African Americans to the Exodus narrative, rekindled their hope for a deliverer, and made them the primary authors of Afro-Atlantic Exodus stories. As early nineteenth-century African American writers and their supporters began to shape new Exodus narratives, they embraced Moses as the model of a deliverer who would lead them to their promised land. In their writings they constituted themselves as God's oppressed people and variously urged free and enslaved blacks to transform their American Egypt into a promised land, fight white racists in a contested American promised land, or emigrate to foreign black promised lands. In the process, some advocated nonviolent resistance, others physical rebellion. Editors of antislavery and black newspapers further encouraged the development of black Exodus stories by publishing articles instructing a national black audience how to transform the language of Exodus into abolitionist and reform rhetoric essential for community building in the African Diaspora. Although writers consistently turned to Moses as the primary leadership model in the early nineteenth century, some created fissures in the Afro-Atlantic Exodus tradition by invoking the Joseph and Joshua stories to characterize new leaders who called for reform in America or homes in foreign promised lands. The black Exodus narratives that emerged failed in fulfilling the promise of emancipation; nevertheless, they fostered racial uplift efforts and nurtured activists who advocated increasingly radical means for African Americans to achieve freedom and equality in the promised land of their choice.

## Exodus, Politics, and Race
### *The United States, a Divided Nation*

George Washington's death in 1799 inspired a proliferation of national Exodus stories that mythologized the Revolutionary War general and first US president as the "American Moses." Prominent theologians throughout the nation, particularly in New England, where many still embraced the Puritan tradition, drew parallels between the two men's upbringing and leadership to emphasize their success in nation building. In *A Funeral Sermon, Preached at Rockaway, December 29, 1799, on the Much Lamented Death of General George Washington* (1800), for example, white Presbyterian minister John I. Carle declares,

> Moses was, under God, almost the sole director in civilian and military departments, to the Israelites, and Washington, by epistolary communication, afforded, unto Congress, much light and assistance. Especially in cases of difficulty and perplexities; and in considerable measure guided our councils while he led our armies.[1]

Other ministers even argued that Washington was a greater man than Moses because he led the American colonists into their promised land.[2] Indeed, the success of the American Revolution and elevation of Washington to Mosaic leadership inspired many white Americans to become more confident and assertive. White writers would later recall the exploits of their Washington Moses to motivate military commanders during the War of 1812, settle disputes between slave and free states in the 1820s, and resolve political conflicts in the late 1820s and 1830s.[3] The memory of a victorious, courageous Mosaic leader assured officials guiding the fledging nation that they, too, would triumph. The United States prospered under the guidance of slaveholding politicians who invoked the Exodus story to chart a course for the new nation.

### Boyrereau Brinch, Nicknamed Jeffrey Brace
### *Reconstructing African Ancestry through Exodus*

Revolutionary War veteran and former slave Boyrereau Brinch turned to a different portion of the Exodus narrative to claim his right to the liberties accorded by the American Moses' successful leadership of the Continental Army and new republic. Brinch was enslaved in Barbados on an English ship engaged in the Seven Years' War and then sold to a New England ship captain who transported him to Connecticut. He was subsequently sold to several different masters, the last of whom was Mary Stiles, a widow in Woodbury, Connecticut, who allowed him to gain literacy. Brinch earned his freedom in 1783 after serving in the Continental Army, and then settled in Vermont. In his narrative, titled *The Blind African Slave, or Memoirs of Boyrereau Brinch, Nicknamed Jeffrey Brace* (1810), written with the assistance of white abolitionist Benjamin Prentiss, Brinch recounts the traditions and customs of his African homeland, the horrors of enslavement in the Americas, and his conversion to Christianity. Within the hybrid text—slave, spiritual, travel, and adventure narrative—Brinch creates a fissure in the Afro-Atlantic Exodus tradition by evoking Exodus to question the integrity of Christians who own slaves, and locates his ancestry in Moses' father-in-law, Jethro, a respected African who aided the Israelites' journey to Canaan. In so doing, Brinch exposes the hypocrisy of Christians who privilege human legislation over biblical admonitions and disputes notions of a perpetual curse that slavery proponents relied on to justify the subjugation of Africans.

Brinch's retrospective overview of the consequences of Israel's disobedience regarding slavery serves as a warning to Christians who engage in the practice despite biblical injunctions against it. He begins by describing the government, customs, and traditions of his people, whom he identifies as the Bow-woo,[4] as well as his own familial history to challenge Christians' characterization of Africans as "savages" whom they can enslave with impunity. Brinch then quotes three Scriptures that reveal the devastating results of Israel's failure to adhere to God's commands against slavery and oppression: Ezekiel 2, God's calling of the prophet Ezekiel to minister to rebellious Israel during the Babylonian captivity just before the destruction of the temple at Jerusalem; Deuteronomy 28, God's warning to Israel regarding the consequences of disobedience, including diasporic dispersal, forced idolatry, and foreign slavery; and Exodus 22, God's admonitions to Israel against the oppression of strangers, widows, and orphans. Although Brinch's evocations of Scripture have been described as "data" that appears "unexpectedly . . . juxtaposed, rather than integrated into the narration,"[5] by beginning with Ezekiel's commission for ministry, he effectively posits himself as the voice of the "stranger" whom Americans have enslaved, claiming biblical authority to rebuke Christians who, like the Israelites, have disobeyed God's prohibitions against servitude. His emphasis on dispersal and slavery as God's punishment for disobedience to divine laws functions as a veiled warning to American slavers that a similar fate awaits them if they persist in the transatlantic slave trade. Brinch augments his indictment of American slavery by citing Mosaic law regarding the treatment of strangers, widows, and orphans, regulations that intimate that the enslavement of strangers is as offensive as the oppression of a nation's weakest citizens.

Brinch contrasts his record of American Christians' hypocrisy with a counternarrative of African prosperity initiated by his people's ancient biblical ancestor Jethro and marred by European incursions into his homeland. He disputes the argument for African servitude based on the Curse of Cain by asserting that Noah and his sons Ham, Shem, and Japheth are "the second original fathers of all human beings" (62). Instead, Brinch then claims Jethro as Africans' progenitor: "As in their religious belief they have a tradition which has been handed down from time almost immemorial, that all the Ethiopian nations, in short that all africans descended from Jethro, the priest of Midean [*sic*]" (31). In the biblical Exodus, Jethro accompanied his daughter Zipporah, Moses' wife, and her two sons to the Israelites' encampment shortly after the recently liberated community entered the wilderness. Moses informed his father-in-law of the Israelites' miraculous deliverance, and Jethro offered sacrifices of thanksgiving to God with Aaron, Moses' brother and Israel's high priest, and other priests. When Jethro witnessed Moses devoting most of each day to mediating the Israelites' disputes, he recommended a court system administered by astute counselors, which Moses implemented.[6] Whereas America's national Exodus stories advanced an aggressive agenda for nation building through the enslavement of Africans, Brinch relies on the biblical story to construct an illustrious history for Africans that precedes the formation of Israelite, European, or American nations. As descendants of Jethro, whose wise counsel enabled Moses to govern the Israelites effectively, Africans, Brinch contends, are best equipped to serve as community-building advisors whose children might intermarry with Europeans rather than labor as slaves. The story of Jethro gives Africans like Brinch a history, culture, and future in America, elevating them to the level of "civilized" and positioning their oppressors as "savages" who have devastated Africans and their communities.

### Gabriel's Co-conspirators
### *Exodus Inspires the Integrated Promised Land of Richmond, Virginia*

While Brinch earned liberty by fighting alongside the patriots in the Continental Army, other enslaved African Americans embraced Exodus as inspiration for post-Revolution revolts to establish their own promised land within the United States. In the summer of 1800, Gabriel and his co-conspirators initiated a six-month recruitment of slaves, free blacks, and sympathetic whites for a rebellion that would transform Richmond, Virginia, into a free and integrated Southern community. Gabriel was born into slavery but learned to read and write. His parents introduced him to Christianity and were spiritual leaders in their community. Thomas Prosser, Gabriel's master, arranged for him to be trained as a blacksmith. Literacy, Christianity, and blacksmithing contributed to Gabriel's sense of independence as he enjoyed new privileges that Virginians provided for slaves after the American Revolution. Inspired by the rhetoric of the American, French, and Haitian revolutions, Gabriel advocated "death or Liberty" to gain political and economic equality for blacks throughout the United States.[7] A torrential rainstorm foiled the conspiracy, which was revealed to authorities by a slave, ironically named Pharaoh. During the trial, several of Gabriel's co-conspirators recalled how the Exodus story had informed the rebellion. They envisioned themselves as emancipated Israelites who relied on revolt to claim their right to establish a home in the promised land of their choice.

Rather than referencing Scripture delineating the Israelites' miraculous Exodus from Egypt, the co-conspirators located themselves within the narrative of the Israelites' wilderness journey. In his testimony during the trials, Ben Woolfork recalled a meeting in which they discussed whether or not they should implement the revolt. According to Woolfork, Gabriel's brother Martin admonished the group to move ahead, reminding them "there was this expression in the Bible, delays breed danger."[8] In opposition to Martin, Woolfork justified delay by positing the group as enslaved Israelites who were seeking divine emancipation: "I told them that I had heard that in the days of old, when the Israelites were in Servitude to King Pharaoh, they were taken from him by the Power of God,—and were carried away by Moses—God had blessed them with an Angel to go with them, But that I could see nothing of that kind these days."[9] Martin's response convinced the conspirators to move ahead: "I read in my Bible where God says, if we will worship Him, we should have peace in all our Lands; five of you shall conquer an hundred, and a hundred a thousand of our enemies."[10] In supporting his case for delay by declaring, "God had blessed [the Israelites] with an Angel to go with them," Woolfork is likely referring to scriptural passages such as Exodus 23:20: "Behold, I send an Angel before thee, to keep thee in the way, and to bring thee into the place which I have prepared." On at least five different occasions, God assured the Israelites that he had sent an angel to lead and protect them during their journey to and settlement in the Promised Land. By characterizing the slaves as being bereft of an angel to lead them, Woolfork situates them within an American Egypt and rejects human leadership. He intimates that an exodus from slavery requires divine intervention rather than human agency, thereby diminishing the success of the American and Haitian revolutions as inspiration for enslaved African Americans in Richmond. Gabriel was neither as powerful as the covering angel Gabriel[11] nor as savvy as the generals George Washington and Toussaint L'Ouverture had been.

Martin acknowledges the similarities between the conspirators' and Israelites' experiences, but in his Exodus narrative Gabriel becomes Joshua, leader of a band of wrongfully enslaved blacks who are reclaiming their freedom and the right to a home in their American Canaan. Martin references God's admonition to the emancipated Israelites regarding the conquest of the Promised Land: "And five of you shall chase an hundred, and an hundred of you shall put ten thousand to flight: and your enemies shall fall before you by the sword" (Lev 26:8). Rather than characterize the group as enslaved Israelites yearning to escape Egypt, Martin creates a fissure in his Exodus narrative by positing the conspirators as emancipated Israelites whom God has instructed to slaughter their proslavery enemies. From this perspective, the conspirators do not need Gabriel to function as a Moses. Rather, by adapting the rhetoric of Exodus for an African American revolution, Martin positions his brethren as freedmen unlawfully held in bondage worse than colonists had experienced under the oppressive rule of King George III. Like the colonists, they will sever ties with their oppressors. Instead of establishing their own republic, however, they will transform the city of Richmond into an integrated promised land within a Southern slave society.

### Thomas Jefferson
### *Exodus-Inspired Nationalism*

Gabriel's failed declaration of independence threatened white Americans' nationalistic dream of a prosperous United States that would flourish under the guidance of proslavery politicians who evoked the Exodus story to chart a course for the young republic. While Gabriel and his co-conspirators plotted rebellion against slaveholders, Thomas Jefferson campaigned in an election that ushered in the Revolution of 1800, when the Federalists lost control of Congress and the presidency. Prior to his election as president, Jefferson received a letter from Virginia governor James Monroe soliciting his advice regarding the punishment for Gabriel and his co-conspirators. Jefferson advised Monroe to expel rather than execute the slaves, reflecting his belief that the rebellion may have been justified. He wrote, "The other states and the world at large will forever condemn us if we indulge a principle of revenge, or go one step beyond absolute necessity. They cannot lose sight of the rights of the two parties, and the object of the unsuccessful one."[12] The oppression of enslaved African Americans did not compel Jefferson to adopt an antislavery platform or liberate his slaves, however.

Five years later, during his second inaugural address on March 4, 1805, the slaveholding President Jefferson turned to the Exodus story as he had during the Revolutionary War to link the future of America to the history of the Israelites. He declared, "I shall need, too, the favor of that Being in whose hands we are, who led our fathers, as Israel of old, from their native land and planted them in a country flowing with all the necessaries and comforts of life." Like the Israelites, who settled in a land "flowing with milk and honey,"[13] Jefferson asserted that the Pilgrims discovered a New World filled with abundant resources essential in developing a prosperous republic. In so doing, he affirmed Exodus as inspiration for America's official story of liberation, migration, conquest, and settlement. To ensure that the inhabitants of their promised land would be white Americans, Jefferson and other prominent white politicians and ministers advocated colonization to displace free blacks to Africa. In the meantime, African Americans shouldered increasing responsibility for providing white Americans' "necessaries and comforts of life."

## Absalom Jones
### *Exodus, Gradual Emancipation, and Free Black Community Building*

Although the young republic grew increasingly dependent on slave labor to support its economic growth, American politicians could not ignore the mounting international outcry against the transatlantic slave trade. In one of his first major actions during his second term, President Jefferson signed a bill that prohibited the nation's participation in the slave trade and levied hefty fines on those who violated its provisions. The British Parliament soon enacted similar legislation. Since neither country eradicated slavery, however, the effect was to increase their reliance on the domestic slave trade. Though the legislation offered only a partial victory for antislavery forces, African American activists held commemorative thanksgiving services on January 1, 1808, the day it took effect. In Philadelphia, African Episcopal rector Absalom Jones preached *A Thanksgiving Sermon* in which he characterized American slaves as ancient Israelites whose cries had moved God to convince politicians in Congress and Parliament to outlaw the slave trade.[14] In the sermon Jones evokes the Exodus narrative to reinterpret the legislation as a divine sign portending the emancipation of the slaves, transforming free black Philadelphians into activists who continually commemorate their victory, aggressively work for civil rights, and extend their community-building efforts to Africa.

By the time he delivered his *Thanksgiving Sermon*, Jones exuded confidence in his Mosaic role as an agent and interpreter of advances in the antislavery cause. He had purchased freedom for himself and his wife, co-led an exodus of African American parishioners from St. George's Methodist Church, defended black Philadelphians from slanderous accusations during a yellow fever epidemic, and petitioned Congress to outlaw slavery, the slave trade, and fugitive slave laws. Jones framed his *Thanksgiving Sermon* with Exodus 3:7-8, God's call to Moses to be the Israelites' deliverer.[15] As Jones encourages his listeners to celebrate the abolition of the transatlantic slave trade, he turns to this Exodus moment to remind them of the Israelites' sufferings during slavery, mingling details from the story with

*The Reverend Absalom Jones, St. Thomas African Episcopal Church, Philadelphia*

descriptions of American slaves' experiences. Yet he shifts emphasis from the Israelites' specific "God of [their] fathers" to the more inclusive "Judge of the world . . . deliverer of the innocent, and of those who call upon His name . . . God of heaven and earth . . . Common Father of the human race" (337). In so doing, Jones redirects attention from a white American Israel's God to the God who functions as a Father, Judge, and Deliverer in responding to the requests and judging the choices of all peoples. When the enslaved Israelites cried for relief, however, God answered their prayers by empowering Moses and weakening Pharaoh through a series of plagues. In Jones' black Exodus narrative, God answered the prayers of slaves and abolitionists when legislators enacted a law that banned the importation of slaves, but did not eradicate the domestic slave trade. Thus Jones posits American politicians as being more obstinate than Pharaoh in their refusal to emancipate the slaves. Unlike the Egyptians, however, US legislators suffered no immediate devastating consequences. And unlike the Israelites, African Americans did not experience a biblical-like Exodus, since they continued to labor in a fragmented nation of slave states and free states.

Yet, in a radical fissure, Jones addresses his brethren's unique Exodus experience by positioning black Philadelphians *within* their promised land to teach them the importance of incorporating faith, commemoration, and action into their community-building efforts. He strengthens his message by doubling a portion of the Exodus story with a New Testament messianic event to position the 1807 legislation as the "first fruits" of "*peace upon earth, and good-will to man*" (338; emphasis in original). When the Israelites left Egypt, Moses instituted Passover, a yearly festival that reminded them of their deliverance from slavery. During their first Passover in the Promised Land, the Israelites presented a sheaf of the first grain they harvested, their "first fruits," to express their faith in the Messiah's resurrection and the ultimate resurrection of all believers.[16] Hundreds of years later, angels heralded Christ's birth by singing "peace on earth" to announce the fulfillment of God's promise of a Savior whose death and resurrection would ransom humanity.[17] Jones offers these rituals as evidence of divine intervention for the emancipation of enslaved Africans, and the establishment of peace and prosperity for the entire black community. When he instructs his audience to "*give thanks unto the Lord*; let us *call upon his name*, and *make known his deeds among the people*," he directs their attention to Psalm 105, which recounts the miraculous deliverance of the Israelites from slavery and settlement in the Promised Land (338; emphasis in original). Jones' biblical allusions also evoke America's first Thanksgiving, when the Pilgrims praised God for safe passage to the New World and the harvesting of their first crops as a sign of divine blessing on their community. He institutes an annual commemoration for free blacks to herald the abolition of the slave trade as a sign of emancipation and equality that will enable African Americans to be exemplary citizens for whom the Exodus story serves as a blueprint for community building.

Like the Israelites, who battled the occupants of Canaan before they could establish their communities, Northern free blacks lived uneasily in a contested promised land. Although Pennsylvania had adopted a policy of gradual emancipation in the late 1700s, slaves and free blacks still faced limited opportunities when Jones preached his *Thanksgiving Sermon*. With the accelerated growth of domestic slave markets after the discontinuation of the transatlantic slave trade, enslaved African Americans in the South were subjected to even greater hardships. Thus, the task of free black Philadelphians was to transform the entire nation into a peaceful promised land. Jones' belief that God had impressed politicians to abolish the transatlantic slave trade informed his assurances to parishioners that God would also answer their prayers and persuade Congress to enact legislation that would emancipate the slaves and provide civil liberties for black citizens. Yet Jones did not expect his brethren simply to wait for divine intervention or congressional measures. He urged them to conduct themselves as model citizens before Congress fully accorded them their rights and privileges as Americans. By supporting the abolition movement, black Philadelphians could exercise their own agency in mitigating their brethren's sufferings. Living frugal and exemplary lives as Christians could help them develop a thriving community. Teaching history to their descendants would instill in young people an appreciation for the sacrifices their ancestors had made to acquire freedom and inspire them to become involved in racial uplift. In short, Jones believed activism, thrift, and education were initiatives that African American should institutionalize in their community.

As a sixty-two-year-old Moses, Jones likely realized he would not live to see the end of slavery, and he recognized the need for continued strong leadership. Instead of encouraging his audience to seek Mosaic leaders, however, Jones creates a second fissure in his black Exodus narrative by instructing his parishioners to shift their attention from the rites of Passover to the beginning of the Exodus narrative for a leadership model in developing vibrant Christian communities throughout the African Diaspora. He muses, "Who knows but that a Joseph may rise up among them, who shall be the instrument of feeding the African nations with the bread of life, and of saving them, not from earthly bondage, but from the more galling yoke of sin and Satan" (340). Joseph had served as Egyptian prime minister and Hebrew savior prior to Israel's enslavement in Egypt. Enslaved and free blacks needed a young leader like Joseph who could function as mediator between the free and slave populations. Jones asserts that such a black Joseph would be missionary-minded and instrumental in Christianizing African nations. He would fulfill his brethren's greatest need for spiritual food and eternal life in black promised lands throughout the African Diaspora.

## Daniel Coker
### *Exodus and Colonization in Africa*

Black Philadelphians heeded Jones' call to commemorate the abolition of the transatlantic slave trade annually and become model US citizens. Their actions did not bring about the desired results, however. Whites resented free blacks' progress, supported discriminatory laws, and continued to rely on slave labor to sustain America's economy. African Americans increasingly began to consider emigration to black promised lands as a more attractive alternative to progressively more difficult survival within the United States. Some free blacks, particularly Paul Cuffee, financed their own colonization schemes, while others, like AME minister Daniel Coker, affiliated themselves with the American Colonization Society (ACS).

A life of setbacks and struggles compelled Coker to seek new opportunities on the ACS's first voyage to Africa. Though born free to Englishwoman Susan Coker and Isaac Wright, an enslaved African, he was subjected to thirty years of indentured servitude because of his mixed-race heritage.[18] He circumvented his fate by escaping to the North, where he earned ministerial credentials from the Methodist Church. While returning to Maryland, the light-skinned young man permanently adopted his half-brother Daniel Coker's name while passing for white to escape detection. Friends in Baltimore purchased his freedom and invited him to teach in a school for free black children. Over the next ten years, Coker would lose his preaching privileges with the AME Church, file for bankruptcy, and face challenges in supporting his family on a teacher's salary. He chronicled his journey to and settlement in Liberia in *The Journal of Daniel Coker, a Descendant of Africa* (1820) and "Daniel Coker, Diary, April 21, 1821–September 21, 1821." Although Coker intimates in his *Journal* that his primary reason for joining the colonization expedition is to Christianize Africans, his view of colonization broadens as he develops closer ties to the ACS agents while traveling in their berth and establishing the settlement in Africa. When he realizes that the other emigrants distrust the agents, he unsuccessfully attempts to bridge the gap between the two groups. Through his manipulation of competing Exodus narratives in his *Journal* and "Diary," Coker demonstrates the

*The Reverend Daniel Coker, educator, abolitionist, and AME minister*

challenges of performing as Moses, positing Africa as the promised land, and presenting race as a presence in biblical reinterpretations.

Coker's first *Journal* entry underscores how the ACS characterizes their voyage as an exodus to give credibility to a venture that many prominent African American activists did not support. In his description of a worship service held while the passengers wait for their voyage to begin, he recalls how white ACS agent Samuel Bacon, a Harvard-educated lawyer and Episcopal minister from Pennsylvania, invokes the Exodus narrative to draw a parallel between the biblical story and African colonization. Coker writes, "This evening Mr. Bacon, read Deut. c. 11 and made some very appropriate and feeling remarks on the same; and I believe that his words were felt by most present" (2). Bacon reads the portion of Scripture in which Moses reminds the Israelites of their miraculous deliverance from bondage and the protection they experienced during forty years of wilderness wandering. Similarly, as the emigrants prepare to leave the United States, Bacon encourages them to go forward fearlessly, obey God's commandments, and teach his laws and their Exodus experience to their children. Bacon thus posits Liberia as the free blacks' new promised land, and America as their Egypt. His appropriation of Exodus to justify the ACS's removal of free blacks from the United States positions people of African descent as an impediment to the nation's aspirations of becoming a promised land for white Americans.

In his *Journal*, Coker acknowledges the mixed motivations of his sponsors and reveals a more realistic view of their community-building plans. Nearly two months after he recorded ACS agent Bacon's appropriation of the Exodus narrative, Coker references the same passage from Deuteronomy 11 in an entry that confirms his view of the voyage as a transatlantic exodus. Like Bacon, Coker positions the emigrants as emancipated Israelites who will share the story of their deliverance with future generations.[19] There is a twist of irony in his reference, however, for Coker hints at the ACS's unscrupulous motive for colonizing free blacks—so they can develop the United States as a slave society. In contrast to Bacon, Coker claims America, not Africa, as African Americans' homeland. Yet the "country that gave them birth" could not truly be their native land because slavery had transformed it into Egypt (20). Furthermore, the promised land that the black emigrants are traveling to is a "bleeding Africa," wounded by the same nation that sponsors their resettlement and relies on them to "heal the wounds" under the guise of colonization (20). Nevertheless, Coker instructs his readers to "tell [the colonization story] to their children, and their children to their children,"[20] just as Moses had commanded the Israelites to teach their descendants about their miraculous deliverance from slavery in Egypt (20). As the emigrants write a new Exodus narrative for their families, Coker encourages them to create a history that casts colonization in a positive light, especially because many of their brethren have denounced the initiative. America has given them life, but the ACS offers them a future—in Africa.

As Coker subtly shifts himself into the role of a Moses, both the emigrants and the agents repeatedly turn to him for guidance and assurance, unwittingly forcing him to assume the responsibility of a mediator. In an entry written after they survive a storm, Coker reports that the emigrants decide to fast and pray for the success of their trip. Echoing the challenges of the biblical Exodus journey, Coker writes, "May He that was with Moses in the wilderness, be with us; then all will be well.—This is a great undertaking, and I feel its importance more and more, daily" (15–16). As a minister, Coker understood the implications of describing their transatlantic journey as a passage through a wilderness. The Israelites' wilderness trek had been the most difficult part of their journey; thousands died because of disobedience to God. His prayerful request for guidance signals his awareness of conflicts aboard the *Elizabeth* and his desire for divine assistance to resolve them. As the ACS agents distance themselves from the emigrants while maintaining control of the colonization plans, however, neither Coker nor the agents realize the limitations of Coker's role as a Mosaic mediator on an ACS-sponsored exodus.

In accord with the Exodus narrative, Coker examines a time filled with murmurings and miracles as the emigrants and agents travel through their wilderness. Initially, Coker is effective in resolving disputes. His job becomes more difficult about halfway through the voyage after the agents inform the emigrants of their plans to set up the colony. The emigrants are particularly displeased over the stipulation that agents will manage the settlement. They had believed the ACS would be a "means of transporting them to a land where they hoped to live free from the intrusions of white domination."[21] The exchange between ACS agents and emigrant leaders becomes so contentious that Bacon fears the "mutinous spirit" might lead to an altercation that will leave the ship without its crew.[22] Once again, Coker acts as a liaison between the groups. Moses had functioned as an intercessor between God and the Hebrews. In contrast, Coker calls the male emigrants aside for a private meeting and convinces all but two to cooperate with the agents. By attempting to resolve differences between the white agents and his brethren, Coker inadvertently elevates the ACS agents to godlike stature and casts the emigrants as disobedient Israelites. Thus, the truce he negotiates can only be a fragile, temporary one.

Nevertheless, Coker's difficulties in mediating conflicts between the emigrants and ACS agents do not diminish his view of himself as a Moses. As they near Africa, he discovers a thriving slave trade. On March 18, 1820, he inscribes a portion of "The Negro's Prayer," a popular antislavery poem,[23] in his *Journal* to express his disappointment:

> When will Jehovah hear our cries?
> When will the sun of freedom rise?
> When will for us a Moses stand?
> And bring us out from Pharaoh's hand? (31)

In offering this prayer for divine aid, Coker affirms his allegiance to the welfare of the African American community. This series of questions positions the "bleeding Africa" that he had described earlier as Egypt rather than Canaan because Europeans and Africans are still engaged in a lucrative slave trade, and he intimates that he could be the Moses whom God will commission to deliver Africans from slavery. Although the US Congress and British Parliament had outlawed the slave trade by 1808, American and European authorities did not aggressively enforce the ban, and business flourished as traders continued to purchase Africans. Coker reminds his readers that the persistent practice of slavery prevents Africa from being Canaan for people of African descent. As a Mosaic leader, he believes he can effectively work for the abolition of the transatlantic slave trade that has destroyed native communities and will threaten the stability of the colony.

The ACS published Coker's *Journal* before death, disease, and defiant emigrants and Africans brought about the failure of its first colony. The agents, emigrants, and Coker had created competing Exodus narratives that were irreconcilable. After two ACS agents died from illness, Coker became the leader of the colony. The emigrants refused to accept his guidance, however. Suspicious of anyone who had worked closely with the ACS agents, they looked instead to Kizzel, a local African leader, for direction.[24] Despite the colony's initial failure, the ACS continued to send emigrants to Africa, including Coker's wife and sons in 1821. Coker and his family soon moved to Sierra Leone, the British colony where his friend Paul Cuffee had settled free black emigrants nearly ten years earlier. In his unpublished "Diary" of this period, a more reflective, experienced Coker muses, "Moses was I think permitted to see the promised land but not to enter in. I think it likely that I shall not be permitted to see our expected earthly Canaan. But this will be of but small moment so that some thousands of African children are safely landed." Unlike Moses, who peered into the Promised Land from Mount Pisgah, Coker was trapped in the wilderness, unable to climb the mountain and catch a glimpse of Canaan. Nevertheless, he experienced some of his vision for an African Canaan when Sierra Leone governor Charles McCarthy appointed him superintendent of the village of Hastings, where he established an AME Church.[25] Black emigrants continued to relocate to Liberia and Sierra Leone throughout the nineteenth century, but the problems that plagued the first settlement persisted, preventing Coker's dream of an African promised land from coming to fruition.

## Exodus and Anticolonization Advocates

From the onset of the ACS-sponsored emigration movement, African American activists and their supporters mounted a public assault against the venture, arguing that the ACS strengthened slavery's grip on the nation by depleting its free black community. They increasingly relied on African American and abolitionist newspapers to circulate their works to wider audiences. Writers for *Freedom's Journal* (1829–1830), the *Weekly Advocate* (later known as the *Colored American*, 1836–1842), and the *Liberator* (1831–1865) facilitated this task. These publications functioned as community-building textbooks, providing rhetorical strategies for attacking opposition, admonitions for well-meaning sympathizers, and practical strategies for implementing reform.[26] Many contributors appropriated episodes from the Exodus story to model how African Americans could develop a national voice to address the diverse needs of their communities.

Some activists evoked Exodus in newspaper articles to expose the ACS's duplicity, challenging the organization to redirect its efforts to the support of African American citizenship in an integrated Canaan. In "African

Colonization" (1832), an article reprinted from *The Friend, or Advocate of Truth* in the *Liberator*, an anonymous writer disputes the ACS's notion of Africa as the promised land for black Americans. The writer argues that readers should not consider Liberia, Canada, or Haiti as promised lands but should focus instead on "the native, vigorous soil of *African intellect*. This is the much neglected and despised land which wants nothing but a proper culture to insure the negro a home in any climate of the habitable globe!" (1; emphasis in original). By shifting the site of the promised land from a geographical space to the human mind, the writer attempts to democratize access to Canaan. Education would enable any American to develop his or her own version of Canaan anywhere in the United States or the world. If the ACS invested in education in America rather than colonization in Africa, the organization could build up the African American community, thereby empowering individuals to become self-sufficient and encouraging the nation to provide equal rights for all citizens. Effective community building for African Americans could occur only when they gained equal access to education and opportunities to develop their intellects.

African American orator and activist Maria W. Stewart, the first American woman to deliver a public political oration, amplified ideas presented in the *Liberator* article by claiming Exodus to suggest a more menacing motivation for the ACS's actions. In her "Address Delivered at the African Masonic Hall" (1833), also published in the *Liberator*, she asserts, "But ah! methinks their hearts are so frozen toward us, they had rather their money should be sunk in the ocean than to administer it to our relief; and I fear, if they dared, like Pharaoh, king of Egypt, they would order every male child among us to be drowned" (69). As Pharaoh sought to check the Israelite slave population by killing newborn baby boys, Stewart believes the ACS would kill all African American males if given the opportunity, thereby reducing the black population and leaving black women more vulnerable to sexual exploitation and poverty. Stewart intimates that the ACS obscures its sinister motivation for the destruction of the race under the guise of social activism, preferring to suffer financial loss rather than invest in resources that would uplift the black community in America. The relocation scheme obscured the ACS's proemigrationist desire to develop a slave society as well as the depth of its disdain for African Americans.

Stewart's fellow activist Bostonian David Walker adopted a more direct rhetorical strategy in his critique of colonization, positing its proponents as scheming Egyptians whose goal was to separate free blacks from their enslaved brethren. In his *Appeal in Four Articles; Together with a Preamble, to the Coloured Citizens of the World* (1829–1830), which he published as a pamphlet and in the African American newspaper *Freedom's Journal*, free black militant activist Walker created a public voice that drew on the religious and political rhetoric colonists had successfully relied on to build the nation, as well as the oral tradition within the African American community.[27] In Article IV of the *Appeal*, titled "Our Wretchedness in Consequence of the Colonizing Plan," Walker critiques arguments by prominent, influential colonization proponents, notably Henry Clay and Elias B. Caldwell, by emphasizing the dehumanizing violence of slavery and asserting that African Americans possess the rights to citizenship because of their humanity and labor. After detailing the cruelties that Christian slaveholders inflict on enslaved African Americans, Walker pairs a portion of the Exodus story with a teaching of Jesus to characterize colonizers as duplicitous, hypocritical slavers: "How cunning slave-holders think they are!!!—How much like the king of Egypt who, after he saw plainly that God was determined to bring out his people, in spite of him and his, as powerful as they were. He was willing that Moses, Aaron and the Elders of Israel, but not all the people should go and serve the Lord. But God deceived him as he will Christian Americans, unless they are very cautious how they move" (75). In the biblical Exodus story, when Moses approached Pharaoh with God's directive to liberate the Israelites to allow them to worship him in the wilderness, the Egyptian ruler offered various emancipation options, and then reneged on his promises when the plagues were stayed. After Moses announced the eighth plague, of locusts, Pharaoh's counselors advised him to acquiesce to God's demand to avoid the destruction of the nation. Pharaoh limited liberation to Hebrew men, however. If Israel's leaders had accepted Pharaoh's offer of emancipation, they would have relegated their brethren to perpetual bondage. Similarly, if free blacks accepted the ACS's invitation to settle in Liberia, they would limit their ability to support the abolition movement and inspire enslaved African Americans to seek freedom. Walker accounts for the lack of "plagues" to punish the sin of slavery in America by acknowledging the presence of sincere Christians: "What would have become of the United States of America, was it not for those among the whites, who not in words barely, but in truth and in deed, love and fear the Lord?" (75). For Walker, greed blinds prosperous slavers to the surety of divine punishments that both Exodus and Jesus affirm. He writes,

> Our Lord and Master said:—"Whoso shall offend one of these little ones which believe in me, it were better for him that a millstone were hanged about his neck, and that he were drowned in the depth of the sea" [Matt 18:6]. But the Americans with this very threatening of the Lord's, not only beat his little ones among the Africans, but many of them they put to death or murder. Now the avaricious Americans, think that the

> Lord Jesus Christ will let them off, because his words are no more than the words of a man!!! (75)

When the disciples asked him who would be greatest in the kingdom of heaven, Jesus instructed them to experience conversion, cultivate childlike humility, and never deceive immature Christians. Walker adapts this admonition for the practice of slavery in America, emphasizing how the system deadens slaveholders' moral and spiritual sensibilities by offering few prohibitions against the abuse and murder of slaves, God's children, in opposition to biblical principles. Walker undermines the colonization plan by exposing the sinister nature of the scheme as a movement that diminishes African American leadership, destroys the black community, and distorts Christian principles. By resisting the ACS's invitation to emigrate, free blacks affirmed their support of their enslaved brethren and their belief that God would provide liberty, justice, and rights for all citizens in a reconstituted, integrated American republic.

## David Walker and Maria W. Stewart
## *The Mosaic Moment for African American Community Building*

A further examination of Walker's and Stewart's appropriations of the Exodus story reveals a practical strategy they employed to impel all African Americans to emulate Moses in establishing strong communities. Both urge their brethren to enact a "Mosaic Moment" in which they choose racial activism rather than pursue worldly pleasure and success. In the preamble to his *Appeal*, Walker provides a comparative analysis of slave systems from antiquity to the early nineteenth century to support his stance that America will suffer divine judgment because its race-based, hereditary slavery practices are more akin to the oppressive institutions associated with the non-Christian slave societies that had experienced devastating losses. In a similar fashion, Stewart relies on the Exodus story to support her assertion that Christian slavers are subject to divine punishment. In her first published writing, *Religion and the Pure Principles of Morality*, she proclaims that "in his own time, he is able to plead our cause against you, and to pour out upon you the ten plagues of Egypt" (19). Later, in "An Address Delivered at the African Masonic Hall, Boston" (1833), she would declare, "But the most high God is still able to subdue the lofty pride of these white Americans, as He was the heart of that ancient rebel" (69). As a female reformer, however, Stewart was not in a position to encourage or sanction insurrection, actions that were outside of the domestic realm that respectable women were expected to occupy and that she had transgressed by becoming a public political speaker. Rather, as a woman of piety who transformed the podium into a pulpit, she directed her readers to depend on divine retribution, not human agency, as their means of deliverance.

Since Walker and Stewart believe white Americans will not show favor to African Americans, they encourage slaves and free blacks to emulate Moses, who rejected Egyptian royalty to share the lot of his enslaved brethren, a decision that led to the Israelites' emancipation. Walker reminds them that Moses "would have become Prince Regent to the Throne. . . . But he had rather suffer shame, with the people of God, than to enjoy pleasures with that wicked people for a season" (13). This choice can be characterized as the Mosaic Moment. Walker exclaims, "O! that the coloured people were long since of Moses' excellent disposition, instead of courting favour with, and telling news and lies to our *natural enemies*, against each other—aiding them to keep their hellish chains of slavery upon us" (13; emphasis in original). Some African Americans—slaves who reported the intimate details of their quarters to their masters, or free blacks who sought favor for themselves without regard for their people—contributed to their community's wretchedness by colluding with the enemy instead of maintaining loyalty to the race. Walker groups race traitors with hypocritical Christians; both are oppressors whose natural inclination is to victimize and destroy African Americans. Thus, he presents American slavery as physical, mental, and spiritual bondage that can only be effaced by a community of Mosaic leaders rather than a singular liberator.

Like Walker, Stewart challenges her readers to embrace their Mosaic moment, but she is more concerned with the majority of free black youth, who follow "the vain bubbles of life with so much eagerness" (8). In *Religion and the Pure Principles of Morality*, Stewart appropriates the Moses story to encourage black youth to become community leaders rather than pleasure seekers, just as Moses had chosen to be the Israelites' leader rather than Egypt's crown prince. She writes, "could I but see young men and maidens turning their feet from impious ways, rather choosing to suffer affliction with the people of God than to enjoy the pleasures of sin for a season" (10). Stewart incorporates the Apostle Paul's declaration of Moses' faith into her admonition to young black Bostonians, enabling them to understand that Israel's revered leader had faced and overcome the temptations of youth (Heb 11:24-26). While Moses resisted the decadence associated with the Egyptian court, black Boston's younger generation struggled to resist the allure of brothels, dance halls, gambling houses, and taverns that nineteenth-century reformers and activists condemned. Stewart presents these enticements as equally attractive for males and females, able to divert both "men and maidens" from becoming Mosaic race leaders. Although she was one of the first black women to speak publicly, she did not envision herself as being the last. By selecting Moses as a role model for black youth, Stewart emphasizes the need for men and women to enter the public sphere and implement community uplift initiatives as well advance the abolition movement.

Stewart soon discovered that enacting a Mosaic moment did not guarantee immediate acceptance or success, particularly for women. In "Mrs. Stewart's Farewell Address to Her Friends in the City of Boston" (1833), she presents a history of female leadership to justify her foray into public political speaking. In explaining her abrupt retirement from the speaker's podium, she explains, "Well was I aware that if I contended boldly for his cause, I must suffer. Yet, I chose rather to suffer affliction with his people, than to enjoy the pleasures of sin for a season" (82). Here Stewart returns to the Mosaic narrative recorded in Hebrews 11, which chronicles the stories of men and women of faith. In so doing, she shifts the focus of Christian leadership from a patriarchal paradigm to a faith-centric calling that any believer could fulfill. Fulfilling this mission would not be easy for anyone, as Stewart indicates, "I must suffer." Gender politics increased the difficulties Stewart and other female reformers experienced in nineteenth-century America.[28] She violated the conventions of a woman's place in the domestic sphere because she believed God called her to public activism. She considered the costs and embraced the challenges associated with public speaking. In so doing, Stewart modeled how nineteenth-century women could speak against injustices and work in their communities, despite the likelihood of rejection, to advance the struggle for freedom and equality.

## The Antislavery and the African American Press
### *Exodus and Activism*

Although Walker and Stewart exemplified the Mosaic life and provided a legacy for future activists, both were criticized for advancing community uplift agendas that were too progressive for their time. During the 1830s, as African American activists shifted their attention to the colored convention movement and increased participation in antislavery organizations, black and antislavery newspaper editors and pamphleteers took a more prominent role in promoting an array of rhetorical strategies drawn from numerous sources to teach readers across the nation how to counter proslavery arguments. This remained a formidable task given the persistence of many leading white theologians and politicians in publicly advocating biblically sanctioned slavery.[29] At times, authors employed comparative analysis effectively to undermine proslavery ideology. At other times, they took a straightforward approach, claiming the authority of biblical scholarship. Finally, some drew direct parallels between slavery in Egypt and the United States to call for a Moses to liberate the enslaved African Americans.

Comparative analysis equipped readers to refute popular proslavery arguments that drew on the Exodus story by emphasizing the inconsistencies between slavery practices recorded in the Bible and those sanctioned in America. The *Colored American* published "Contrast between the Mosaic Servitude and American Slavery" (1837), which had been published in *The Anti-Slavery Record* (1835) and attributed to a *Review of Nevins' Biblical Antiquities*, in which the anonymous author itemizes and compares eight characteristics of laws regulating slavery in America and among the Israelites. The writer's point-by-point analysis of Mosaic specifications that Americans followed clearly indicates that in creating a national Exodus story to recast the United States as God's Israel, Americans appropriated Mosaic law to develop a slave society that breached nearly every regulation regarding biblical servitude. *The Anti-Slavery Record* had presented the material in a double-column format, with Mosaic characteristics on the left side and American on the right, emphasizing the deepening rift between the pro- and antislavery factions, as well as the gap between free and slave populations in America.[30] Yet it also represents a more complex rendering of early nineteenth-century Exodus narratives. At least two other forms of Exodus stories were circulating in America at this time: national narratives by white writers and community-building stories by Afro-Atlantic writers. Indeed, the national stories by white authors were also lurking in the white space and were the most pervasive and influential in charting the course of the nation. However, the racial line separating the American and the Mosaic stories of slavery represents Afro-Atlantic Exodus narratives that could bridge the gap by exposing the degradation of American slavery and emphasizing the slave's humanity.

Newspaper readers also discovered how to adapt classical forms such as the apology in comparative analyses of different types of Exodus stories that could advance the antislavery cause. Writers who advocated this rhetorical strategy embraced the Exodus narrative to challenge claims about the harshness of nineteenth-century slavery and to argue that slaveholders' obstinacy could lead to the destruction of the nation. In "An Apology for Pharaoh" (1827), republished in *Freedom's Journal*, the anonymous author asserts that Egyptian slavery was milder than American slavery, and that Pharaoh had greater justification for enslaving the Israelites than did masters of African American slaves, an argument that David Walker amplified in his *Appeal*, published two years later. By encouraging readers to compare the Hebrews' plight with that of enslaved blacks in America, the writer leads them to see that God had punished a "pagan" ruler for refusing to emancipate his people. In effect, white masters were worse than Egyptian slaveholders, and would certainly be held more accountable for establishing a brutal system of hereditary slavery that fractured families and impaired individuals.

By providing instruction in exegesis, newspaper editors further increased their readers' ability to transform the Exodus story into a rhetorical weapon that undermined proslavery arguments. In "Biblical Exposition, by Thomas Scott" (1839), which had been published in the *Emancipator* and reprinted in the *Colored American*, the author presents Scott's exegesis to condemn slave owners,[31] and quotes Scott's commentary on Scripture regarding Mosaic laws that regulate slavery, including the death penalty for those who steal and enslave a man (Exod 21:16), the death penalty for anyone who steals and sells his brethren (Deut 24:7), and the mandate to protect fugitives and allow them to live wherever they choose (Deut 23:15-16).[32] In effect, Scott intimates that whites and blacks are members of an American family that is being destroyed by the slave trade, just as Cugoano had argued in his eighteenth-century Joseph story. African American activists could thus cite commentary from a well-respected white theologian to undermine the influence of proslavery Christians who refused to follow biblically sound principles to build a nation that protected the rights of all peoples.

Still other newspaper writers took the opposite approach, emphasizing a parallel between slavery in Egypt and America as they urged readers to confront politicians and demand emancipation. Cornish suggests this strategy in a fictionalized "Dialogue between Moses, Pharaoh and Others" (1838) that he reprinted in the *Colored American*. As the conversation progresses, Pharaoh's arguments against emancipating the Israelites reflect those advanced by American presidents: "I did not bring this people hither. I found them in my possession on taking the throne of my father." Like Pharaoh and his advisors, American legislators and proslavery advocates of the 1830s offered excuses to perpetuate slavery, much as they had in the late eighteenth century when Absalom Jones and others confronted them with antislavery petitions. By equating the Egyptians' obstinacy with American slavers' defiance, the writer asserts that Christian slaveholders are waging a losing battle against God. Newspaper editors urged community activists to appeal for the slaves' freedom, confident that God would intervene if government officials did not cooperate, just as he had when Pharaoh denied Moses' petitions for the Israelites' freedom. These Exodus narrative strategies enabled Afro-Atlantic writers and their supporters to move their struggle for recognition as American citizens from the local and regional levels to national forums by way of the lecture hall, conventions, and Congress.

## Proslavery Advocates
### *Exodus Justifies Slavery*

Despite newspaper editors' efforts to incorporate Exodus narratives into their moral suasion strategy, they were unable to check the flow of biblically based proslavery arguments published by prominent white community leaders, particularly theologians and politicians.[33] Disagreements among abolitionists regarding the effectiveness of moral suasion versus militant action limited the stories' effectiveness. In *The South Vindicated from the Treason and Fanaticism of Northern Abolitionists* (1836), prominent South Carolina politician William Drayton epitomizes the biblically based Exodus stories circulated by slavery proponents to counter the effect of antislavery narratives that drew on the same rhetoric. Drayton declares, "The book of Exodus produces many conclusive evidences of the direct sanction of slavery" (90). He cites numerous scriptural passages that slavery advocates repeatedly relied on to identify slaves as property, exclude foreign slaves from the covenant promises, and make slaves of the "strangers" who abided with them. He strengthens his argument by deconstructing biblical injunctions such as the Golden Rule from the New Testament, which abolitionists asserted should compel the master to treat the slave as he wished to be treated (98). Drayton argues that slaves were children under the care of benevolent masters to whom the rule did not apply. His public endorsement of this argument, coupled with his refusal to investigate the impact of the slavery on individuals, helped sustain the system and the proslavery cause.

## Temperance Reformers and Women's Rights Activists
### *Exodus and Community*

As the proslavery and antislavery activists debated the efficacy of Exodus to support their respective causes, contributors to black and antislavery newspapers focused on divine and Mosaic laws governing emancipated Israelites to broaden the scope and appeal of their national community-building efforts. During the Second Great Awakening in the early nineteenth century, church growth sparked the establishment of numerous voluntary societies to spread Christianity and initiate moral reform in the United States and abroad.[34] Temperance advocates also initiated national campaigns that prohibited alcohol consumption and saloon construction, often out of concern regarding the negative impact of alcoholism on marriage and the family.[35] Contributors to newspapers evoked the Exodus narrative to posit America as a promised land where reform, particularly the temperance and women's rights movements, functioned as an essential component of community-building efforts.

Newspaper editors played a critical role in enabling African Americans to construct the Exodus story as a bridge between the racial uplift and temperance movements. The *Colored American* highlighted this connection in "Temperance Celebration" (1837), an article that reports the opening festivities of the Marlboro Hotel in Boston, operated by white American temperance reformer Nathaniel Rogers. As guests offered toasts with sparkling iced water, white American poet John Pierpoint sang an "Ode" in which he transformed Moses into a temperance man who advocated abstinence as the only means for Americans to enter their promised land. Pierpoint argues that God always provided water when he established new communities, beginning with Adam and Eve in the Garden of Eden. To emphasize further the central role of water in building healthy communities, he pairs the Edenic story with the portion of the Exodus narrative in which Moses struck the rock to provide water for the Israelites. By highlighting Moses' role in the miraculous provision of water, Pierpoint intimates that Mosaic leaders' relationship with God gives them access to divine power to supply their brethren's temporal needs. Thus, restaurant owners like Rogers who served water rather than alcohol need not worry about losing business. When Moses provided water for the newly emancipated Israelites, they "rushed" to drink the beverage. Similarly, as African Americans embarked on the road from slave to citizen, they should follow the Israelites' example and patronize restaurants that served water.[36] In so doing, they could distance themselves from a beverage associated with the institution of slavery and invest their resources in businesses that sustained strong communities. Saloons exposed all Americans to a potentially devastating practice, but could be even more destructive for African Americans by distracting them from community uplift, diminishing the ranks of activists, and undermining their ability to attain citizenship.

The Exodus narrative not only provided Mosaic leaders with new strategies for building temperate communities, it also suggested innovative means to acknowledge the contributions of women to the reform movement. The anonymous author of "Right of Petition" (1838), published in the *Colored American*, reminds women of their civic duty to petition in his praise of Representative John Quincy Adams' speech against the gag rules that Congress had imposed to quell the flow of antislavery petitions. Adams believed that everyone, including slaves, had the legal right to lobby Congress. The author reports that Adams chastised Representative Benjamin Chew Howard, a four-term Maryland Democrat, for asserting that "women have no right to petition Congress on political subjects." Adams challenged Howe's stance by recalling the Israelite women's pivotal role in the celebration following their emancipation from slavery.[37] Instead of discouraging the women, Moses allowed the celebration and recorded their action in Exodus to inspire future generations. Adams interpreted the Israelite women's song as a political act that inaugurated the birth of their nation. He illuminated his argument through the retelling of a series of biblical stories in which Hebrew women played major political roles after the Israelites settled in the Promised Land. He included the judge Deborah, Queen Esther, the wealthy and wise Abigail, and the prophetess Huldah.[38] Adams conflated his list of female biblical leaders with the names of women who had distinguished themselves in secular history, particularly from Rome and Sparta, a rhetorical strategy that Maria W. Stewart had employed in her "Farewell Speech." By citing these examples of female leadership, he reinforced the need for women's involvement at all levels of community building, from supportive roles at home to management positions in the government. Some women, like Miriam, who served Israel with her brothers Aaron and Moses, could fill administrative roles alongside male leaders. Others could initiate petition drives to Congress or organize public demonstrations. Like Moses, men had a responsibility to affirm women's participation and ensure the preservation of their collective history in order to inspire young men and women to contribute to African Americans' community-building efforts.

Women also took a leading role in encouraging members of their sex to be involved in the political process. In "Appeal to Christian Women of the South" (1836), white abolitionist Angelina E. Grimké addresses Southern women directly, linking the story of Esther to the narrative of Exodus to compel her spiritual sisters in the South to become liberators of enslaved and oppressed African Americans. She urged them to "send petitions up to their different legislatures, . . . to abolish the institution of slavery; no longer to subject *woman* to the scourge and the chain, to mental darkness and moral degradation; . . . no longer reduce *American citizens* to the abject condition of *slaves*, of 'chattels personal;' no longer to barter the *image of God* in human shambles for corruptible things such as silver and gold" (25–26; emphasis in original). Grimké lends credence to her appeal by reminding her readers of her affinity with them both as a woman who was born into Charleston's prominent slaveholding Grimké family and as a member of the community of Christian believers who is following biblical admonition to "speak those *truths in love*"[39] (1; emphasis in original). Grimké's truths focus on the veracity of biblical arguments for slavery, and she offers Southern Christian women biblical exegesis that undermines proslavery arguments. After citing the creation of man and his God-given dominion over animals to support the equality of the human species and insisting that the Curse of Canaan was limited to the Canaanites, Grimké explores the practice of slavery among the Israelites. She then lists the six different ways Israelites could become slaves and asks her readers to conduct a comparative analysis of Hebrew and American slavery to discern if the systems are equivalent, just as the author had modeled in "Contrast between the Mosaic Servitude and American Slavery." In so doing, she seeks to empower Southern women by insisting that they examine the evidence for themselves instead of accepting the dogmas disseminated by proslavery ministers and advocates. To facilitate their study, Grimké analyzes the points, interjecting "No!" after each type of servitude except the regulation that focuses on fathers selling their daughters into slavery: "A father might sell his children as servants, i.e. his *daughters*, in which circumstance it was understood the daughter was to be the wife or daughter-in-law of the man who bought her, and the *father* received the price. In other words, Jewish women were sold as *white women* were in the first settlement of Virginia—as *wives, not* as slaves. Ex. xxi, 7" (5; emphasis in original). Here Grimké links Mosaic law to colonial regulations to draw a stark contrast between arranged marriages and human trafficking of slaveholders' daughters. Grimké creates a fissure in her Exodus narrative by framing her appeal to Southern women with the story of Esther, the Hebrew orphan who became the Queen of Persia. When the Jews were threatened with annihilation, Esther's uncle Mordecai urged her to petition the king on behalf of her people. She responded, "and so will I go in unto the king, which is *not* according to law, and if I perish, I perish" [Esth 4:16] (25). By inviting Southern women to see themselves as Esther, Grimké takes the role of a Mordecai in acknowledging their position as the "weaker sex" in society. Yet she asks them to come to the aid of the slave as women of faith who exhibit a willingness to break the law and to die for the cause of abolition. In effect, she reconfigures the South as a slave society facing destruction, which can be averted only through the direct intervention of white Southern Christian women.

## Conclusion

In the early nineteenth century, an increasing number of African American activists and their supporters appropriated specific portions of the Exodus narrative to develop community-building strategies for African Americans within America and abroad. Despite its inspirational nature, however, the Exodus story did not enable them to accomplish their goals between 1800 and 1840. Revolts failed. Neither America, Africa, nor Haiti became a promised land. Slavery flourished and the oppression of African Americans increased. While Exodus-inspired proslavery rhetoric proliferated and national Exodus narratives helped to stabilize and enlarge the republic for many white citizens, Afro-Atlantic Exodus narratives remained fragmented and unfulfilled. Nevertheless, Exodus stories by black writers and their supporters nurtured existing communities, inspired attempts to create new communities in the African Diaspora, offered innovative rhetorical strategies to combat slavery and oppression, and continued to sustain the prolonged, difficult battle for civil liberties.

CHAPTER THREE

# Exodus in the Era of Manifest Destiny (1840–1861)

*We do but follow out our destiny,*
*as did the Ancient Israelite—and strive,*
*Unconscious that we work at His decree,*
*By Whom alone we triumph as we live!*

—William Gilmore Simms, "Progress in America"

*We had well find fault with the children of Jacob, for leaving Egypt, as the colored Americans, for leaving the hell of the continent and the piety of demons.*

—"The Free People's Hate of the People Enslaved"

*If Moses authorized slavery, then he also authorized polygamy, concubinage, and divorce; none of which do we now believe to be right.*

—"Bishop Hopkins on Slavery"

*All three, polygamy, divorce and slavery, were sanctioned by the law of Moses. But under the gospel, slavery has been sanctioned in the church, while polygamy and divorce have been excluded from the church.*

—Thornton Stringfellow, "The Bible Argument; or, Slavery in the Light of Divine Revelation"

By 1840 nearly two and one-half million African Americans suffered in slavery, while more than three hundred thousand free blacks languished under laws that severely restricted their liberty.[1] African American leaders and their supporters maintained their demands for freedom, while the majority of white politicians remained invested in strengthening the national economy through Southern slavery, Northern industrialization, and westward expansion rather than joining the movement for emancipation and equality. National discourse continued to posit the United States as a promised land. Yet as Congress persisted in enacting legislation that regulated rather than eliminated slavery, it seemed to African Americans that the United States was Egypt.

During the 1850s, congressional legislation and scientific racism initiated serious setbacks in racial uplift efforts that reignited the Exodus-inspired integration versus emigration debate within the African American activist community. The revised 1850 Fugitive Slave Act demanded that citizens capture and return runaway slaves. The Kansas-Nebraska Act of 1854 undermined the gains made by free-state advocates by forcing residents of new territories to determine whether to enter the union as a slave or free state. The US Supreme Court's *Dred Scott* decision of 1857 denied enslaved African Americans citizenship. Racist sentiments published in books such as George R. Gliddon and Josiah C. Nott's *Types of Mankind: or, Ethnological Researches* (1854) offered "scientific" justification for racial hierarchies that strengthened black codes and quashed African Americans' hopes for equality. In effect, these developments reaffirmed the nation's status as Egypt by stripping African Americans of their rights and humanity, subjecting the entire community to slavery.

In search of promised lands, African American authors and their supporters of this period, like their predecessors, sustained the momentum of the racial uplift movement by relying on a variety of traditional and innovative rhetorical strategies to decenter national Exodus stories. Some writers evoked episodes in the Exodus narrative to anoint themselves and others as Moses figures, or to transform Mosaic leaders into multifaceted sacred heroes who would identify African Americans as God's people, initiate emigration enterprises, spearhead antislavery efforts, justify slave revolts, or warn white Americans of divine punishment for enslaving African Americans. Many authors conflated the language of Exodus with secular/republican discourse to present Mosaic leaders as civic-minded revolutionaries who demanded emancipation, claimed citizenship, supported migration, or planned insurrections.

The location of the promised land was also on the minds of these authors. In their Exodus stories, some looked for a Moses who would transform the United States or Canada into African Americans' Canaan. Others set their sights on homes in a black Atlantic Diaspora, including Central and South America, Haiti, and Africa, where they hoped to settle among people who abhorred slavery. Still other writers viewed the United States as simultaneously Egypt and promised land because slavery and discriminatory laws constrained the African American experience in the nation. Finally, a few authors created fissures in this era's dominant Mosaic narratives by appropriating the Joseph and Joshua stories to emphasize militant action, such as a massive Southern slave revolt, and a neglected populace, such as free black Northern laborers, which abolitionists had ignored. Ultimately, these Afro-Atlantic Exodus narratives represent the varied, persistent attempts of African Americans and their supporters to achieve freedom and equality for the African American community, efforts that remained unfulfilled yet thrust the nation to the brink of war over states' rights and slavery.

## White American Writers
### *Founding Fathers as Exodus Heroes*

While black activists appropriated various Exodus narratives to implement their racial uplift initiatives during the 1840s and 1850s, white writers embraced the biblical story to characterize white Americans as a superior race destined to enjoy civil and religious liberty in their own homeland and spread democracy into western territories. Editors of national periodicals affirmed and disseminated patriotic sentiments that posited pivotal moments in the young republic's history through the lens of Exodus. For example, in "American Puritanism" (1843), an anonymous writer for the *New Englander and Yale Review* characterizes separatist English minister John Robinson as a Moses who was "not permitted to enter with [the Puritans into] the promised land," for Robinson died before he realized his desire to emigrate to America (357–58). In a review of the *Cyclopedia of American Literature* (1856) published in *Putnam's Monthly Magazine*, another anonymous author associates the genesis of American literature with the arrival of the Pilgrims, who "brought the love of learning, with their household treasures, to the promised land of religion and freedom" and "handled the pen with no less facility than the axe and the musket" (170). Editors affirmed the continued efficacy of Exodus for America's national identity by highlighting its relevance to the War of Independence. In "Memoirs of Generals Lee, Gates, Stephen, and Darke" (1858), published in *Harper's New Monthly Magazine*, an anonymous author recounts the exploits of major generals who served in the Continental Army during the American Revolution. He describes soldiers who opposed General George Washington as disobedient Israelites who rejected their "true chief" during their wilderness journey and favored General Horatio Gates to "lead them by a short and pleasant route into the Promised Land," a reference to Gates' decision to take a direct route through Loyalist territory to a disastrous defeat at Camden, South Carolina (506). In so doing, the article's author establishes Washington as Moses and situates the American Revolution in the wilderness rather than Egypt, affirming the American colonists' self-liberation from English rule but identifying the internal struggles for leadership as the colonial army's greatest threat. By sustaining the circulation of national Exodus stories to construct a history for the young republic, periodical editors encouraged their readers to continue identifying with a biblical narrative that could empower them to control their own destiny with the guidance of Mosaic leaders and the development of national literature. Yet these official stories failed to acknowledge the presence of Afro-Atlantic people or other marginalized groups such as Native Americans within the United States or the importance of their contributions to the growth from thirteen colonies to an independent nation.

## Henry Box Brown
## *An Unwilling Moses*

By the 1830s, continued oppression and marginalization led African American activists to initiate their own revolution by declaring independence from white abolitionists and reformers through the implementation of their own radical racial uplift efforts. Some anointed themselves or others as Moses figures who would emancipate slaves and settle African Americans in promised lands within and without the United States. They include Henry Highland Garnet, who eulogized David Walker as a Moses-David figure in "Sketch of the Life and Character of David Walker" (1848) and encouraged the slaves to enact Mosaic principles in demanding pay for labor in *Address to the Slaves of the United States of America* (1843). Others, such as Ebenezer James, Frederick Douglass, and Osborne Anderson, focused on various types of Mosaic leadership. In his letter to the *North Star* (1849), white Quaker abolitionist James links the Exodus story to Old Testament prophecy to create a jeremiad that characterizes the North as Egypt and urges Douglass to become a Moses for enslaved blacks. Douglass reveals how he enacted various Moses roles in the *Narrative of the Life of Frederick Douglass, an American Slave, Written by Himself* (1845), "What to the Slave Is the Fourth of July?" (1852), and *My Bondage and My Freedom* (1855). In *A Voice from Harper's Ferry: A Narrative of Events at Harper's Ferry* (1861), African American activist Anderson places John Brown's raid on Harpers Ferry within the contexts of Exodus and historical revolutions to justify Brown's reliance on violence to elevate and emancipate enslaved African Americans.[2] These competing, conflicting Exodus narratives widened the rifts within the activist community and encouraged the search for a leader who could achieve the goal of emancipation and equality they all desired.

*Resurrection of Henry Box Brown at Philadelphia*

Henry Box Brown's daring escape in a crate via express railway from Richmond, Virginia, to Philadelphia brought him to the attention of abolitionists who were searching for a Moses figure with national appeal. Brown soon joined the antislavery circuit and, after the enactment of the 1850 Fugitive Slave Act, followed the path of other popular fugitive slaves, including William Wells Brown and William and Ellen Craft, who sought refuge in England, where they published narratives and won more acclaim. Instead of settling into the conventional role of lecturer, however, Brown created a variety show that featured performances of slave songs, reenactments of his journey to Philadelphia, and viewings of his "Mirror of Slavery," a moving scroll of paintings depicting the history of servitude through the experiences of a "Nubian family" forced into slavery in Africa and brought to the United States, as well as the story of Brown's escape from slavery.[3] He reportedly developed a rather sophisticated educational, entertaining, and even subversive program, but his showman style troubled the British abolitionist community, particularly after he staged a reenactment of his railroad journey.

In the introduction to the second edition of Brown's *Narrative* (1851), Thomas Gardiner Lee, a British minister and reformer, appropriates the

Exodus story to encourage readers see enslaved African Americans as Israelites and to force the independent-minded Brown into the traditional role of Moses, more in keeping with the image of the godly, conservative activist that English abolitionists had in mind.[4] Lee introduces Brown as a potential Moses figure by turning his readers' attention to the plight of the Israelites in Egypt. He writes,

> [W]hen we consider that Great Being who beheld the Israelites in their captivity, and beholding, came down to deliver them is still the same; have we not reason to believe that he will in his Providence raise up another Moses, to guide the now enslaved sons of Ham to the privileges which humanity, irrespective of colour or clime, is always at liberty to demand. (6)

As God had sent Moses to emancipate the Israelites, Lee believes God will send a pious Moses to guide enslaved African Americans to freedom. Like Absalom Jones, who assured his congregation that God had seen the oppression of enslaved Africans and impressed Congress and the British Parliament to outlaw the international slave trade, Lee argues that God is aware of the slaves' suffering and will emancipate them. Lee does not simply draw a parallel between the experiences of enslaved Israelites and African Americans, however. He refutes the commonly held belief that slaves were cursed descendants of Ham by declaring that blacks are members of the human family, and all human beings—African Americans, Englishmen, and Americans—have the right to demand liberty. When human beings enslave others, God always sends a deliverer.

Numerous Moses figures had stepped forward to demand freedom for slaves, employing every means from petitions to revolt. Rather than blindly accept anointed or self-appointed Moses figures, however, Lee encourages readers to consider Brown's escape as a sign that the fugitive slave could be a divinely appointed Moses. He suggests, "It may be that the subject of the following narrative has a mission from God to the human family. Certainly the deliverance of Moses, from destruction on the Nile, was scarcely more marvelous than was the deliverance of Mr. Henry Box Brown from the horrors of slavery" (7). Although Moses' rescue from an ark and Brown's ingenious escape in a crate may appear similar and divinely appointed, Lee's comparison strips Brown of human agency. The biblical Moses was dependent on his mother, Jochebed, who created his ark; his sister, Miriam, who watched over him as the ark floated in the river; and the Egyptian princess who rescued and named him and groomed him for the Egyptian throne. In contrast, Brown left his wife and children in the South, shipped himself north in a crate, adopted the name Henry Box Brown, and joined the antislavery movement, not as the slaves' deliverer but as a shrewd businessman. By placing Brown in an ark, Lee recasts the autonomous abolitionist as a dependent baby Moses who must rely on the British Antislavery Society, which "adopted" Brown, established him in a foreign country, named him "Moses," and groomed him to be his people's deliverer.

By the time Lee wrote his introduction to the *Narrative*, however, Brown had been touring with his "Mirror of Slavery" panorama and giving lectures for six months. Although Brown was devoted to abolition, he preferred crowded amusement halls to the staid antislavery lecture venues. Brown soon learned that the British Antislavery Society was as conservative as its American counterparts, with strict ideas about how their protégés should conduct themselves.[5] Brown refused to be contained. Instead of becoming Moses, he exercised his autonomy by touring on his own, rejecting offers to purchase and bring his family to England, and marrying an Englishwoman. When he returned to the United States after the Civil War, he arrived as Professor H. Box Brown, the magician.[6]

## Frances E. W. Harper
## *The Mosaic Model for African American Citizenship*

In contrast to Lee and other abolitionists who anointed Moses figures to liberate enslaved African Americans, some activists advocated the Mosaic Moment, when individuals chose community activism rather than the pursuit of personal pleasure. In her influential essay "Our Greatest Want" (1859), published in the *Anglo-African Magazine*, Frances E. W. Harper shifts the focus of the activist community from the search for singular, patriarchal leadership to the necessity of collective individualism by encouraging each reader to experience a Mosaic Moment that would weaken the South economically, politically, socially, and religiously. Although many Mosaic figures had worked to free the slaves, Harper questions whether a Mosaic leader existed: "We have millions of our race in the prison house of slavery, but have we yet a single Moses in freedom. And if we had, who among us would be led by him?" (160). Harper issues her plea despite the activism of John Brown, Martin Delany, Frederick Douglass, Henry Highland Garnet, William Lloyd Garrison, and David Walker, as well as Harriet Tubman, who had functioned as Moses figures for African Americans. None of these influential activists had garnered support for a national antislavery movement, however. With the enactment of the 1850 Compromise, the political landscape shifted dramatically, casting all African Americans as potential fugitive slaves, affirming the continued existence of slavery in new western territories, and exacerbating internal conflicts that fractured fragile coalitions brokered by black and white activists who advocated competing agendas for the advancement of the cause.

To resolve these challenges, Harper lauds Moses as Americans' consummate role model for personal and community activism. She writes, "He is the first disunionist we read of in the Jewish Scriptures. The magnificence of Pharaoh's throne loomed up before his vision, its oriental splendors glittered before his eyes; but he turned from them all and chose rather to suffer with the enslaved, than rejoice with the free. He would have no union with the slave power of Egypt" (160).[7] By characterizing Moses as a "disunionist," Harper emphasizes his refusal to embark on a path that would force him into a sociopolitical alliance with Egyptian taskmasters that required a repudiation of his faith. In so doing, she affiliates herself with the disunion ideology advocated by Garrison and other abolitionists who believed the North should sever itself from the South and establish an independent nation.[8] Harper's evocation of the Moses narrative adds a spiritual dimension to this approach, however. Rather than look for a Moses to emancipate the slaves or initiate reforms, Harper directs her readers to emulate Moses' act of faith by abstaining from affiliations with slavers. In 1856 African American activist Robert Purvis had enacted a Mosaic Moment in publicly identifying himself as a "Disunion Abolitionist" and declaring, "'No Union with Slaveholders is our Motto.' . . . Not simply politically and religiously should we dissever ourselves from them, but commercially and socially."[9] Such commitments could ultimately lead to direct engagement with enslaved African Americans, for Moses not only gave up access to Pharaoh's court, but he launched his abolition initiative from within the Israelite community and devoted the remainder of his life to their welfare.

Harper broadens her appeal by emphasizing similarities between Moses' choice and the choices faced by Americans, tempted to collude with the enemy under the guise of preserving the union. She writes,

> When we have a race of men whom this blood stained government cannot tempt or flatter, who would sternly refuse every office in the nation's gift, from a president down to a tide-waiter,[10] until she shook her hands from complicity in the guilt of cradle plundering and man stealing, then for us the foundations of an historic character will have been laid. (160)

Harper's depiction of a "blood stained government" conjures images of a tyrannical regime rather than a democratic republic. By singling out the president and a tidewaiter, occupations unavailable to African Americans in the mid-nineteenth century, Harper stresses the need for influential white

Americans to embrace the Mosaic Moment. In refusing to associate with slavery proponents and racist officials or to patronize businesses that relied on slave labor, African Americans could develop a formidable network of Mosaic citizens whose collective impact would undermine the viability of the institution of slavery and force its demise.

### Harriet Wilson
### *African American Joseph in Egypt, North*

Although Moses remained the most popular figure in African American and national Exodus stories, various activists, politicians, and religious leaders turned to the Joseph story during the early nineteenth century in developing standards of perseverance, faith, and ingenuity for leaders and reformers. Seeking to capitalize on the story's popularity, Virginia governor Henry A. Wise claimed that his political enemies had treated him like a Joseph: "The Reubens have tried to sell me into Egypt for my dreaming."[11] Numerous newspaper editors quickly criticized Wise for incorrectly characterizing his foes as Reuben, the sibling who had vainly attempted to protect Joseph from his brothers' jealous wrath. Other writers were more successful in their appropriations of the story, referencing Joseph in calls for a deliverer out of the enslaved African American community or in debates that questioned the veracity or affirmed the validity of biblically based proslavery arguments. One respected organization, the influential American Sunday School Union, abandoned its affirmation of the story's indictment of American slavery in its book series *Jacob and His Sons* (1832), compelling black abolitionist and fugitive slave William Wells Brown to advocate the withdrawal of financial support for the organization.[12] Perhaps the most influential Joseph reference appeared that same year in Harriet Beecher Stowe's *Uncle Tom's Cabin*, when the narrator informs readers that the protagonist "often compared his unfortunate lot, in the bondage into which he was cast, with that of Joseph in Egypt."[13]

The Joseph story, a riveting account of betrayal, slavery, redemption, and restoration, compellingly reflected the plight of slaves as well as the dreams of free blacks who believed a better day would come for their posterity. When introducing its new correspondent, African American Attorney George B. Vashon, the *Frederick Douglass' Paper* lauded the young man's father, prosperous Pittsburgh bathhouse owner and barber John B. Vashon, as a Joseph because he had provided a college education for his son, hoping such preparation would enable the young man to escape the drudgery of manual labor. The writer asserts, "This work requires something of that faith, by which Joseph foresaw the exodus of Israel out of Egypt, and gave commandment concerning his bones."[14] In the biblical Exodus story, Joseph instructed the Israelites to carry his remains with them when they began their journey from Egypt to Canaan. Vashon exercised faith by preparing his son for a career in a promised land of opportunity that he, like Joseph, could only imagine. By choosing a career in law, the young Vashon equipped himself with the tools he would need to challenge the social and legal restrictions that impeded the fulfillment of his father's wishes as well as his own dreams for success.

The Joseph narrative also appealed to the often-overlooked free black indentured servants, particularly in Northern abolitionist strongholds, where contract labor was still a common practice in the nineteenth century. Domestic work remained a central component of this system of servitude, disproportionately affecting African American women like Harriet E. Wilson. After surviving twelve years of indentured servitude in Milford, New Hampshire, Wilson published *Our Nig; or, Sketches of the Life of a Free Black* (1859), a fictionalized account of her life through the eyes of Frado, a biracial young woman who is deserted, exploited, and ignored by both family and community. Wilson adapts the conventions of popular genres—autobiography, sentimental novel, and slave narrative—in this experimental book, whose sales she hoped would lift her out of poverty.[15] She links the memory of the imprisoned, forgotten Joseph to the reality of her experience as an oppressed, neglected indentured servant to position the North as Egypt, expose abolitionists as hypocrites, and re-envision African Americans as primary arbiters in preserving their history.

Wilson's appropriation of the Joseph story set in the slave society of Egypt compels readers to reconsider their perception of the North as free territory for African Americans. In the final sentence of the last chapter of *Our Nig*, she declares, "Frado has passed from [the Bellmonts'] memories, as Joseph from the butler's" (72). In the biblical narrative, Joseph was sold into slavery in Egypt, where he labored in Potiphar's household. After being falsely accused of raping his master's wife, he was imprisoned for about two years, languishing longer because the butler, who regained his position in accordance with Joseph's interpretation of a dream, forgot to mention his benefactor to Pharaoh.[16] The Joseph story enables Wilson to remember and reimagine her life as part of sacred and secular history as she seeks to make herself a visible and vital member of a Christian community that disparages her because of its low perception of her domestic labor and race. The North had become Egypt for free blacks in the 1820s, long before the passage of the 1850 Fugitive Slave Act. Although she casts the Bellmonts, the prominent white family for whom she worked, as the butler in Joseph's story, she gives them the authority of Egyptian taskmasters who force her to experience years of slavelike servitude.

Wilson's characterization of herself as Joseph not only positions the Bellmonts as her butler-taskmasters, but it recasts her mother, Mag, as Joseph's brothers, who betray their relative into servitude, and Northern abolitionists as the butler who forgets his fellow prisoner. In the preface to *Our Nig*, Wilson writes that she was "deserted by kindred." Her mother, whose options are limited by white America's adoption of Victorian ideals regarding virtuous womanhood, abandons her daughter to servitude with the Bellmonts. Wilson suffers the additional indignity of betrayal by abolitionists who profess commitment to racial uplift. Like the butler who was released from prison and forgot Joseph, some activists had escaped the drudgery of day labor or domestic work but neglected those left behind. The "good anti-slavery friends at home," who devoted themselves to liberating slaves while ignoring oppressed free black indentured servants, did not fully understand the necessity of addressing racism in the North, particularly its effect on female domestics. Wilson's experience revealed that the absence of slavery did not engender equal opportunities for African Americans. She published her story in part to convince free black Northerners to demand more equitable labor conditions, and to convince abolitionists that the future of the race was inextricably linked both to the abolition of slavery and to the elevation of impoverished free blacks.

Bereft of benefactors, Wilson creates a Joseph narrative that stresses her reliance on human agency, rather than Providence, to release herself from the prison of poverty by publishing a book that privileges her version of her experience with the Bellmonts. She promises readers that "she will never cease to track them until beyond mortal vision" (72). Whereas Joseph interprets dreams, Wilson claims the ability to keep the Bellmonts under surveillance until their deaths. After she fulfills her service contract, she struggles to release herself from the prison of poverty resulting from years of abuse and overwork. By immortalizing the Bellmonts' misdeeds in *Our Nig*, Wilson prevents them from reclaiming a place of honor in their community, as the butler was able to do after he recommended Joseph as a reliable interpreter of Pharaoh's dreams. Wilson encourages her community to read, remember, and retell the story of an indentured servant who not only survives, but confronts and exposes her oppressors, and then sells hair tonics to support herself and her child—a direct challenge to prevailing notions of slothful and idle free black domestics.

## Exodus and Manifest Destiny
### *The West for Whites, Africa for Blacks*

While African American authors such as Wilson debated the best strategies to address worsening conditions for both enslaved and free blacks, US government officials focused on westward expansion. This Manifest Destiny–inspired enlargement of the nation's borders nurtured white Americans' visions of their homeland as Canaan. In the mid-nineteenth century, editors of prominent periodicals played a central role in circulating national Exodus stories that established Southern colonies and western territories as extensions of the Pilgrims' promised land. A review of Georgia Historical Society cofounder William Bacon Stevens' *A History of Georgia, from Its First Discovery by Europeans to the Adoption of the Present Constitution* (1848), published in the popular literary magazine the *North American Review*, epitomizes this strategy. The reviewer highlights Stevens' assertion that the "Garden of Georgia" rivaled the attractiveness of Virginia and South Carolina. According to Stevens, "[James] Oglethorpe, in particular, was quite enthusiastic in his description of the climate, soil, production, and beauties of this American Canaan."[17] Stevens conflates images of the Garden of Eden with the Promised Land to create a perfect setting for the emergence of the American republic. Two years later *Harper's Monthly Magazine* published an article in which white editor and illustrator Benson J. Lossing describes Daniel Boone as a Moses figure,[18] gazing from a mountaintop to survey land that would become Kentucky: "That eminence was the Pisgah from which those pioneers of civilization looked into the glorious promised land."[19] By situating Boone on Mount Pisgah, where God allowed Moses to view the Promised Land he was forbidden to enter, Lossing affirms a narrative of settlement and expansion of an American Canaan that will continue long after Boone's exploration and life have ended.

Such recollections of the providential establishment of colonies in the New World encouraged white Americans to continue the physical, ideological, and rhetorical work of converting unexplored western territories into their promised land.[20] To commemorate the annexation of Texas into the Union in 1845, the highly respected political-literary monthly the *United States Magazine and Democratic Review* published William Gilmore Simms' "Progress in America: Or, a Speech in Sonnets, on Great Britain and the United States; Not Delivered Either in Parliament or Congress" (1846). Simms, a white South Carolinian politican and writer who advocated the annexation of Texas, equates the United States' acquisition of Texas with the Israelites' conquest of the Promised Land:

> We do but follow out our destiny
> As did the Ancient Israelite—and strive,
> Unconscious that we work at His decree,
> By Whom alone we triumph as we live! (92)

By dissociating his view of the providential establishment of an American promised land from British-American disputes over western territories, Simms affirms US citizens' right to enact westward expansion as the God-ordained route to prosperity. The anonymous author of a review published in the *North American Review* of Thomas Falconer's *The Oregon Question; or, a Statement of the British Claims to the Oregon Territory, in Opposition to the Pretensions of the Government of the United States of America* (1846) adopts a similar stance in describing Oregon Territory as the "promised land" for white settlers (228). Expansionists were determined to limit opportunities for prosperity to white Americans, however. When Texas became a state, its population included thirty thousand enslaved African Americans. In 1849, ten years before Oregon entered the Union in 1859, its white residents enacted the Oregon Exclusion Law, A Bill to Prevent Negroes and Mulattoes from Coming to, or Residing in Oregon. The law allowed blacks who lived in the territory to remain, but banned new black emigrants, except those accompanying whites on business. In 1844, Oregon's provisional government had outlawed slavery but forced African Americans to leave the territory or face punishment.[21]

The focus of the debate regarding the African American presence in the West eventually shifted back to colonization as a means to settle both the enslaved and free black populations in a promised land outside of America. *Godey's Ladies Journal* editor Sarah J. Hale helped popularize this plan through the publication of her novel *Liberia: or, Mr. Peyton's Experiments* (1853), in which she characterizes former slaves as unfit freedmen who can only find happiness through emigration to Liberia. Thomas Bangs Thorpe also identifies Africa as African Americans' Canaan in his novel *The Master's House; or, Scenes Descriptive of Southern Life* (1854), in which a white Southern preacher offers his vision of an exodus through the Atlantic Ocean for the sons of Ham.[22] Additionally, prominent politicians such as Abraham Lincoln recalled the success of early colonization efforts to support the revival of the practice of resettling African Americans in Africa. In his eulogy of influential statesman Henry Clay (1852), Lincoln invokes the Exodus narrative to portray the founder of the American Colonization Society as a leader who could enable the nation to avert the fate of Egyptian slavers: "Pharaoh's country was cursed with plagues, and his hosts were drowned in the Red Sea for striving to retain a captive people who had already served them more than four hundred years. May like disasters never befall us!" (271). He conveys a sense of the nation's danger in enslaving African Americans then offers a means of averting destruction, "If as the friends of colonization hope, the present and coming generations of our countrymen shall, by any means, succeed in freeing our land from the dangerous presence of slavery; and, at the same time in restoring a captive people to their long-lost father-land, with bright prospects for the future" (271). Lincoln inverts the national Exodus narrative by casting American slaveholders as Egyptians, enslaved African Americans as Israelites, and Africa as Canaan—for people of African descent. Within a decade, however, the Civil War would lead some activists to characterize Lincoln as a Pharaoh presiding over a plague-infested American Egypt whose army suffered devasting losses because of the nation's refusal to liberate enslaved African Americans.

## James T. Holly
## *Haitian Canaan*

The Fugitive Slave Act of 1850 convinced many African Americans to support activists who advocated emigration to foreign promised lands. Emigration proponents organized a series of conventions to discuss and develop their plans, exposing a major rift within the black activist community regarding the best means to achieve civil liberties. Frederick Douglass, for example, favored the continuance of struggle within the United States, while black emigrationist and poet James M. Whitfield insisted that it was "the destiny of the Negro, to develop a higher order of civilization and Christianity than the world has yet seen. I also consider it part of his 'manifest destiny' to possess all the tropical regions of this continent, with the adjacent islands."[23] The resulting efforts by a variety of Northern activists sparked a spate of competing Exodus narratives, notably Mary Ann Shadd's *A Plea for Emigration; or, Notes of Canada West* (1852) and Martin R. Delany's *The Condition, Elevation, Emigration, and Destiny of the Colored People of the United States* (1852), which presented Africa, Canada, Central America, and the Caribbean as promised lands that offered civil rights, economic opportunities, and safe homes. Influential white writers such as Harriet Beecher Stowe in *Uncle Tom's Cabin* (1852) complicated this debate by depicting the North and Canada as optimal promised lands for fugitive slaves, and Africa as a site for Christianizing and colonizing people of African descent.

The mounting challenges of assimilation into Canada, coupled with nationalistic sentiments stoked by continued admiration for the successful Haitian Revolution, compelled some black emigrationists to shift their sights

*James Theodore Holly, Episcopal minister and emigrationist*

to the tropical isles. Episcopal minister and abolitionist James Theodore Holly epitomized this transition, for he had advocated colonization in Liberia and migration to Canada before promoting settlement in the West Indies.

After obtaining an education in Washington City (now the District of Columbia) and New York and then finding few opportunities for advanced academics or employment, Holly flirted with colonization before he wrote letters to Henry Bibb's Canadian newspaper *Voice of the Fugitive* in support of emigration to Canada. He soon joined Bibb in the Canadian West, where he helped to publish the *Voice of the Fugitive*, develop the Refugee Home Society, and promote emigration.[24] By the mid-1850s, Holly had become an Episcopal priest and selected Haiti as the ideal destination for black emigrants because slaves had "sprung by their own efforts, and inherent energies from their brutalized condition, into the manly status of independent, self-respecting freemen at one gigantic bound; and thus took their place at once, side by side with nations whose sovereignty had been the mature growth of ages of human progress" (185). After failing to gain authorization from the Episcopal Church to become a missionary to Haiti, he worked directly with the Haitian government and its agents to recruit emigrants.[25]

In "Thoughts on Hayti" (1859), a six-part series of articles published in the *Anglo-African Magazine*, Holly appropriates the language of Exodus to introduce a Pan-African vision of Haitian emigration as the spiritually ordained means for restoring self-identity in African Americans. Holly characterizes the biblical Exodus as emigration to infuse the miraculous liberation with black nationalist yearnings. He writes,

> Emigration alone . . . is God's divinely appointed method of national regeneration, if we be allowed to deduce a legitimate conclusion from the great deliverance, that He effected for his people Israel, when He led them forth from Egyptian bondage, with a high hand and an outstretched arm. (241)

Although Holly describes emigration as a spiritual quest, he invites readers to apply deductive reasoning in constructing a parallel between the means by which a community of slaves became the nation of Israel and the means by which enslaved African Americans could attain freedom and develop a national identity. By equating emigration with nationalism, Holly rejects abolition and assimilation as the most effective racial uplift strategy and the United States as African Americans' rightful homeland.

Emigration is an essential step in the regeneration process for Holly because it protects African Americans from the divine judgments that Exodus and other biblical narratives portend for nations like America because of the sin of slavery. He believes America had tested the limits of divine patience through its failure to uphold the Declaration of Independence and Constitution for three generations.[26] Holly constructs a black jeremiad by pairing the story of Exodus with a well-known biblical narrative to emphasize the surety of destruction for evildoers and a means of preservation and prosperity for the righteous. He asserts that African Americans

> must escape as Lot . . . lest like the wife of Lot, they should be turned into signal monuments of Divine vengeance; or like that Slavish generation of Israelites, who hankered after the flesh pots of Egypt, be doomed to wander in the wilderness of darkness and error until they are all slain by the avenging hand of God, with but two left to bear witness that such a degenerate race ever existed. (242)

Holly conflates the story of the Israelites' desire for the meat of Egypt rather than manna from heaven with that of their punishment of wandering forty years in the wilderness for accepting the ten spies' report that the Promised Land could not be conquered. He cites biblical narratives, like the story of Lot's wife, who was turned into a pillar of salt when she defied the angel's command not to look back on her home in Sodom as her family escaped the city's destruction, as evidence of the surety of divine justice for disobedience. By juxtaposing unrepentant, slaveholding America with defiant, disobedient biblical figures, Holly suggests that African Americans risk complicity through their close proximity to slavers. Thus, disassociation from evildoers rather than separation of the races is the motivation for emigration and national restoration.

Emigration to Haiti did not guarantee nationhood, however. The émigrés could fail if they repeated the mistakes the Jews made after entering Canaan. Holly argues, "The Jews being thus without national prestige in the world, have been the scorn and derision of all the nations of the earth" (365). After the conquest of Canaan, the Israelites experienced prosperity and blessings, but disobedience of God's commands led to oppression and captivity. Holly admonishes African Americans to avoid the Israelites' fate by obeying God's call to emigrate to Haiti and develop "a *strong, powerful, enlightened and progressive negro nationality, equal to the demands of the nineteenth century, and capable of commanding the respect of all the nations of the earth*" (365; emphasis in original). Holly introduces the concept of a "New Negro" long before Sutton Griggs, Alain Locke, and other early twentieth-century African American writers and intellectuals adopted the term. He envisions a black nation whose military, political, and intellectual prowess would earn African Americans the esteem they could never receive in the United States, despite their personal and professional accomplishments and their contributions to the nation's development and success.

Few African Americans heeded Holly's call in "Thoughts on Hayti." Dissuaded by the difficulties of adjusting to a tropical climate, making a living in an agricultural economy, and abandoning their enslaved brethren, most remained in the United States or relocated to Canada. Emigration to Haiti did not bring the results Holly expected. Many of the emigrants returned to the United States after fulfilling their four-month commitment to live and work on the island, and most of the members of Holly's extended family died shortly after their arrival in Haiti. Sorrow did not break his commitment to emigration, however. Although his dream of a community of African American expatriates with a new Negro identity never materialized, Holly remained in Haiti, became a Mason, built schools and institutions, and was ordained the first African American bishop in the Episcopal Church.

## Martin R. Delany
## *Black Nationalistic Diasporic Exodus Imaginings*

Like Holly, black emigrationist Martin R. Delany advocated several different emigration options during the 1850s, including the Americas, the Canadian West, and Niger in Africa. One of his early plans for emigration coalesced after his dismissal from Harvard Medical School due to the complaints of racist white classmates and the passage of the 1850 Fugitive Slave Act. He outlined the scheme in *The Condition, Elevation, Emigration, and Destiny of the Colored People of the United States* (1852). Delany politicizes emigration by presenting the Israelites' Exodus as a precedent for the subsequent emergence of nation-states established by emigrants, as evidenced by "the Exodus of the Jews from Egypt to the land of Judea; in the expedition of Dido and her followers from Tyre to Mauritania; and not to dwell upon hundreds of modern European examples—also in the ever memorable emigration of the Puritans, in 1620, from Great Britain, the land of their birth, to the wilderness of the New World" (159). Delany historicizes African Americans' response to racism in America to justify their motivation for migration and their right to choose a destination. In these biblical, mythological, and historical iterations of migration, leaders of oppressed groups initiated relocation to a foreign land where their people established prosperous communities. Thus, Delany establishes himself as an astute visionary who offers an emigration plan through which people of African descent could achieve nationhood.

Although Delany was unsuccessful in convincing African Americans to implement his emigration plan, he continued to explore its potential through the creation of a fictionalized radical Moses who enacts his vision for the development of a Pan-African community. In *Blake, or the Huts of America* (1859–1861), a novel that was serialized in the *Anglo-African Magazine*, protagonist Henry Blake travels through the United States, Canada, Africa, and Cuba recruiting co-conspirators for a regional slave insurrection. As a free black from Cuba who was illegally forced into slavery in the American Delta, Blake aptly represents the slave and free black experience in the Americas and enables Delany to examine the possibilities for the development of militant national leadership and a Pan-African community that African American activists such as Douglass in *The Heroic Slave* (1852) and other authors such as Stowe in *Uncle Tom's Cabin* had been unable or unwilling to explore.

In chapter 7 of the novel, when the oppressive forces of slavery destroy Blake's family, Delany signals Blake's transformation into a militant Moses by reinterpreting a pivotal moment in the Exodus narrative as a call to action. As Blake angrily contemplates his response to the news that his wife, Maggie, has been sold, his father-in-law, Daddy Joe, rebukes his son-in-law's rebellious attitude, admonishing him to "'stan' still an' see de salbation'" (21). In the biblical narrative, Moses encouraged the Israelites, when they were trapped between the Egyptian army and the Red Sea, "Fear ye not, stand still and see the salvation of the LORD" (Exod 14:13). God sent a wind to create a path for them through the water, but their Egyptian oppressors drowned when attempting to pursue them. After the Israelites had settled in Canaan and King Jehoshaphat faced the Ammonite and Moabite army, the prophet Jahaziel offered a similar admonition: "set yourselves, stand ye still, and see the salvation of the LORD with you" (2 Chr 20:17). The Israelites, led by singers, marched to the battlefield, and God sent "ambushments" to defeat their enemies. In both incidents, the Israelites trusted God to fight and win their battles. During the antebellum period, advocates from within both the abolition and proslavery communities directed enslaved African Americans to obey their masters and wait on God for deliverance. Delany examines this approach by presenting a slave within a fictive community who rejects such injunctions. Blake declares, "That's no talk for me. . . . I've been 'standing still' long enough—I'll 'stand still' no longer. . . . 'Now is the accepted time, today is the day of salvation'" (21). To position enslaved African Americans as Christians who must enact their faith, Blake conflates the stories of God instructing the Israelites to wait for timely deliverance with the Apostle Paul advising the Corinthians to accept salvation without delay. While acknowledging his belief in divine aid, Blake asserts his need for immediate justice. In Delany's fictional black Exodus narrative, enslaved African Americans claim biblical authority to defy hypocritical Christian slaveholders because they are destroying slave families while urging bondsmen and women to wait passively for divine intervention. Like Moses, who killed a taskmaster and fled to the wilderness, where he gained the skills essential to leading his people through the Red Sea and into their own wilderness experience, Blake kills an overseer, crosses the Red River into Mississippi, begins his journey through the wilderness, and accepts the challenge of Mosaic leadership.

Blake initiates his Exodus by embarking on a journey through the Deep South to seek out enslaved African Americans who are courageous enough to liberate themselves. This change of direction occurs after he sings a verse from Isaac Watts' hymn "There is a Land of Pure Delight" (1709):

> Could I but climb where Moses stood,
> And view the landscape o'er;
> Not Jordan's streams, nor death's cold flood,
> Could drive me from the shore! (69)

The hymn recalls the portion of the Exodus narrative in which God directed Moses to climb Mount Pisgah to look over the Jordan River and into the Promised Land as he neared the end of his wilderness journey.[27] Delany makes a slight but significant change in the last line of hymn, inserting "drive" for "fright" to affirm Blake's courage and determination to attain liberty. Blake's contemplation of a solitary journey to freedom while his people languish in slavery compels him to implement a plan for their liberation, however, for Exodus intimates a communal experience initiated through divinely appointed Mosaic leadership. Delany depicts him as an avenging Moses: "From plantation to plantation did [Blake] go, sowing seeds of future devastation and ruin to the master and redemption to the slave, an antecedent more terrible in its anticipation than the warning voice of the destroying Angel in commanding the slaughter of the firstborn of Egypt" (83). Unlike Moses who delivered a warning to Pharaoh that God would kill the Egyptians' firstborn if Pharaoh refused to liberate the Israelites, Blake transforms slaves into soldiers who will wield the dual-edged swords of justice and liberty in emancipating themselves.

As Blake travels throughout the South building his army, Delany presents him as a Mosaic savior-judge capable of unifying an enslaved African American community that maintains varied visions of how their liberation should be accomplished. When two community elders, Aunt Dolly and Uncle Nathan, meet Blake, they receive him as a savior. Aunt Dolly exclaims, "'God bless de baby!'" (73). At the end of their conversation, Uncle Nathan offers a prayer, "'Now Laud!' with uplifted hand . . . 'My eyes has seen, and meh yeahs heahn, an' now Laud! I's willing to stan' still an' see dy salvation!'" (73). Aunt Dolly and Uncle Nathan rejoice, as did Anna and Simeon when Joseph and Mary brought the baby Jesus into the temple for his dedication service.[28] While Aunt Dolly sees Blake as the slaves' long-awaited savior, Uncle Nathan proclaims him to be their deliverer as well. Together they affirm their faith in Blake as the divinely appointed means through which the slaves will achieve liberation. As Blake continues to travel, he meets Samson and his wife, Dursie, who describe the fugitive "as the messenger of deliverance foreshown to them," recalling the judges Samson and Deborah, whom God sent to rescue the Israelites from their enemies after they settled in the Promised Land (85). By giving Blake the authority of a judge, Delany enables him to mete out justice on behalf of his people. Thus, Blake exhibits the qualities of savior, deliverer, and judge when he utters the biblical injunction to "stand still and see the salvation," assuring all slaves who have been looking for a divinely appointed leader that he will give them a sign when the time is ripe for their exodus from slavery through insurrection.

Blake gains the devotion of the enslaved black community by revealing how they can disempower the slaveholder by seizing his wealth to finance their revolt. He finds a blueprint for his strategy and assurance of its success in the story of Exodus:

> God told the Egyptian slaves to "borrow from their neighbors"—meaning their oppressors—"all their jewels," meaning to take their money and wealth wherever they could lay hands upon it, and depart from Egypt. So you must teach them to take all the money they can get from their master, to enable them to make the strike without a failure. (43)

In the biblical story, the Egyptians gave liberally to the departing Israelites because they were happy to rid themselves of a people who had brought devastation to their nation.[29] By directing his followers to steal from their masters *prior* to the insurrection, however, Blake empowers slaves to implement the first phase of their rebellion, building their confidence to accomplish the violent attacks that will follow and establishing their community with the fruits of their own labors.

By connecting the cause of enslaved African Americans in the South with their needs of their brethren in the Diaspora, Delany transforms Blake into a Pan-Africanist Moses seeking to establish an autonomous diasporic community. After Blake finishes his Southern tour and leads a group of family members and friends to freedom in Canada, he travels to Cuba, where he is eventually reunited with his wife and son. He seeks more recruits for his insurrection during a trip to Africa and in Cuba. Men and women of African descent throughout the Diaspora acknowledge his leadership and pledge to participate. At the end of the novel, Blake is appointed "Commander in Chief of the Army of Emancipation" (256). Yet we have not learned if Blake and his co-conspirators are successful in carrying out their revolt, for the final chapters of the novel are missing. Nevertheless, Delany seems to intimate that the successful nineteenth-century Mosaic leader must be committed to family and community, and skilled at building a Pan-African coalition to combat slavery and racism throughout the world. In the antebellum period, however, this type of leader seemed to exist only in fiction.

## Provincial Freeman
### *African American Joshua for Southern Slave Revolt*

Before Delany published his fictional account of a Pan-Africanist Moses, another writer had avowed the existence of a fugitive slave revolt leader in Canada who was plotting a large-scale insurrection throughout the South. Mary Ann Shadd and the Reverend Samuel Ringgold Ward published the account in the militant weekly black newspaper the *Provincial Freeman*, which they coedited and distributed in Canada. In an article titled "Wisdom and Her Children" (1855), an anonymous writer creates a fissure in the Afro-Atlantic Exodus narrative by characterizing the revolt leader as a black Joshua whose existence and strategy is justified by social reform movements, biblical liberation narratives, and historic military initiatives. The writer argues that enslaved African Americans can expect a deliverer because God always sends reformers to remedy injustices in society. He asserts, "If wisdom is the use of the best means to attain certain ends; then most beautifully is the wisdom of God seen in *his* adaptations of means to accomplish his purposes. . . . How strikingly does such a truth appear, in God's giving existence to, and the preparation of *a man* for *every* age and its reforms!"

(emphasis in original). The nineteenth century was a time of great reform movements. *Freeman* readers would have been familiar with the activities of Frances Harper and Sojourner Truth in the women's movement, Susan B. Anthony and Frances Willard in the temperance movement, Charles Grandison Finney and Francis Asbury in the evangelical movement, and Douglass and Garrison in the antislavery movement. Some readers may have benefited from these efforts in their flight from slavery and settlement in Canada. The writer reminds readers that reformers are God-appointed agencies for aligning societies with his will. Hence, the writer argues, God had initiated nineteenth-century reforms, including the abolition movement, which assured the success of reformers and their initiatives.

The writer presents Exodus as the foundational story for the history of human liberation from oppressive political systems that shifts the role of the reformer from savior to military leader:

> As Jacob had a Joseph,—so his children had a Moses. IF the Philistines had a Goliath,—so Israel had a David. If the American colonies had a *despotic* George,—they had also a *democratic* Washington. If Europe had a Napoleon the I,—she had her Wellington too. If Turkey has a *foe*, in the Russian Czar,—so she has a *friend*, in the British Queen. AS THE AMERICAN SLAVE HAS A WHITE CAPTOR,—SO HE HAS A BLACK DELIVERER!

He characterizes "sacred" and "secular" events as part of a singular historical record of oppression and liberation. He begins with the Israelites' early history, when Joseph delivered his father, Jacob, from famine by settling him and his extended family in Egypt, and Moses directed Jacob's descendants' transformation from a community of slaves to the nation of Israel. The writer abruptly shifts to a series of if-then statements that contrast formidable foes—Goliath, King George III, Napoleon, the Russian Czar Nicholas I, and a white captor—with unlikely military heroes—David the shepherd, General George Washington, the Duke of Wellington, Queen Victoria, and a black deliverer. The writer racializes the conflict between the slaves and their oppressors, however, introducing an element of black nationalism into their struggle. The "captor" functions as a representative of the American government and the "deliverer" of its dispossessed citizens. Because military leaders had arisen to protect the Israelites, American colonists, and European nationals from hostile forces, enslaved African Americans could also expect a deliverer. By locating the genesis of all sociopolitical reform in the Exodus story, the writer transforms American slaves into a people beloved of God who are worthy of deliverance. By contextualizing their deliverance within the milieu of biblical and world military history, he argues for their right to emancipate themselves.

Focusing specifically on colonial America, the writer conflates an episode from the Exodus narrative with pivotal points in the young republic's history to argue for the inevitability of the emergence of the slaves' deliverer. According to the writer, the revolt leader "reminds one of *the Joshua*, of Americans, the Ajax of the *Seminoles*," who is in a "campaign for freedom or the grave" (emphasis in original). The writer bolsters his claim by recalling how military leaders had guided the colonists to victory over the British. During the American Revolution, some colonists had hailed George Washington as the patriots' Joshua after his triumphs on the battlefield secured the promised land of America. In the early nineteenth century, Native Americans had extolled Ajax for his valor during his people's initial victories over the US military in Florida. Like Joshua, Washington, and Ajax, the black deliverer would lead the slaves in a fight over a contested promised land. The writer characterizes this fight as a "campaign for freedom or the grave," echoing the rhetorical strategies of Gabriel, Douglass, Garnet, and other African American activists who evoked Patrick Henry's motto, "Give me liberty or give me death," to equate the slaves' quest for emancipation with the colonists' revolution for independence. He distinguishes African Americans' revolution from that of the colonists by affiliating it with the Native Americans' struggle for political and cultural autonomy within the nation.

Like Washington and the Israelites' Joshua, the black Joshua desires recognition for slaves as men and citizens, but he does not seek to establish an independent nation. The writer creates a black jeremiad that draws on biblical narratives and world history to equip the divinely appointed "obscure general" with the wisdom to execute a successful Southern slave revolt. He explains, "It is time for the oppressor to know, that the slave is a man, and if need so require, let the weapons of death teach him what he would not learn without them, and in this righteous work may the 'weak be as David, and David as the Angel of the Lord,' and the obscure general come forth, and lead his people on to *victory*!" (emphasis in original). In the biblical record of the Israelites' Babylonian captivity, Zechariah prophesied, "In that day shall the LORD defend the inhabitants of Jerusalem; and he that is feeble among them at that day shall be as David; and the house of David *shall* be as God, as the angel of the LORD before them" (Zech 12:8). God promised to defend and strengthen his people, destroy their enemies, and develop a society of equals, a prophecy that was fulfilled on the day of Pentecost and in the early Christian Church. Unlike Washington, who led the colonists' revolution against the British, and Joshua who directed the Israelites' conquest of Canaan, the black Joshua would initiate a slave insurrection that would liberate African Americans, destroy recalcitrant slaveholders, and establish an integrated land of freedom for *all* citizens. But the slaves' victory would come through human agency augmented by divine intervention. After years of pleading for emancipation and equality, some African American activists desired militant action. After securing liberty, however, African Americans would need divine power to eradicate racist attitudes and practices that blocked their path to citizenship.

## Conclusion

Mid-nineteenth-century African American activists and their supporters turned to the Exodus narrative to address the complex concerns of enslaved and free black communities, which needed an arsenal of rhetorical and practical tools to map varied paths from slavery and oppression to emancipation and equality. Although African Americans met annually in colored conventions to discuss and construct initiatives to combat racism and eliminate slavery, they could not agree on a strategy to achieve their goals and eventually fractured into assimilationist and emigrationist factions. The Moses story dominated Afro-Atlantic Exodus stories that emerged from both groups, however. Assimilationists anointed leaders to deliver enslaved African Americans, encourage the slaves to liberate themselves, or unite all Americans in fighting for freedom and equality. After the passage of the 1850 Fugitive Slave Act, emigrationists posited themselves as Moses figures who urged African Americans to relocate to foreign promised lands, but they could not agree on a destination. The majority of emigrationists emigrated to Canada, where they experienced freedom but encountered racism and discrimination. Another writer questioned the existence of Mosaic leadership and urged Americans, both male and female, to enact a Mosaic Moment that would enable them to dissassociate from slavers even if their choice led to disunion. As the African American community grew and the promise of various Exodus narratives remained unfulfilled, other authors embraced different episodes of the biblical story to address the needs of neglected segments of the African American community. These attempts to construct Afro-Atlantic Exodus stories that would advance racial uplift objectives did not enable black activists to obtain their goals. By 1861, as the divided nation tottered toward civil war, unable to reconcile its desire for slavery with African Americans' demands for civil rights, black authors and their supporters turned again to the story of Exodus and searched for new means to sustain their hope for the freedom and equality of all citizens through adaptations of the accounts of the Israelites' four-hundred-year enslavement in Egypt and protracted journey to the Promised Land.

CHAPTER FOUR

# Exodus, the Civil War, and Reconstruction (1861–1877)

*Abraham Lincoln and not Jeff. Davis becomes the Pharaoh of the mystic Egypt.*

—Henry M. Turner, "The Plagues of This Country"

*Lincoln was mild, and meek and good,*
*Like Moses who on Pisgah stood;*
*He thought upon the peaceful plan,*
*That must take place throughout the land.*

—Jacob Rhodes, "The Nation's Loss: A Poem on the Life and Death of the Hon. Abraham Lincoln, Late President of the United States, Who Departed This Life, in Washington, D.C., April 15, 1865"

*I feel as if I could laugh to scorn all the long line of malignant slave traders who have defiled and devastated this wretched coast of Africa, and fling in their teeth the gracious retort of Joseph: "As for you, ye thought evil against us, but God meant it unto good, to save much people alive."*

—Alexander Crummell, "A Sermon, Preached in Trinity Church, Monrovia, Liberia, West Africa, to the Barbadian Emigrants, May 14, 1865"

*We have a woman in our country who has received the name of "Moses," not by lying about it, but by acting it out* (applause)*—a woman who has gone down into the Egypt of slavery and brought out hundreds of our people into liberty.*

—Frances E. W. Harper, "We Are All Bound Up Together"

During the early 1860s, the events leading to the outbreak of the Civil War compelled African American activists, white abolitionists, proslavery advocates, and white writers to develop distinct Exodus narratives to advance their disparate agendas for emancipating or subjugating African Americans. Economic policy disparities between the North and South, particularly taxation, continuing disagreement regarding states' rights and slavery, and the election of Republican Abraham Lincoln were the major catalysts for secession in South Carolina, which eventually led eleven states to withdraw from the Union. As the crisis intensified, African American writers maintained their reliance on Exodus to demand liberty and civil rights. Antislavery activists still turned to the story to augment their efforts to end slavery and elevate freedmen, primarily through moral suasion, and to counteract the proslavery argument that cited Mosaic law as justification for the continued existence of human bondage. White authors remained invested in the biblical story to establish themselves as God's New Israel and promote westward expansion. While many white Americans prospered in their Canaan, however, African Americans languished in oppressive Egypt-like conditions within the young republic.

Although the North took up arms against the secessionist South, they did not immediately advocate equal treatment of African Americans. Nevertheless, the Civil War and Reconstruction encouraged African American activists and their supporters to create fragile, short-lived new national Exodus narratives for both white and black citizens. President Lincoln proved unreliable, however, issuing the Emancipation Proclamation for enslaved African Americans in Confederate states, but also publicly advocating colonization and initially banning the recruitment of African Americans for the Union Army. African Americans variously viewed Lincoln as Pharaoh and Moses, depending on the stances he took toward emancipation and the elevation of slaves and freedmen. But the assassination of Lincoln brought him Mosaic martyrdom and ushered the nation to the brink of unprecedented unity in a reconstructed republic. Other writers anointed figures such as Andrew Johnson as Joshuas who could facilitate the nation's transition into its new status as Canaan.

In the biblical narrative, Exodus required leaving the land of bondage and included the destruction of former oppressors. African Americans faced the daunting challenge of transforming their Egypt into a promised land still populated by proslavery advocates who had been forced to abandon a way of life they had been willing to die to maintain and presided over by politicians like the duplicitous Johnson, whose fidelity to the freedmen was questionable. Ultimately, the failure of Reconstruction under Johnson's leadership led to the revival of the three-pronged approach to American Exodus stories. African Americans reappropriated the biblical narrative to reformulate their struggle for citizenship and search for new leadership to revitalize their protracted journey to an American promised land.

## Exodus and Slavery on the Eve of the Civil War

The secession crisis of 1861 revived and intensified the controversy regarding Exodus and slavery. New, influential voices from the North and Europe figured prominently in the debate. In "The Bible View of Slavery" (1861), a sermon delivered on the "day of Humiliation, Fasting, and Prayer throughout the Union" declared by President James Buchanan, Unionist Rabbi Morris Jacob Raphall became an unlikely ally of proslavery advocates by affirming many of their biblically based justifications for slavery, particularly the Curse of Canaan and Mosaic law.[1] Editors of antislavery newspapers such as the *New-York Tribune* and the *Liberator* and publishers of popular periodicals such as the *New Englander and Yale Review* helped integrate the sermon into national discourse regarding slavery as a principal cause for America's Civil War.[2] After the war began, abolitionists found an ally in Oxford University history professor Goldwin Smith, publisher of *Does the Bible Sanction American Slavery?* (1863), a three-point argument against slavery from a moral and historical perspective that disputed many of the points regarding Exodus and slavery that Raphall had defended. Editors of prominent national magazines, including the *North American Review* and the *Living Age*, published favorable reviews of Smith's antislavery treatise, lauding it as irrefutable evidence that slavery in Israelite communities did not justify the institution's existence in America.[3] These texts reflected the continuing ideological debate regarding slavery that spilled onto the battlefield, as both proslavery and antislavery advocates viewed Exodus and the Civil War as essential to their cause.

## John S. Rock
### *Southern Egyptians, Northern Israelites*

As the Civil War commenced, African Americans appropriated the language of Exodus to identify their foes and friends and mark a clear route to emancipation and equality. In his speech "What if the Slaves Are Emancipated" (1862), African American abolitionist and lawyer John S. Rock assured the Massachusetts Antislavery Society that slavery had caused the war and its elimination was the only means to restore the Union.

*John S. Rock, attorney, educator, dentist, doctor, and abolitionist*

Rock evokes the Exodus story to cast Southerners as Egyptians and Northerners as potential Israelites, whose victory is contingent on heeding God's warnings and inviting African Americans to join the Union Army. Rock relies on a complex series of biblical narratives to call for divine liberation of the slaves and punishment of their oppressors. He asserts, "I think I see the finger of God in all this. Yes, *there* is handwriting on the wall: *I come not to bring peace, but the sword. Break every yoke, and let the oppressed go free. I have heard the groans of my people, and am come down to deliver them!*" (367; emphasis in original). Rock first alludes to the message God etched with his finger on the wall of King Belshazzar of Babylon's palace during Israel's captivity, informing the king that he had been judged, deemed evil, and punished by foreign invasion. He then doubles the story with a recollection of Jesus' words that wielded the sword of the gospel to thwart the Jews' expectation of an earthly kingdom. Rock further complicates his indictment of America by recalling the words of Isaiah, who chastised Israel for oppressing its own people after experiencing prosperity in the Promised Land. Finally, he cites the Israelites' cries for deliverance, which moved God to initiate their Exodus from Egypt.[4] In so doing, Rock closes off every possibility for Americans to escape condemnation, for the Bible situates God as a fair judge who violently overthrows oppressive individuals and regimes. Unlike Absalom Jones, who quoted Scripture regarding the Israelites' cry to Jehovah to posit the 1807 law outlawing the international slave trade as a harbinger of the slaves' *eventual* liberation, Rock intimates that it signals the *imminent* emancipation of enslaved African Americans. He adds, "I thank

God I have lived to see this great day, when the nation is to be weighed in the balances, and I hope not found wanting" (368). Rock directs his audience's attention back to Belshazzar, whom God had punished. If Americans heed Rock's warning, they can avert national destruction.

Americans could ensure their redemption by viewing the war through the lens of the Exodus narrative. Rock asserts, "Jeff Davis is to the slaveholders what Pharaoh was to the Egyptians, and Abraham Lincoln and his successor, John C. Frémont, will be to us what Moses was to the Israelites. I may be mistaken, but I think the sequel will prove that I am correct" (368). In characterizing the South as a monarchy ruled by a Pharaoh, Rock alleges that Southerners' desire for a slave society negates their belief in democratic governance. In effect, secession reverses the gains of the Revolution, placing all Americans at risk of becoming subjects rather than citizens. As Moses figures, President Lincoln and General Frémont can provide an Exodus experience for both African Americans and white Americans by exerting legislative and military powers against Confederate Egyptians that restore and preserve the democracy.

The interracial community of Israelites in the North would need to rely on an integrated army to assure victory, however. Although African Americans were willing to fight for emancipation, President Lincoln initially prohibited the enlistment of black soldiers. Rock asserts, "As the Government has not had the courage to receive the help that has been standing ready and waiting to assist her, we will now stand still, and see the salvation of our people" (368). During the Exodus, the Israelites relied on God to deliver them from the Egyptian army when they faced the impossible task of crossing the Red Sea. Conversely, Rock intimates that African Americans were prepared to wield their own weapons in the war for liberation. Earlier in his speech, he declares, "I have faith in God and gun-powder and lead and believe we ought not to be discouraged" (368). Having acknowledged the multiple means God employs to liberate his oppressed people, Rock endorses war as the divinely appointed agency for African American emancipation.

### Henry M. Turner
### *America as Egypt, Lincoln as Pharaoh, and the Civil War as Armageddon*

Some African American activists did not share Rock's confidence in Lincoln as a Mosaic leader. During the early years of his presidency, Lincoln often seemed inconsistent in his support of emancipation and equality for African Americans. Black activists, notably David Walker in his 1828 *Appeal* and James T. Holly in his 1859 "Thoughts on Hayti," had warned

*Bishop Henry M. Turner, AME Church*

Americans that God would punish the nation for the sin of slavery. As the Civil War drew near, other writers, inspired by the millennial fever that swept the nation during the Second Great Awakening from 1790 to 1845, issued similar pronouncements. In a dispatch to the *Christian Recorder* titled "The Plagues of This Country" (1862), AME minister and correspondent Henry M. Turner conflates the language of Exodus with the discourse of apocalyptic prophecy to posit himself as a trustworthy interpreter of events that signal the abolition of slavery rather than the end of the world.

Turner recasts the Civil War as retribution for slavery, placing the conflict within a spiritual realm governed by divine justice and mercy. He writes,

> There seems to be a very singular correspondence existing between the war in the United States and the Egyptian plagues. I suppose no one, in the face of so many evidences, will question the practicableness of the assertion, that this war is being waged through a providential interposition for the benefit of some portion of discarded humanity.[5]

Turner's readers would have been familiar with biblical interpretations of current events, for the *Christian Recorder* regularly published sermons, religious essays, political commentary, and moral admonitions. Turner attributes secession and its aftermath to providential intervention rather than man's rebellion, placing the South under divine control and boosting the confidence of his readers in a favorable outcome for oppressed African Americans.

Turner lends credence to his Exodus-inspired interpretation of the causes of the Civil War by contextualizing his message with the influential millennial teachings of prominent nineteenth-century preachers. He reminds his audience that Baptist William Miller, Methodist Joseph Cross, and Lutheran Joseph A. Seiss in America; Church of Scotland minister John Cumming; and Methodist Edward B. Elliot in England had inspired worldwide interest in their interpretations of biblical prophecies regarding an apocalypse.[6] Turner asserts that all lost followers because they incorrectly predicted events associated with the Second Coming of Christ. He offers a new explanation of apocalyptic prophecies concerning falling stars and a blood-red moon as harbingers of the terrors that African Americans experienced after the enactment of the 1850 Fugitive Slave Act and the sociopolitical ruptures within America that led to secession. Rather than identify African Americans' oppressor as Pharaoh, Turner asserts, "And then to crown this *hell-forged* schism, Jeff. Davis, elder brother to Pluto, was inaugurated in all his bestial vices to preside over a power organized for the purpose of crushing down the manliness of as loyal hearts as ever owned fealty to the God of heaven" (emphasis in original). Turner thus characterizes the South as Hades and establishes a confrontation between the forces of good and evil that requires divine intervention for resolution.

Turner is equally critical of the North, however, constructing the region as a slave society ruled by an Egyptian monarchy. He argues, "Abraham Lincoln and not Jeff. Davis becomes the Pharaoh of mystic Egypt (American slavery). And however unwilling to comply with a dispensation of liberation, nature's God calls from heaven, echoed too by five million of the mystic Israelites, (abject slaves) in peals of vivid vengeance, *let my people go.*" In the Exodus story, God heard the cries of the enslaved Israelites and sent Moses to tell Pharaoh, "*let my people go.*"[7] Turner's Exodus story mingles enslaved Africans' earthly cries with the divine mandate from heaven, signaling the certainty of divine justice and the necessity of their participation in avenging their wrongs. Lincoln's refusal to liberate the slaves qualifies him for pharaonic leadership and transforms America from a Christian community into a mystical realm. In effect, God intervenes to eliminate a manmade institution that enslaves physically as well as spiritually. The abolition of slavery is the means whereby America's Christian church and democratic government are restored.

Exodus is the lens for Turner's examination of the republic's failure to emancipate, enlist, or encourage African Americans as the cause of the early setbacks that plague the Union Army. He cites five actions that provoked divine displeasure:

| *Action* | *Plague* |
| --- | --- |
| President Lincoln refused to emancipate the slaves. | Confederate forces attacked Fort Sumter and also killed soldiers of the Sixth Massachusetts Regiment in Baltimore. |
| General Irvin McDowell, with presidential approval, prohibited the enlistment of black soldiers. | Confederate soldiers defeated the "American Egyptian" (Lincoln) at Bull Run. |
| President Lincoln voided General John C. Frémont's order to shoot rebels and free their slaves. | General Nathaniel Lyons died, Lexington fell, and General Franz Sigel's army was demoralized. |
| General Henry Halleck replaced General Frémont and proclaimed enslaved African Americans to be disloyal spies for the Confederacy, forbade their entrance into Union territory, and returned them to their masters. | The USS *Merrimack* sailed from Norfolk, destroyed lives, ships, and property, and nearly demoralized the entire nation. |
| General David Hunter ordered slaves in South Carolina, Georgia, and Florida to be freed, but President Lincoln rescinded the order and returned them to slavery. | Members of the Federal First Maryland regiment were killed, General Stonewall Jackson captured thousands of prisoners and humiliated General Nathaniel Banks, and the Union Army experienced other brutal cruelties. |
| | The liberation of the oppressed. |

In the Exodus story, God sent ten plagues that wreaked havoc throughout Egypt and challenged the efficacy of the polytheistic Egyptian religion.[8] Turner's Exodus story features six plagues for an obstinate US president and Union Army officers who exacerbate rather than alleviate the precarious condition of slaves and freedmen. Instead of facing supernatural disasters, however, the North is plagued by losses to Confederate soldiers whom they deem rebels. Turner further complicates his interpretation of the Civil War by linking the story of the plagues in Egypt to the prophecies of Revelation. He declares, "The sixth plague—the sixth phial or vial—or the sounding of the sixth trumpet is just ahead. What Miller and other prophet writers have been seeing, and the great revolution which is to rack the earth and convulse the nations about the year 1866, is the liberation of the oppressed." In the final plague of the Exodus story, all firstborn humans and livestock died in households whose inhabitants did not brush lamb's blood on their doorposts.[9] In Revelation, when the sixth angel blows his trumpet and pours out the contents of his vial, the Euphrates River will dry up and Armageddon, the battle of the great day of God Almighty, will begin, restoring harmony and peace on earth.[10] Like Pharaoh, Abraham Lincoln loses his beloved sons, Union soldiers, because of his refusal to emancipate and elevate African Americans. Yet Turner shifts his readers' focus from the nation's plagues to its Armageddon—the Civil War—to effect the slaves' emancipation. Armageddon brings both the elimination of evil and the restoration of equality, pitting both Confederate and Union armies in a battle against divine, undefeatable forces.

Turner reinforces his apocalyptic message to the North with accounts of historic events that remind readers of the inevitability of the overthrow of oppressive regimes. He declares that "the inexpressible tortures inflicted upon ancient Egypt, the cruelties of Antiochus to the Jews, the devastation of Jerusalem by the Roman Generals Titus and Vespasian, the bloody streets of France in 1792, will all hardly bear a comparison to what will befall this nation." Turner makes no distinction between punishments God inflicted on oppressive governments and those he allowed his people to suffer to support his contention that autocratic leaders always face reprisals. Claiming a rich heritage as God's New Israel, white Americans relied on biblical and historical precedence for developing an economy dependent on the labor of millions of enslaved people of African descent. Turner suggests that both the Confederacy and the Union will suffer more devastation than the Egyptians, Jews, Greeks, Romans, or French because they rejected their founding libertarian principles and ignored biblical and historical lessons regarding the fate of tyrannical rulers and disobedient believers.

## Sergeant-Major Milton M. Holland
### *Abraham Lincoln as African Americans' Moses*

Shortly after the *Christian Recorder* published Turner's warning of continued devastation if the North refused to liberate African Americans, President Lincoln authorized the establishment of Company A, First South Carolina Volunteer Infantry, the longest-serving regiment of African American soldiers in the Civil War. Prominent activists, notably Martin Delany, Frederick Douglass, and John Brown, had long advocated for the inclusion of African Americans in the military as a means to achieve rights and display their courage and patriotism. Eventually, more than three hundred and eighty-six thousand African Americans fought in the Civil War. Some turned to the Exodus narrative to sustain their hope for victory. Milton M. Holland recruited black soldiers for a Massachusetts regiment but African American attorney John Mercer Langston convinced them to join Ohio's 5th US Colored Troops. Sergeant-Major Holland reported their exploits and challenges on the battlefield in letters to his hometown paper, the *Athens (Ohio) Messenger.*[11]

In a letter published near the end of the war, Holland characterizes Lincoln as Moses and black soldiers as patriots to demand equitable benefits for his troops. He writes, "Though we should fall struggling in our blood for right and justice, for the freedom of our brothers in bondage, or fall in defense of our national color, the Stars and Stripes, our home and fireside will ever be protected by our old friend Gov. [David] Tod, by the loyalty of Abraham Lincoln, our Moses, and the all-wise God that created us." Holland's repeated reliance on the collective pronoun "our" conveys his company's confidence in a democracy's military that rewards loyalty and valor. His "old friend" Governor Tod had initially resisted giving African Americans such opportunities. When Langston volunteered to recruit African Americans for an Ohio regiment, Governor Tod responded, "Do you not know, Mr. Langston, that this is a white man's government; that white men are able to defend and protect it, and that to enlist a negro soldier would be to drive every white man out of the service? When we want you colored men we will notify you."[12] Governor Tod notified Langston two years later, authorizing the organization of and promising equal pay for the 127th Ohio Volunteer Regiment, later renamed the 5th United States Colored Troops. Pay disparity persisted in the ranks, however, with African American soldiers earning

*Sergeant-Major Milton M. Holland, Union Army 5th US Colored Troops, from Athens, Ohio*

ten dollars and white soldiers thirteen dollars. In his letter, Holland publicly confronts his "old friend," challenging him to rectify the situation, for the troops' valor in battle displayed their unquestionable commitment to the state, nation, and oppressed citizens. In expressing his expectations for support from President Lincoln as their commander-in-chief, Holland turns to the Exodus narrative to equate the duty of the US president to African American troops with the fidelity of Moses in guiding Israel to the border of Canaan. During the Civil War, military personnel were often required to sign a "Union Loyalty Oath" pledging "loyalty and allegiance to the Union."[13] For Holland, loyalty was reciprocal. To ensure the success of the war, Ohio's governor and America's president needed to align their commitment to black servicemen with that of the "all-wise God." As members of the human family, black Union soldiers served God and country and challenged US officials to honor their patriotism by providing equitable military benefits for the families of African American veterans.

### Henry Highland Garnet
### *Reconstruction Architect of a New National Exodus Story*

In January of 1865, Congress took its first major step in guaranteeing equitable treatment of African Americans by approving the 13th Amendment, which abolished slavery, and sending it to the states for ratification. William H. Channing, chaplain of the House of Representatives, and several Republican congressmen invited black abolitionist and Presbyterian minister Henry Highland Garnet to speak at a religious service commemorating the historic legislation. Garnet had joined black abolitionists Mary Ann Shadd Cary, Delany, Douglass, and Mercer in pressuring Lincoln to authorize black regiments, and then recruiting and demanding equitable treatment of black soldiers who fought in the Civil War. Garnet further exhibited his commitment to the troops by volunteering to serve as a military chaplain in New York and organizing a Ladies' Committee for the Aid of Sick Soldiers to help soldiers who suffered from the harsh conditions on Rikers Island, where they received training.[14] While supporting the war effort, he continued his pastoral duties at Shiloh Presbyterian Church in New York. In 1864 he accepted an appointment at the 15th Street Presbyterian Church in Washington City as the Senate approved legislation to abolish slavery. In his sermon "Let the Monster Perish," delivered on February 12, 1865, in the Hall of the House of Representatives, Garnet decenters white Americans' national Exodus narrative by establishing Mosaic law as precedent for American law and the Hebrews' transformation from a community of slaves to the nation of Israel as a model for America's reconstruction.

Garnet conflates the Moses story with republican discourse to argue for the incompatibility of slavery and democracy. He characterizes Moses as "the greatest of all lawgivers and legislators," who declared, "Whoso stealeth a man, and selleth him, or if he be found in his hand, he shall surely be put to death."[15] Garnet intimates that US politicians should have modeled their legislative initiatives on Mosaic law. Because they did not, "The destroying angel has gone forth through his land to execute the fearful penalties of God's broken law." Like Turner, Garnet turns to the portion of the Exodus story in which God sent a series of plagues, culminating in the death of all firstborn children and livestock, as a means to interpret the consequences of legalizing slavery through a war that killed nearly four hundred thousand soldiers, destroyed numerous communities, and devastated the South's infrastructure.

Nevertheless, many Americans did not view slavery as the cause of their misfortune. Garnet evokes the Exodus story to support his argument that slavery must die before legislators can rebuild the nation. He asserts,

> The nation has begun its Exodus from worse than Egyptian bondage; and I beseech you that you say to the people that they go forward. With the assurance of God's favor in all things done in obedience to His righteous will, and guided by day and by night by the pillars of cloud and fire, let us not pause until we have reached the other side of the stormy and crimson sea.

In the Exodus narrative, God directed the Israelites to embark on their journey to the Promised Land, guided by a pillar of fire and cloud, a symbol of his presence and power. When the colonists won independence from England, Benjamin Franklin and Thomas Jefferson urged the founding fathers to adopt a seal featuring a pillar of fire and cloud leading the nation. Garnet reminds Congress that they are responsible for setting the course for the nation, and can achieve success only if they follow biblical principles of equality for all Americans. The path to a slave-free society will be difficult, even violent, however, for the nation will pass through a "stormy and crimson sea." Americans who had achieved independence through a bloody revolution should not expect an easy transition to a new society that will guarantee the rights of citizenship to a formerly enslaved population.

Like Moses, Garnet provides instruction on how a fractured nation could regain its power and develop unity. Near the end of his sermon, he quotes a verse from the poem "Exodus" by Adeline T. Whitney to encourage legislators to emulate key figures in the biblical narrative as they construct a new national Exodus story for the nation:

Show us our Aaron, with his rod in flower!
Our Miriam, with her timbrel-soul in tune!
And call some Joshua, in the Spirit's power,
To poise our sun of strength at point of noon![16]

In Garnet's new national Exodus narrative, Americans are beginning their journey from Egypt to the promised land at the end of the Civil War. They will need an Aaron, godly ministers like Israel's high priest, to provide spiritual guidance as they develop a democratic republic for all citizens. In recalling Miriam's leading role in directing the Hebrew women's song of praise to God for drowning their Egyptian oppressors in the Red Sea, Garnet affirms the contributions of American women by advocating and honoring their participation in the political process. Finally, he recommends a Joshua, who commanded the sun to stand still in his battle with the Amorites, as a guide for Americans in their conquest of Canaan. Garnet intimates that the battle against proslavery advocates and racists would continue and courageous leadership would be essential for combating new methods of oppression. However, he omits the verse from the poem in which Whitney positions Moses within the pillar of cloud communing with God. As the first African American to speak to Congress, Garnet assumes this Mosaic role in emerging from his own communion with God as a respected Presbyterian minister to admonish legislators to fulfill their responsibilities by collaborating with ministers, women, and activists during the nation's exodus from slavery.

## Jacob Rhodes
### *Lincoln as America's Moses*

The assassination of President Lincoln temporarily halted writers' efforts to narrate the nation's journey from Egypt to Canaan, but preachers, poets, and the public revived the potential for a national Exodus by eulogizing him as a Mosaic leader who had set the nation on the path to the promised land. Some viewed Lincoln as African Americans' Moses because of his administration's engagement in a war that ended slavery. In *Thirty Years a Slave and Four Years in the White House* (1868), Elizabeth Keckley, a former slave who worked as a modiste and traveling companion for First Lady Mary Todd Lincoln, recalls, "The Moses of my people had fallen in the hour of his triumph . . . whom I had worshipped as an idol—looked upon as a demi-god" (190). She elevates Lincoln to godlike stature because the Mosaic president had helped the nation accomplish what no other leader had been willing or able to do: free the slaves, outlaw slavery, and preserve the Union. Universalist minister Richard Eddy adopted a similar approach in his eulogy "The Martyr of Liberty," presenting Lincoln as a multifaceted, godlike Mosaic figure, worthy of the freedman's worship. He asserted that as former slaves experienced citizenship, they would "remember this one President—their life-long friend—the martyr to their liberty. And as the Moslem to Mecca; as the Hebrew to Mount Sion; as the Christian to Gethsemane, so shall the black man turn to the grave of Abraham Lincoln, and say with deep emotion, 'There lie the ashes of our Moses, of our good Father Abraham, our Emancipator!'" (18). Contributors to black newspapers played a prominent role in shifting perceptions of Lincoln from African Americans' Moses to America's Moses. In "Xenia Correspondence," a letter to the *Christian Recorder* (1865), Annie M. Smith reports, "Crowds gathered in the streets, with melancholy countenances and downcast eyes; not a smile was to be seen—all hearts were sad on account of the assassination of our noble and praiseworthy President,—our modern Moses." In describing Americans' reaction to Lincoln's death, Smith recalls mournful groups that likely included black and white citizens. Smith and other writers appropriated the Moses story to depict Americans' response to the news of Lincoln's death as a communal experience of grief that could unify the nation.

Ultimately, most authors remembered Lincoln as a complex Mosaic figure who variously exhibited the characteristics of a good man, martyr, patriot, friend, pioneer, Father Abraham, savior, and messiah in his relations with black and white Americans. Like editors of popular periodicals who circulated national Exodus stories prior to the Civil War, white Northern Protestant preachers wielded enormous influence in promoting new national Exodus narratives by publishing their eulogies for a national audience. In a marked departure from the approach of ministers who posited slaveholding President George Washington as white Americans' Moses following his death, Henry Fowler, C. B. Crane, Charles Lowe, Joseph E. Rankin, Joseph A. Seiss, and other white Northern Protestant pastors presented Lincoln as a Mosaic president for all Americans. The eulogies frequently appeared in bibliographies of Lincolniana, materials celebrating the life and legacy of the president, ensuring the continued circulation of national Exodus narratives. Andrew Boyd compiled one of the most comprehensive listings, *A Memorial Lincoln Bibliography being an Account of Books, Eulogies, Sermons, Portraits, Engravings, Medals, etc., Published upon Abraham Lincoln, Sixteenth President of the United States, Assassinated Good Friday, April 14, 1865* (1870). It included "The Nation's Loss: A Poem on the Life and Death of the Hon. Abraham Lincoln, late President of the United States, who Departed this life, in Washington, D.C., April 15, 1865," by African American writer Jacob Rhodes. In his poem, Rhodes posits Lincoln as a multifaceted Mosaic president who relied on the bonds of friendship to solidify relationships with varied constituencies while eradicating slavery to restore the Union.

Rhodes signals his vision of the nation's collective grief in the title of his poem. By asserting that Lincoln's death is "The Nation's Loss," he not only assuages the grief of a mourning nation but he also bridges racial and sectional divides. Rhodes offers several different means for all Americans to view Lincoln's death as their loss. He asserts that "like the Saviour he was sold, / For shining silver or for gold." Rhodes likens those associated with Lincoln's assassination to Judas, who betrayed Jesus to the Jewish leaders for thirty pieces of silver. Betrayal is the ultimate act of disloyalty for both Christians and patriots. In presenting Lincoln as a Christ figure, however, Rhodes imbues him with a providential mission to save America from the sin of slavery. Thus, he taps into the nationalistic sentiments of enslaved, oppressed, and free Americans, encouraging all to see Lincoln as the fulfillment of their hopes for a savior whose death has brokered the solution to disunion.

Like the Savior, who was known as the sinner's friend, Lincoln is depicted by Rhodes as Americans' friend. Rhodes creates a series of scenes that display Lincoln's relationships with Americans from varied socioeconomic backgrounds:

> The cities all, both great and small,
> Were draped with mourning one and all,
> In honor of their worthy friend.

He reminds readers of Lincoln's wife, Mary Todd Lincoln, who will suffer distress "until she meets her friend on high / Where they will never, never die." He describes Lincoln as a man whose "many friends both far and near / Will drop a sympathizing tear." Yet when Rhodes describes Lincoln's relation with "Four millions of the human race, / Redeemed from bondage and disgrace," he twice characterizes the slain president as their "dear friend." His final image of friendship is in heaven, where "friends of freedom" will be reunited with their "worthy friend." By characterizing Lincoln's familial and political relationships as friendships, Rhodes personalizes readers' perceptions of the president, encouraging them to view his actions favorably. Yet he also stokes nationalistic yearnings by reconfiguring heaven as a reunion of patriots rather than saints.

When Rhodes finally evokes the Exodus narrative near the end of his poem, he positions Lincoln as a Moses figure but gives him a Reconstruction role. He writes,

> Lincoln was mild, and meek and good,
> Like Moses who on Pisgah stood;
> He thought upon the peaceful plan,
> That must take place throughout the land.

Unlike Moses, who ascended Mount Pisgah to receive a vision of the Israelites' Promised Land, Rhodes' Mosaic Lincoln ponders a plan for the transformation of war-torn America into a peaceable state. By depicting Lincoln's life as a Moses story, Rhodes offers a means for mourners to understand how the eradication of slavery is essential for the long-term viability of a democracy. He explains:

> The affliction to the nation sent,
> Should lead them truly to repent;
> And teach us all throughout the land,
> To bow submissive to His hand.

For Rhodes, the path to peace lay in acquiescence to God's will. In calling the nation to repentance, he emphasizes the complicity of the North in financing slavery, the culpability of the South in seceding to protect their right to continue the practice, and the hypocrisy of Americans who refused to take a stance on the issue.

For those who could not envision Lincoln as a savior, friend, or Moses, Rhodes suggests that they acknowledge him as a martyr. He writes that Lincoln had "gone to join the martyr's band, / Around the throne at God's right hand." Rhodes is likely evoking John the Revelator's description of martyrs as judges sitting around the throne of God.[17] Religious martyrs faced death because of their fidelity to God in the face of persecution. As a Mosaic president, Lincoln engaged the forces that threatened national stability through the oppression of enslaved African Americans. Rhodes memorializes him as a martyred Moses, enabling Americans to transform tragedy into triumph by viewing the slain president as a hero whose death initiated the rebirth of a republic that guarantees freedom, justice, and equality for all citizens.

## American Activists and Ministers
### *Andrew Johnson as Potential Joshua, Unfaithful Moses, and Duplicitous Pharaoh*

After effectively memorializing Lincoln as a revered Mosaic leader, black and white writers attempted to complete the nation's new national Exodus narrative. As vice president, Democrat Andrew Johnson was the most likely candidate for Joshua, who in the biblical narrative guided the Israelites across the Jordan River after Moses' death and directed the conquest of the

Promised Land. His earlier characterization of himself as African Americans' Moses and his administration's repressive policies toward the black community inhibited the construction of the new Exodus narrative, however, as writers variously envisioned him as Joshua, Moses, and Pharaoh, leading to the bifurcation of the national Exodus story into separate racialized narratives.

White Protestant ministers were the foremost proponents of national Exodus stories featuring Johnson in the leading role of Joshua. In a eulogy delivered at the South Baptist Church in Hanford, Connecticut, the Reverend C. B. Crane assured mourners that "Andrew Johnson is the Joshua whom God has appointed to consummate the work which our dead Moses so nobly commenced."[18] Others like white Presbyterian pastor Henry Fowler were even more emphatic, declaring, "Andrew Johnson will lead us into the promised land!"[19] Some joined Congregational minister Pliny H. White of Vermont in expressing doubt, however, suggesting that "Andrew Johnson may be the Joshua to finish the uncompleted work."[20] The ministers relied on the trajectory of the Exodus journey from Egypt to Canaan to delineate a clear path for Americans from the devastation of war and the instability of government to the restoration of a peaceful, prosperous republic under the leadership of a courageous Joshua. Some attempted to mitigate the fears of African Americans who questioned the trustworthiness of a Democratic president, given his party's support of slavery and the Confederacy. The Reverend Kendrick, speaking to the congregation of an AME Church in Xenia, Ohio, assured his audience, "Don't fear Johnson, for he is a Joshua of old, who will lead us out of this struggle. I have all confidence in Andy Johnson; he is a friend to all Union-loving men, but will not show much mercy towards the traitor in heart or sentiment."[21] Kendrick acknowledges African Americans as citizens, fully integrated into the nation because of their loyalty to the Union. Patriotism erases racial differences among citizens in his new Exodus narrative, separating them from all who exhibit or encourage rebellion.

As mentioned, the transformation of Johnson into a Joshua was complicated by the fact that he had earlier cast himself as Moses for African Americans. Approximately six months prior to Lincoln's assassination, then–Vice President Johnson delivered a speech to black residents of Nashville, Tennessee, in which he expressed sympathy for their plight and conveyed his desire for a Moses to arise and lead them "to their Promised Land of peace and happiness." The crowd responded, "'You are our Moses! . . . we want no Moses but you!' . . . 'Well, then,' replied [Johnson], 'humble and unworthy as I am, if no other better shall be found, I will indeed be your Moses, and lead you through the Red Sea of war and bondage to a fairer future of peace and liberty.'"[22] By couching his aspirations in the language of Exodus, Johnson raised the hopes of his audience that their emancipator had arrived. As a former governor and state senator who remained loyal to the Union after his state seceded, Johnson was a familiar and somewhat heroic figure for black Tennesseans. By intimating that African Americans needed a federal representative like himself to ensure their safe passage into an authentic American Canaan, Johnson incorporated African Americans into a national narrative informed by the rhetoric of revolution, which created opportunities for them to become citizens who enjoy "life, liberty, and the pursuit of happiness."

When Johnson assumed the responsibilities of the presidency after Lincoln's assassination, however, he enforced policies that favored former Confederates, unfitting himself for leadership as the nation's Moses or Joshua. Johnson granted amnesty, pardon, and property to former Confederates but vetoed the Freedmen's Bureau Act of 1865, the Reconstruction bills, and the Civil Rights Act of 1866. Black activists derided Johnson's failure to keep his promise to "lead them to freedom and happiness" in an American Canaan. Frances E. W. Harper directed her mixed-race audience at the Eleventh National Woman's Rights Convention in New York in May of 1866 to consider whether Harriet Tubman, a fugitive slave conductor of the Underground Railroad and Civil War scout and nurse, or the duplicitous Johnson had earned the moniker Moses (219). She contrasted the bravery of an African American female liberator with the cowardice of a "lying" president to emphasize character, rather than race or gender, as the key trait in determining effective sociopolitical leadership. The national press affirmed black activists' assessment of Johnson's duplicity in characterizing himself as black America's Moses. In the political cartoon, "Andrew Johnson's Reconstruction, and How It Works" (1866), published in *Harper's Weekly Magazine*, white political cartoonist Thomas Nast depicted Johnson as Shakespeare's Iago and a black Union veteran as Othello the Moor, who is flanked by Johnson's slogans "I am your Moses" and "Treason is a crime that must be made odious" and surrounded by scenes that signal the ineffectiveness of Reconstruction. In critiquing Johnson's leadership style, Nast inadvertently marginalized African Americans. By positing the African American veteran as a Moor, Nast characterized the soldier's brethren as outsiders whose liberty had to be curtailed to protect white Americans' freedom and purity.

Johnson's failure to fulfill expectations to be a Joshua for the nation or a Moses for African Americans led black activists and their supporters

*"Andrew Johnson's Reconstruction, and How It Works,"*
*by Thomas Nast,* Harper's Weekly *(1866)*

to reconfigure the nation as Egypt and the president as Pharaoh. In 1866 Frederick Douglass delivered a series of speeches that identified Johnson as Pharaoh because of his refusal to support legislation that provided civil liberties for African Americans. In "The Issues of the Day: An Address Delivered in Washington, D.C., on 10 March 1866," Douglass declared, "What shall be said of him who promised to be the Moses of the colored race, if he becomes their Pharaoh instead? Why, this must be said of him: that he had better never have been born" (123). In his "Great Speech," published in the *Christian Recorder* in January of 1867, Republican senator Charles Sumner of Massachusetts joined Douglass in characterizing Johnson as Pharaoh after the executive appointment of former Confederates to federal government posts: "[Johnson] is a usurper, who, promising to be a Moses has become a Pharaoh." Douglass and Sumner crafted *reverse* Exodus narratives, signaling America's repudiation of the values of freedom and justice that are essential to the effective working of a democracy.

Black Mason Grand Master Lewis Hayden offers a more complex critique of Johnson as Moses in *Caste among Masons: Address before Prince Hall Grand Lodge of Free and Accepted Masons of the State of Massachusetts, at the Festival of St. John the Evangelist, December 27, 1865*. Infusing his Exodus narrative with the powerful oratory of the Apostle Paul to challenge the authority of a rogue president, Hayden declares that Johnson "was to be our Moses to lead us to liberty and equality; instead of which, I fear he will prove to be the Pharaoh of our day. In this we ought not to be deceived; for it is plain that he who undertakes to be the friend of the black man in this land of Negro haters, will not have the Negro haters all over the country singing praises to him, as you see they are now doing to our said Moses" (9). Like Frances E. W. Harper, who accused Johnson of lying about his role as Moses, Hayden cites Johnson's duplicity as evidence of his untrustworthiness to implement essential reforms during Reconstruction. Hayden then relies on biblical authority to circumvent the limitations of legislation enacted to protect federal officials from censure by citizens: "Were it not that we are forbidden to speak against those in authority, I should say, the Lord rebuke thee and deliver us from such a Moses" (10). Hayden references the Apostle Paul's appearance before the Jewish council, when the high priest Ananias commanded that the Apostle be slapped on the mouth after asserting that he had lived in good conscience before God. Paul warned Ananias of punishment for actions that were contrary to God's law. When rebuked for reviling the high priest, Paul responded, "I wist not, brethren, that he was the high priest: for it is written, Thou shalt not speak evil of the ruler of thy people" (Acts 23:1-5). Hayden places himself in the role of the

Apostle Paul, a Roman citizen, in expressing his desire for Johnson to receive a divine rebuke and removal from office, just as God had punished Pharaoh. He was fearless in his rebuke and angry at his treatment, yet respectful of authority. For Hayden, oppressive policies toward African Americans had led Johnson to become the embodiment of evil.

## African American Activists
### *American Politicians and Citizens as Mosaic Leaders*

Johnson's disappointing performance as a Moses for African Americans did not diminish the community's need for a Mosaic figure to facilitate the legal process for acquiring civil rights. To sustain their struggle, some black activists directed their brethren's attention to other white politicians who had honorably served as Mosaic leaders. When Ohio congressman and Congregational minister Owen Lovejoy died in March of 1864, James L. N. Bowen, a descendant of slaves who served in the Civil War and later became one of the first African Americans to earn a medical degree at Howard University,[23] eulogized Lovejoy as a "a friend, . . . a true and tried friend—a friend that has been with us in adversity as well as in prosperity—a friend, who, in the dark day of slavery, when we groped in darkness like that of Egypt which could be felt, he was with us, and like Moses, helped to lead us to the promised land."[24] After the murder of his brother, Elijah Lovejoy, by a proslavery mob, Owen Lovejoy developed his reputation as a "true and tried friend" by supporting the antislavery efforts of the Congregational Church, offering his home as a station on the Underground Railroad, and winning election to public office to advance the goals of the abolition movement. Other activists developed an expanded vision of Mosaic leadership for American citizens. In 1865 Garnet helped organize a Fourth of July celebration for the Colored People's Educational Monument Association in Washington, D.C., which had been established to honor Lincoln's memory. Charles Sumner wrote a letter encouraging his "fellow-citizens" to have "patience, and confidence" in President Johnson, who had promised to be their Moses, but he also assured them that Northerners would be their Moses and Congress would act on their behalf during its next session.[25] He intimated that Mosaic character enables national leaders and local citizens to change the legal and social infrastructure of the nation to ensure African Americans' rightful place as equals in society.

Rather than look for leadership outside the African American community, Frances Harper challenged her brethren to redirect their efforts into individually developing Mosaic character. She had long acknowledged Moses as a role model for African Americans, recommending that they reflect his disunionist strategy during the Civil War and reject President Johnson, whose duplicitous deportment undermined his claim to the Mosaic leadership legacy. As the nation entered the Reconstruction era, Harper turned her attention back to the Moses story to devise a road map for African Americans to follow during the next phase of their arduous journey from slavery and oppression to freedom and equality. In her epic poem *Moses, a Story of the Nile* (1869), Harper retells the Moses narrative with an emphasis on the role of women in shaping his life and establishing the nation of Israel.[26] Her novel *Minnie's Sacrifice* (1869) features dual mixed-race Mosaic protagonists, Minnie and Louis Le Croix, who are raised as white children but regain their racial consciousness through unexpected encounters with their African American families. Both texts enable Harper to refashion the biblical Moses story into a Afro-Atlantic Exodus story that presents the politicization of African Americans as the means for developing a conscious, Christian community within a reconstructed nation.

Harper encourages her readers to view the Civil War as indisputable proof of God's justice for the oppressed and the equality of humanity. Unlike Henry M. Turner, who constructed a parallel between the plagues of Egypt and Revelation and the North's actions to explain the outbreak of the Civil War, Harper evokes Exodus as the crisis ends to encourage Americans to see the devastation of the nation as divine punishment for slavery and an opportunity for restoration. Harper presents Exodus as a conflict between God and his agents, Moses and Aaron, and Pharaoh and his magicians and priests. Depicting the plagues of Egypt, she presents them in quick succession, a relentless assault that decimates the political, religious, social, and physical structure of the nation. In *Moses, a Story of the Nile*, for example, "millions of frogs" overrun the "worshiped Nile," "pathway of priests," and Pharaoh's bed, trays of bread, ovens, and pans (30). The frog invasion represents God's loathing toward a dehumanizing system that permeates every aspect of society, for millions of American slaves were bound by an institution sanctioned by preachers and politicians who relied on their labor for sustenance and wealth.

The abolition of slavery did not guarantee African Americans a liberated consciousness or easy transition into a life of freedom, however. In *Moses, a Story of the Nile*, when the Israelites face their first crisis, the pursuit by Pharaoh's army as they leave Egypt, they cry to Moses, "Were there no graves in Egypt that thou hast / Brought us here to die?" (33). When the wilderness journey becomes difficult, they repeatedly rebel and reminisce about the "flesh pots" of Egypt, even when they reach the border of the Promised Land. The narrator explains, "For when the chains were shaken from their limbs / They failed to strike the impress from their souls" (39). Harper suggests that proclamations and amendments only define the legalities of liberty. While she acknowledges God as the slave's liberator, she insists that the oppressed exercise agency in excising the debilitating effect of slavery on one's mind.

To facilitate this process of creating consciousness, Harper issues a call for race workers to serve as community and nation builders. She posits her invitation through pivotal moments in the texts when her protagonists face crossroads that force them to choose between identifying themselves as a member of an oppressed race and assimilating into the dominant culture. For Harper, this transformation of individuals, community, and nation is best accomplished through a matrifocal influence. In the biblical narrative, Moses' story unfolds chronologically. He is adopted by an Egyptian princess, entrusted to the care of his mother during his formative years, and then groomed for leadership in Pharaoh's household. His consciousness is raised as he witnesses an Egyptian overseer abuse an enslaved Israelite. In part I of *Moses, a Story of the Nile*, "The Parting," Harper introduces the story in medias res, with Moses informing his adopted mother of his decision to leave Pharaoh's palace and dwell in Israel's huts. Moses declares:

> . . . I go to join
> The fortunes of my race, and to put aside
> All other bright advantages, save
> The approval of my conscience and the meed
> Of rightly doing. (3)

Conversely, in *Minnie's Sacrifice*, coprotagonists Louis Le Croix and Minnie are forced to choose either to pass for white or to identify with African Americans when their African heritage is revealed. Minnie's father, St. Pierre Le Grange, a Louisiana planter, had protected his daughter from his wife's wrath by sending her to live in Philadelphia with white Quakers Thomas and Anna Carpenter, who had kept her racial identity secret. Minnie discoverers her African heritage when she encounters an African American woman who provides evidence of maternal lineage. Minnie declares, "So, when I found out that I was colored, I made up my mind that I would neither be pitied nor patronized by my former friends; but that I would live out my own individuality and do for my race, as a colored woman, what I never could accomplish as a white woman" (72). Minnie locates the advantages to African American identity in both heightened individual consciousness and service to the race. Her coprotagonist, Louis Le Croix, experiences a more circuitous route to racial consciousness after his white family adopts him, at the insistence of his white half-sister, Camilla Le Croix, for he remains in the

South, advocates slavery, and joins the Confederate Army. After his enslaved grandmother Miriam reveals his African heritage by showing him his manumission papers, he says, "I see it all. I can never raise my hand against my mother's race" (59). Both protagonists experience an awakening of racial consciousness informed by renewed connections to their mothers. In emphasizing following one's conscience, making up one's mind, and sharpening one's ability to see, Harper presents race work as intellectually driven rather than culturally informed. By uplifting their own community, African Americans would elevate themselves individually as well. In reworking the Moses narrative into stories of racially conscious African Americans, Harper not only draws on nineteenth-century sentiments regarding the role of the mother in child rearing. She challenges the two-hundred-year-old law that dictated children would "follow the condition of the mother."[27] Harper posits a distinction between physical condition and intellectual consciousness, however. Through the influence of mother figures who had experienced slavery, African American children would cultivate a consciousness that valued fidelity to one's race. The means by which the nation sought to subjugate African Americans becomes the method through which they were empowered.

## Alexander Crummell
### *Reunion, Reconciliation, and Restoration via a Pan-African Exodus in America and Abroad*

Buoyed by the war effort and congressional initiatives that abolished slavery, guaranteed citizenship, and provided suffrage, Harper, Douglass, Garnet, and other activists affirmed African Americans' exodus from slavery to freedom in the United States through the Mosaic story. The editorial staff of the *Christian Recorder*, published by the AME Church, created a major fissure in the African American Exodus tradition, however, by emphasizing the Joseph story as inspiration for slaves and freedmen who faced formidable odds in affirming their humanity, unifying their community, and achieving their political goals. In the biblical narrative, Joseph's brothers sold him to Ishmaelite traders who transported him to Egypt, where he eventually experienced the fulfillment of his boyhood dreams when he was appointed prime minister. During the Civil War, one writer pointed readers to Joseph's transformation from betrayed brother to Egyptian ruler in asserting his belief that "God can and will work out all His purposes concerning individuals and nations."[28] As the AME Church experienced exponential growth after the war, a contributor admonished readers to heed Joseph's counsel to his bickering brethren in avoiding infighting in "'See That Ye Fall Not Out by the Way.'"[29] Another writer lauded Joseph as the first of many admirable men who seized "an opportunity for the vindication [of] his manhood" by earning the trust of his captors and being rewarded with freedom and a position of authority.[30] Such leadership depended on "radical punctuality," according to the Reverend J. H. Cole in his sermon on "Punctuality." He chides listeners who respond "I can't" when asked to contribute their talents to church work, encouraging them to imagine how Joseph's story might have turned out differently if he had complained, "I know not the language of the people" when invited to be Egypt's prime minister.[31] In looking to the Joseph story, African Americans gained inspiration from a wrongfully enslaved young man who realized his dreams and achieved success within the land of captivity. As Joseph figures in the United States, African Americans functioned as reinterpreters of the American dream through their trust in divine intervention to right the wrongs of slavery, their commitment to establishing community leaders and institutions, and their willingness to help rebuild the nation.

As African American activists and their supporters struggled to achieve integration and equality during and after the Civil War, the colonization versus integration debate reemerged, pitting politicians, preachers, activists, and citizens against one another in ideological battles regarding emigration to Haiti, Liberia, or Central America as the most effective solution for America's race problem. In 1862 President Lincoln had stoked the debate by appointing Episcopal minister James Mitchell as commissioner of emigration for repatriating African Americans and advocating colonization in Central America during a White House meeting with a "deputation of Negroes."

*The Reverend Alexander Crummell, Episcopal priest, missionary, educator, and activist*

Congress had also signaled its support of colonization by appropriating over half a million dollars to repatriate African Americans.[32]

Although the majority of African Americans in the United States following the Civil War devoted their attention to acquiring civil liberties, other peoples of African descent in the Americas embraced colonization as a means to better their condition and achieve more autonomy. In 1865 Joseph S. Atwell helped organize the Barbados Company of Liberia and embarked upon a successful fundraising tour. The ACS was receptive to the venture, and John P. Crozier, president of the ACS Philadelphia chapter, tapped a fund that had been established to support resettlement of African Americans in Haiti and Central America to finance the voyage. Within a year, the ACS chartered the *Cora* to transport 346 Bajan emigrants to Liberia. The group was responding, in part, to Liberian President Daniel Warner's promise to provide the opportunity to "build up a African nationality" and to "twenty-five acres of fresh, fertile land . . . to each family and of ten acres to each individual."[33] African American Episcopal priest Alexander Crummell welcomed the émigrés to Liberia.

Crummell had opposed colonization until he worked in Liberia in 1853 as a missionary and realized the potential for Christian converts in a Pan-African community. He later served as professor of intellectual and moral science at Liberia College. In "A Sermon, Preached in Trinity Church, Monrovia, Liberia, West Africa, to the Barbadian Emigrants, May 14, 1865," published in the *Christian Recorder*, Crummell evokes the Exodus story to infuse colonization with Pan-Africanist sentiments by positing migration as the divinely ordained means of fulfilling the destiny of African peoples.

Crummell begins with a traditional Exodus narrative, comparing the Barbadian emigrants' arrival in Africa to the Israelites' resettlement in Canaan. He describes Israel's migration as "colonization," however, and reminds his listeners that the Hebrews left Egypt at "God's bidding" to settle in Canaan. Crummell conflates emigration and colonization, assuring his audience that both are "among the commonest movements of mankind," evidenced by the experiences of Adam's descendants and Noah's family, as well as the historic migrations of various peoples, including the "Malay family," the "Celtic race," Pacific Islanders, and Phoenician explorers. For Crummell, resettlement offers evidence of God's design in populating the earth in distinct nations. He relies on biblical and historical migrations to bridge the chasm between voluntary movement and forced resettlement, thereby erasing the stigma of colonization. Crummell affirms the émigrés' choice as compliance with God's will, which unleashes blessings that flow from obedience in their new homeland.

The history of the transatlantic slave trade complicates Crummell's narrative, however, situating Africa as both the Egypt where slavery originated and the Canaan where nationhood is accomplished. He adapts the story of Joseph to re-envision the trade as beneficial for Africa. Crummell explains, "I feel as if I could laugh to scorn all the long line of malignant slave traders who have defiled and devastated this wretched coast of Africa, and fling in their teeth the gracious retort of Joseph: 'As for you, ye thought evil against us, but God meant it unto good, to save much people alive.'" When Joseph unexpectedly encountered his brothers, who had traveled to Egypt to purchase food during a famine, he allayed their fears of retribution by assuring them that God counteracted their harmful intentions by placing him in a position to save his family and the nation. Crummell shifts the focus of redemption exclusively to African slave traders, however, emphasizing the necessity for reconciliation between the perpetrators of slavery and the survivors of brutal West Indian bondage to facilitate nation building. He explains,

> For that, I maintain, that is, "to save much people alive," that is the great mission of our race to this coast: to turn this heathen population "from darkness to light, and from the power of Satan unto God, that they may receive forgiveness of sins, and inheritance among them who are sanctified by faith (Acts xxvi. 18)."

Crummell augments the story of Joseph with a reference to the biblical account of the early church in Acts of the Apostles to redefine the nineteenth-century Joseph figure as a savior who rescues a people from a spiritual famine triggered by the slave trade. Although the ACS recruited emigrants to cultivate the land and convert Africans, Crummell emphasizes evangelism as their chief goal. In effect, he commissions the Bajan émigrés as missionaries devoted to the saving of souls to bring about reunion and reconciliation with their African slavers and the restoration of their homeland.

Unlike the Israelites, who entered a lush Promised Land with a strong infrastructure, Liberian emigrants discovered a swampy countryside tainted by disease, death, and devastation. In the biblical Exodus narrative, God instructed the Israelites to offer the first harvest of the land as a sacrifice of thanksgiving for the fulfillment of God's promise. As Crummell welcomes the Bajan émigrés to Liberia, he assures them, "Ye have done right well in coming up here to Holy Communion this morning; in offering your 'first fruits' on 'coming into the land which the Lord your God has given you.'" The emigrants' participation in Communion enables them to offer a gift of praise in acknowledging God's care during their unusually pleasant transatlantic voyage and to receive instructions for settlement in the land. Crummell steels them for the difficult transition by positing the land as a gift from God. The Bajans may have needed such assurances; because Barbados was not officially affiliated with the ASC and they had embarked on the ACS-financed journey without the six-month provisions usually provided émigrés. Crummell invites them to look beyond the paucity of their personal resources and the desolation of the landscape by sharing his vision of an African Canaan:

> Schools, and churches and Christian colleges will spring up throughout thy borders. . . . The Lord God shall hasten the number of His elect, and the tide of salvation, sweep along in one broad, mighty current, shall bear along the mighty masses of thy people to salvation and to glory; and then "Ethiopia," from the Mediterranean to the Cape, from the Atlantic Ocean to the Indian, "shall soon stretch forth her hands unto God."

Crummell cites schools first, providing an opportunity for education denied most slaves. Operating their own churches would enable them to ensure the dissemination of the Gospel and the establishment of a faith community to support their work and nurture believers. In emphasizing "Christian colleges," however, Crummell maintains his focus on the essential role of missionaries in rebuilding Africa. He references a scriptural passage regarding Ethiopia that abolitionists often cited as evidence of the eventual elevation of people of African descent as a metonym for a transformed continent that will emerge from the devastating slave trade as a bastion of education and piety.

## Conclusion

Exodus narratives that had held so much promise at the beginning of the Civil War yielded disappointing results for black men and women who yearned to experience the rights and privileges of citizenship that many white Americans had enjoyed for nearly one hundred years. African Americans found themselves in an increasingly unstable society, where presidents could shift from being Pharaoh to Moses, or Moses to Pharaoh, depending on whether it was more politically expedient to support or neglect them. Confederate soldiers could fulfill the role of Egyptian oppressors and then regain their status as respected businessmen, community leaders, and politicians who possessed a deeper desire to marginalize people of African descent. Black Americans who had once viewed themselves as enslaved Israelites felt dispossessed, having gained freedom without protection from white supremacists who often resorted to violence to terrorize and subdue them. Even when white authors included African Americans in their new national narratives, they often identified blacks as foreigners—Ethiopians or Moors—rather than American citizens, while inviting European immigrants to enjoy the bounties of their American Canaan. Some white writers even advocated an exodus of the African American community to foreign promised lands. Rather than provide a journey from slavery to freedom or marginalization to equality, these unfulfilled Exodus narratives marked a path from bondage to a land of broken promises that pushed African Americans further than they had ever been from the border of their American Canaan. Yet the lure of Exodus proved irresistible as new writers rekindled the hope of their brethren by refocusing their experience through the lens of the Joseph narrative, a story of dreams fulfilled in a strange land.

CHAPTER FIVE

# AFRICAN AMERICANS IN THE NADIR (1877–1900)

*The "Exodus" implies two things, the perfect emancipation of an enslaved people, and the immediate destruction of their enslavers, and both accomplished by a miracle, in which the former, as a race, is forever separated from the latter as a race. These ideas became facts in the case of Egyptian bondage—they can never be realized in the case of American slavery.*

—Daniel Payne, "Evergreen Cottage,
Near Wilberforce University, Xenia, O."

*Exodus is medicine, not food; it is for disease, not health—it is not to be taken from choice, but necessity. In anything like a normal condition of things, the South is the best place for the negro. Nowhere else is there for him a promise of a happier future. Let him stay there if he can, and save both the South and himself to civilization.*

—Frederick Douglass, "The Negro Exodus from the Gulf States"

*The characters of the Old Testament I most admire are Moses and Nehemiah. They were willing to put aside their own advantages for their race and country.*

—Frances E. W. Harper, *Iola Leroy; or, Shadows Uplifted*

*[T]he railroad locomotive will furnish the "pillar of cloud by day and the pillar of fire by night" which is to guide the great exodus of the poor from the crowded communities of the Old World and the New into this promised land.*

—J. A. Wheelock, "The New Northwest"

The failure of Reconstruction thwarted black and white writers' attempts to create new national Exodus narratives that would have developed a more perfect union for all American citizens. Reconstruction had ushered in an era of unparalleled economic, educational, political, and social gains that signaled the transformation of the United States into a promised land, particularly for its African American populace. Within a decade, however, white Americans had marginalized African Americans by presenting "the Negro Problem" as a popular topic in monthly magazines that targeted white middle-class readers, and they attempted to solve the "problem" by enacting codes that curtailed African American citizens' rights, lynching blacks in record numbers, and perpetuating stereotypical images of African Americans in minstrel shows, plantation literature, and other cultural productions. The African American community struggled to survive in a period characterized as "the Nadir," "the lowest point in the quest for equal rights."[1] Although African Americans established numerous colleges, women's clubs, and benevolent societies to uplift the race, unemployment, poverty, and discrimination decimated the community. African Americans further faced a formidable obstacle when the US Supreme Court legalized "separate but equal" facilities in its 1896 *Plessy v. Ferguson* decision, effectively barring them from the American promised land of equality. As their newfound freedoms disappeared, African Americans wondered if they were waiting on the border of the promised land, wandering in the wilderness, or journeying back to Egypt. The increasing circulation and influence of white supremacist ideologies fragmented America, even limiting opportunities for immigrants and lower-class whites to experience economic advancement and social mobility. Nevertheless, a new generation of white writers sustained the national Exodus narratives while American manifested itself as an increasingly imperialistic, industrialized world power.

From the end of Reconstruction to the dawn of the twentieth century, African American writers returned to the Exodus narrative to reconstitute the nation as an inclusive, integrated society. They invoked the Joseph and Moses stories to affirm and advise leaders who preserved the community's commitment to activism by encouraging their brethren to continue demanding civil rights and social equality as they confronted the challenges of the Nadir. Other writers were more interested in searching for a promised land than in identifying a leader, however, reigniting the debate that pitted integration, emigration, and migration factions against one another. New Exodus-inspired strategies, rather than the persistent concerns about Exodus leaders and promised lands, were on the minds of still other African American activists who appropriated the Exodus narrative as a blueprint for new guides to racial uplift that could address African Americans' concerns and aspirations in the early twentieth century. Although the promise of freedom and equality offered by Exodus stories remained unfulfilled during the Nadir, the biblical narrative empowered a new generation of writers to sustain the struggle and lay the foundation for the modern Civil Rights Movement.

### AME Bishop Abraham Grant
### *Joseph Affirms Prosperity in the Pit*

During the end of the nineteenth century, as racial discrimination and violence escalated throughout the nation, African Americans found inspiration in the story of Joseph, which chronicled the transformation of the beloved son of the Israelites' patriarch Jacob into a favored slave who became a powerful ruler in Egypt. In reports from field correspondents, articles by reporters, and lessons developed for Sunday School classes, the *Christian Recorder* held up Joseph as a model of integrity for businessmen yearning for promotion, of faithfulness for young people seeking to be Christ-like, of hope for families broken by disunity, and of perseverance for anyone struggling through adversity. AME Bishop Abraham Grant's transfiguration from slave to influential minister likely informed his admiration of Joseph, for he declared "there is no character in the Bible more interesting to me than that of Joseph."[2]

In the mid-1850s Grant escaped from slavery in Florida with his brother Alex and two other slaves but was captured and sold in Georgia. After the Civil War, Grant returned to Florida, where he joined the AME Church, took classes at Cookman Institute in Jacksonville, and received government appointments as inspector of customs and county commissioner. During a reunion with his former master, Frank Rollinson, Grant forgave the impoverished, elderly man, offered to care for Rollinson in his home, and promised to delivery his eulogy. In 1873 Grant became a licensed AME minister and was soon ordained as a deacon and elder. In addition to his pastoral work, he established schools, served as trustee for several colleges, presided over AME conferences, labored extensively throughout the United States, Europe, Mexico, and West Africa, and was elected bishop of the AME Church in 1888, one of five, out of the first thirty bishops, who had been born slaves.[3]

While the nation seemed paralyzed by problems of the color line, the AME Church nurtured its membership, encouraged church growth in America and abroad, and employed a variety of means to engage its members in social protest. The *Christian Recorder*, its monthly national newspaper, was a particularly effective tool for challenging racial oppression and

*Bishop Abraham Grant, D.D., AME Church, and his wife, Florida Grant*

disseminating racial uplift strategies to the African American community. The 1900 account of the ordination service for the Reverend George Gay Daniel as deacon and elder to equip him for mission service in the Danish West Indies epitomizes the church's view of the interconnectivity of racial empowerment and spiritual nourishment.[4] In his ordination sermon, Bishop Grant embraces the Joseph narrative to teach his audience how to prosper in adversity, critique the federal government's inconsistency in addressing their racial concerns, and equip the Reverend Daniel for the challenges of foreign mission service.

Grant frames his message with a focus on the role of Providence in Joseph's life, noting that "[t]he Lord was with Joseph, and he was a prosperous man."[5] He reminds his audience that Joseph experienced prosperity during his enslavement in Egypt. Joseph's success under the debilitating conditions of slavery encourages both the congregation and the missionary to expect similar favor from God in their civil rights struggle and mission work. In effect, Joseph's fidelity to God infused his slave labor with a missionary spirit in Egypt. Similarly, despite persistent adversity within the United States throughout the nineteenth century, the AME Church had prospered. In *A History of the African Methodist Episcopal Church*, historiographer Charles Spencer Smith recounts the institution's "state of prosperity," "increased prosperity," and "future prosperity" from its founding in 1816 through the end of its developing years in 1922.[6] The church's prosperity stemmed largely from its rapid expansion throughout the United States and into foreign fields under the leadership of its first bishop, Richard Allen, a former slave. With indisputable evidence of the veracity of the Joseph narrative in the history of the AME Church and his own experience, Grant enables his audience to acknowledge their prosperity despite the unfavorable environment created by the nation's failure to protect the rights and privileges of citizenship for African Americans.

Although Grant faults the US president as the major impediment to African Americans' prosperity, he identifies the church, business, home, and government as critical sites where the community should nurture effective leaders. He warns against favoritism, however, admonishing, "If there is a father or mother in this church tonight who has a favorite among his children, my advice is, not to let the other children know of it. The jealousy consequent upon known favorites affects the family, the Church, the State. It was the case with Joseph's brethren. His father's present of a coat of many colors to Joseph affected his brethren: and then his dreams. He didn't seem to interpret those dreams. They did." In the biblical narrative, Joseph's brothers plotted to murder him but them sold him into slavery because his multicolored coat distinguished him as his father's favorite child and his divinely inspired dreams portended his eventual ascendancy over his family. To warn against resorting to violence to solve national and international disputes, Grant contrasts the debilitating dissension within Jacob's family with the original plan for racial harmony through the creation of Adam. By 1900, racial violence was rampant in America. For example, during the last decade of the nineteenth century, an average of one hundred lynchings of African Americans were reported annually.[7] Indeed, Grant remarks, "If Joseph had lived in our day he would have perhaps been lynched." During his enslavement in Egypt, Joseph was imprisoned after being falsely accused of rape by his master's wife. During the Nadir, African American men were lynched for "any mesalliance existing between a white woman and a colored man [which] is a sufficient foundation for the charge of rape."[8] Grant links America's violent mechanism for the social control of African Americans to its participation in the Spanish-American War, contrasting the gospel of "peace on earth, good will to men" that the AME Church advocated with the bloody warfare that "civilized nations" engaged in to advance imperialism in Cuba and the Philippines. Grant asserts, "The very thing Aguinaldo is contending for is the very thing George Washington contended for—Independence!" After Filipino revolutionary leader Emilio Aguinaldo assisted the United States by directing a successful guerilla war against Spain, he served as the president of the provisional government. United States president William McKinley did not acknowledge him as the rightful leader, however, and excluded him from final negotiations with Spain regarding Filipino sovereignty, which led to the Philippine-American War. As Grant preached his ordination sermon, Aguinaldo languished in the Philippines, having lost his influence among a revolutionary army that was ill-equipped to face the formidable US military. Grant draws a parallel between white Americans' refusal to give African Americans equal rights and the nation's war with Spain and its imperialistic notions regarding the Philippines, emphasizing the duplicity of a nation that staged a revolution for independence and a civil war to emancipate slaves but engaged in warfare that led to the annexation of the Philippines. The Joseph story offers a cautionary tale for politicians regarding the dangers of deceit in dealings with minority populations in America and throughout the world.

Indeed, Grant offers his strongest critique of the federal government, holding the US president responsible for the increasing deterioration in race relations in the nation. In his overview of the Joseph story, he asserts that the young man's fidelity is grounded in his father's love for and commitment to his family, which symbolizes the connection between the character of leaders and their followers. Grant contrasts the Cleveland administration, which kept its promises to African Americans, with the McKinley administration, which exudes "a suavity of manner, a bowing and scraping which greets you everywhere, and it will make almost any promise you want. . . . The President, however, is looked upon as a friend to the race." President McKinley acquiesced to white Democrats, who controlled most Southern statehouses by the end of the nineteenth century and enacted legislation to disenfranchise and marginalize African Americans. He favored white Democrats for federal appointments and refused to address African Americans' concerns regarding their loss of civil rights and the escalation of racial violence. Furthermore, McKinley devoted more attention to bringing freedom to millions abroad in the Spanish-American War than to ensuring the rights of millions of African American citizens whose civil liberties were being violated by the Democrat-controlled Southern statehouses and the US Congress.

The deterioration of conditions for African Americans under the McKinley administration leads Grant to adapt the Joseph story as a model of spiritually driven sociopolitical empowerment of a people who prosper despite oppression. He asserts,

> Joseph was taken out of the pit and sold into Egypt and though a slave the Lord was with him and he rose to office even in his slavery. He obtained favor in the eyes of Potiphar, who made him ruler of his house, and the Scripture narrative declares that the

> house was blessed because of Joseph's presence therein. A nation is sometimes blessed because of a good man.

Grant then offers Prime Minister William Gladstone, who brokered a peace treaty between Great Britain and the Boers in South Africa, as an example of the effect a good man can exert on a nation. After Gladstone's death and Britain's second war with South Africa, however, the Boers were defeated and subjected to colonization. Grant suggests that the AME Church can exert a more lasting influence than Gladstone's through mission work in Africa: "As true as I stand upon this floor tonight I believe that through this people here represented, Africa is to be blessed! The Catholic compiler says there are twelve hundred thousand homes owned by our people today. We may be like Joseph in the pit, but we will nevertheless put our hands in God's hands and make for the journey." Grant argues that the presence of the AME Church in America has fostered African American prosperity, evidenced by the increase in African American home ownership, a central component of the American dream. He suggests that mission work will effect a similar outcome in foreign fields, bringing spiritual nourishment as well as fostering material prosperity for African peoples whose nations have been decimated by the slave trade and European colonization. Grant then reminds the audience of the reunion of Joseph's family in Egypt and their settlement in the lush land of Goshen, which portends the reunion of an Afro-Atlantic family and eventual affluence of the community in fertile lands throughout the African Diaspora.

## AME Bishops, Paul Laurence Dunbar, and Frances E. W. Harper *Moses as Role Model for Leaders and Laity*

Despite the Joseph narrative's efficacy in enabling African Americans to sustain their hopes and dreams throughout the Nadir, the Moses story offered some authors greater inspiration for leadership as well as character building for everyday citizens. Moses types figured prominently in Exodus stories by an array of authors, including a contributor to the *Daily Phoenix* who lauded gubernatorial candidate Frank J. Moses as a "true Moses" in South Carolina, and Robert Smalls, who celebrated Union Army general David Hunter as the Moses of enslaved South Carolinians because he liberated them before the enactment of the Emancipation Proclamation.[9] Members of the AME Church also affirmed Moses as a model for spiritual leadership, particularly for the bishop, its chief elected officer. In his church history *The Budget: Containing Biographical Sketches, Quadrennial and Annual Reports of the General Officers of the African Methodist Episcopal Church* (1884), Benjamin

W. Arnett memorializes Richard Allen as belonging "to the constellation of moral and religious reformers; he is to the Negro race what Moses was to the Jews in Egypt; what Luther was to the Germans; what Wesley was to the English" (5). By linking Allen to two central religious reformers, Arnett suggests that the establishment of the AME Church signaled a radical shift in America's Christian community that would not only liberate African Americans but would usher in an era of reform that would advance the race. He elevates Allen from the role of church leader to the position of race reformer whose initiatives exerted a long-term, international impact. The Reverend D. H. Bowen adopted a different strategy in identifying Bishop Moses B. Salter as a Moses who worked within the AME community. In a two-part report to the *Christian Recorder* in May of 1895 on Bishop Salter's visit to eastern South Carolina, Bowen reports on the triumphs and challenges the Florence, South Carolina, district faced in building up church membership, finances, and facilities. He characterizes South Carolinian Bishop Salter's visit to the district as akin to the biblical Moses' return from Midian to lead the Israelites to the land flowing with milk and honey. Bowen reports that they responded,

> Lead, on, bold Moses,
> we're your boys,
> Your calls we'll all obey.[10]

Bowen's allusion to the biblical narrative suggests that members of the Florence district look to Bishop Salter as a divinely inspired leader who can unify and fortify the church. In his poem "The Progress of Liberty," James Madison Bell similarly lauds AME bishop Jabez Pitt Campbell as a Moses who served as their "prophet and guide" during his two-year tenure from 1864 to 1868.[11] During the Civil War, Campbell not only built up the church but openly criticized Lincoln's commitment to abolition and decried the discrimination black soldiers experienced.[12] As Moses figures, AME bishops succored the church body, affirmed the African American community, challenged national leaders, and exerted an international influence through foreign missions.

Paul Laurence Dunbar also upheld the Mosaic tradition in African American Exodus narratives in his poem "An Ante-bellum Sermon" (1895), which features a dialect-speaking preacher who conveys his understanding of the transformative nature of Scripture for the oppressed. In his engagement with the plantation tradition, Dunbar, to direct African Americans to embrace the vision of Mosaic community leaders rather than promises of government agencies in achieving their racial uplift goals, suggests a parallel between the injustices African Americans suffered during the Nadir and the oppression they experienced during slavery. In the poem, Dunbar decenters the national Exodus narrative through a slave preacher who prophesies the arrival of an avenging messianic Moses who will restore slaves to their rightful status as freeborn citizens. Such a figure would have been appealing to African Americans during the Nadir, for they had lost many of the rights they had gained during Reconstruction. The slave preacher takes what he describes as a "Bibleistic" approach to freedom, appropriating the Exodus narrative to characterize his enslaved brethren as God's children, worthy of divine liberation. He links biblical rhetoric to republican discourse in claiming African Americans' right to freedom, asserting that God allowed Pharaoh to see "Dat de people he put bref in,— / Evah mothah's son was free." He further argues, "the Lawd's intention / Evah sence de worl' began / Was dat His almight freedom / Should belong to evah man." In effect, the preacher issues his own version of the Declaration of Independence for slaves, echoing the sentiments of the founding fathers but aligning himself with Gabriel's co-conspirators, David Walker, Henry Highland Garnet, Frederick Douglass, and Afro-Atlantic writers who claimed a proclamation that liberated those born into American slavery. In 1895 African Americans needed to make a similar declaration, for Black Codes enacted throughout the South restricted their rights and curtailed their freedoms.

The preacher instructs his enslaved brethren to rely on the biblical language-world to articulate their desire for freedom, but their experience in the United States calls for the development of a new Exodus narrative featuring a more militant Moses. When he describes their eventual liberation, the slave preacher couples the Exodus story with prophecies from Revelation to herald the coming of a messianic deliverer for enslaved African Americans. He had begun his sermon by reminding his audience that God emptied "down on Egypt / All de vials of [his] powah" when Pharaoh refused to free the Israelites. As he nears the end of his sermon, the slave preacher declares that God will sound "his thundah" and "Gab'el's ho'n" to signal his intent to free the slaves. White Christians had taught slaves that they would experience emancipation in heaven. In contrast, the preacher insists that their deliverance will be brought about by a powerful Moses who

> [I]s a-comin',
> An' he's comin', suah and fas'
> We kin hyeah his feet a-trompin'
> We kin hyeah his trumpit blas'.

The words the preacher associates with the arrival of their emancipator echo the terms that John, the author of Revelation, relies on to describe Christ's Second Coming and judgment. On their "reck'nin' day," the slaves will be recognized "ez citiz" " rather than saints. Unlike the Israelites, enslaved African Americans sought freedom, civil rights, and liberties in their native land. Revelation's prophecies reveal the destruction of sinners, including slaveholders, in hell, and the reward of the righteous, a sin-free world. Slavery had become so entrenched in American society that it could be abolished only through an apocalyptic appearance of a messianic deliverer. Like Henry Turner, who analyzed the Civil War through the lens of Exodus and the millennial prophecies of Revelation, Dunbar refashions fragments of biblical narratives to construct an Exodus story that speaks to the experiences of oppressed African Americans in both slavery and freedom. Frederick Douglass, whom Dunbar revered and many had lauded as Moses, died in 1895, the year Dunbar published his "Ante-bellum Sermon." Thus Dunbar's fashioning of a messianic slave preacher may have reflected the yearnings of many members of the African American community for a new Mosaic leader to address the race problem.

Unlike Dunbar or contributors to the *Christian Recorder* who focused on Mosaic leadership, Frances E. W. Harper continued to develop and enlarge the application for her concept of the Mosaic moment for all members of the African American community. Shortly before the Nadir, she published "A Factor in Human Progress" (1885), which lauds Moses as a model of self-sacrifice whose preference for the hardships of the wilderness journey over a life of luxury in Egypt enabled him to lead the Israelites in becoming a nation that proffered a legacy of science, art, and spirituality. However, she provided a practical application of the Mosaic principle in *Iola Leroy or, Shadows Uplifted* (1893), a Reconstruction novel that outlines how African Americans could respond to the challenges of the Nadir. The novel focuses on Iola's family and other light-skinned African American characters born of enslaved mothers who experience a Mosaic Moment when they must choose to pass for white or identify themselves as African Americans. For her protagonist, Iola, Harper couples the Moses story with biblical allusions and mythological imagery to reconstruct the quadroon figure as a mixed-race woman working within African American communities rather than a tragic mulatto pining in white society. As Iola labors among the wounded soldiers during the Civil War, she rejects the marriage proposal of Dr. Gresham, a white physician who insists that she pass for white in order to become his wife. When recalling Iola's choice, her new suitor, Dr. Frank Latimer, a mulatto physician, explains,

> But I know a young lady who could have cast her lot with the favored race, yet chose to take her place with the freed people as their teacher, friend, and adviser. . . . She had been fearfully wronged, and to her stricken heart came a brilliant offer of love, home, and social position. But she bound her heart to the mast of duty, closed her ears to the siren song, and could not be lured from her purpose. (263)

Harper suggests that for light-skinned, mixed-raced African Americans, true favor came from identification with and service to the race. Iola's experiences as a slave temper her talented-tenth-like role within the community, enabling her to develop close relationships with the freedmen. Harper complicates Iola's Mosaic moment with an allusion to the *Odyssey*, in which Odysseus instructs his men to stuff their ears with beeswax to block out the Sirens' song and to tie him to the mast to enable him to resist the lure of the music. In describing Iola as binding her heart to duty and closing her ear to the Siren song of interracial marriage, Dr. Latimer posits Dr. Gresham's marriage proposal as a seduction more ruinous than the abuse Iola experienced as a slave. Like Iola, Dr. Latimer was offered the choice of passing as white, but his option lay in professional acclaim brokered through the patronage of his white paternal grandmother.

Iola is equally enamored of Dr. Latimer, but locates her attraction to him in biblical standards of masculinity grounded in Old Testament heroes. She explains, "[T]he characters of the Old Testament I most admire are Moses and Nehemiah. They were willing to put aside their own advantages for their race and country. Dr. Latimer comes up to my ideal of a high, heroic manhood" (265). Unlike Moses, who grew up as the adopted son of Pharaoh's daughter while the Israelites were enslaved, Nehemiah served as the king's cupbearer in the Persian court while Israel was in exile. Whereas Moses forfeited the throne of Egypt to emancipate enslaved Israelites, Nehemiah gained support from the Persian ruler to return to the desolate land of Israel and complete the work of rebuilding the wall around Jerusalem.[13] As a Mosaic Nehemiah, Dr. Latimer eschews assimilation in white American society yet associates with whites to advance the cause of African Americans.

## African American Exodus in the Age of European Immigration

Although American writers remained fascinated with the role of Joseph and Moses figures in Exodus narratives, they continued to explore the experience of Exodus itself in their migration stories. After Reconstruction, white writers frequently posited the United States as a dominant world power that welcomed European immigrants as the newest members of God's American Israel. Millions of Europeans moved to the United States in the nineteenth and early twentieth centuries, attracted by the promise of economic opportunity and religious freedom in a democratic republic. Although immigrants often experienced discrimination, white writers romanticized emigration to America as an Exodus journey, just as they had during the Civil War era. For example, in "The New Northwest" (1898), published in *Harper's New Monthly Magazine*, J. A. Wheelock asserts that "the railroad locomotive will furnish the 'pillar of cloud by day and the pillar of fire by night' which is to guide the great exodus of the poor from the crowded communities of the Old World and the New into this promised land," the New Northwest—Minnesota, North Dakota, South Dakota, Montana, Oregon, and Washington (310). Unlike European immigrants who had migrated to the West via trails and canals during the Gold Rush, those who entered America after Reconstruction joined other recent settlers on a transcontinental journey to the fertile lands of the New Northwest Canaan. The rapid expansion of national transportation networks and growth of western port cities such as Portland and Seattle shifted the impetus for exodus from religious freedom to economic opportunities for peoples of European descent. The railway system facilitated the ease of their journey and insured the success of their business ventures.

While some white authors invoked the biblical story to create a place for European immigrants in their national Exodus stories, others were more concerned with excluding African Americans from white Americans' promised land. In *An Appeal to Pharaoh: The Negro Problem, and Its Radical Solution* (1889), Carlyle McKinley argues that the US government should deport African American citizens to atone for the nation's error in sanctioning slavery. McKinley was not the first to suggest the removal of blacks from the United States. From the Revolutionary War to the Civil War eras, Thomas Jefferson, Robert Finley, and Abraham Lincoln had recommended colonizing African Americans as a viable emancipation and deportation policy. To justify his scheme, McKinley asserts that the United States made four mistakes in its relationship with African Americans: bringing them to the nation, keeping them in America, leaving them in slavery too long, and giving them suffrage rights. The nation could redeem itself by sending African Americans to Africa, forcibly if necessary (29–32). Although McKinley accepts the biblical injunction "God hath made of one blood all nations of men, for to dwell on the face of the earth," he stresses the latter part of the verse: "'[He] himself *hath determined the bounds of their habitation!*'" (197; emphasis in original). For McKinley, the boundaries between whites and blacks are as wide as the Atlantic Ocean. White Americans could regain

God's favor and occupy their promised land only by expelling African American citizens.

## Reaffirmation of the National Exodus Stories

Some white Americans, notably Henry Ward Beecher, continued to encourage the development of an inclusive national narrative, however. Beecher, the brother of Harriet Beecher Stowe, was one of the most influential preachers and reformers of the nineteenth century. He published his sermons and lectures, along with pamphlets and books, extending the power of his pulpit across the nation and around the world. The 1891 *Patriotic Addresses in America and England from 1850 to 1885, on Slavery, the Civil War and the Development of Civil Liberty in the United States*, a collection of Beecher's works edited by John R. Howard, includes a variety of orations that link the story of Exodus to the history of America, particularly during the Civil War. In his Thanksgiving Day sermon "Modes and Duties of Emancipation" (1861), which is categorized as a "Patriotic Address," Beecher recast the 1850s as the Northern states' journey from the Red Sea to the promised land, a transformation that equipped them to do battle with the Confederate states in the Civil War (339). As the war began, he presented "The Ground and Forms of Government" (1862) to affirm the Northern states' efforts to restore self-government through the Civil War as a march to the promised land (396). As the war drew to a close, Beecher eulogized Abraham Lincoln as a martyr who died on the border of his American promised land (701–3). Beecher also outlined his vision for reconciliation between the Southern and Northern states in a series of texts that were featured in the "Reconstruction of Southern States" unit. He composed the works while serving as chaplain of the Soldiers' and Sailors' Convention, formed to facilitate the integration of the Southern states back into the Union. In a text dated August 30, 1866, Beecher describes freedmen as travelers from the "Egypt of ignorance to the promised land of civilization," a journey that all "uncivilized" peoples have undertaken (741). Near the end of his life, Beecher posited himself as a type of Mosaic leader in "Retrospect and Prospect," a Thanksgiving Day sermon preached November 27, 1884, after Grover Cleveland, whom he supported, was elected president. Beecher asserted, "Moses after forty years of toil, was allowed to see the promised land from afar off only. Less worthy, yet more blessed, I am spared to go over with the rejoicing tribes into the land flowing with milk and honey" (836). Beecher viewed Exodus as a narrative that spoke to the experiences of many different Americans and attempted to use the story to foster the development of a more inclusive nation.

Other white writers embraced Exodus to affirm traditional national Exodus narratives introduced by Puritan writers and adopted at pivotal points in American history. In *The Story of America: Containing the Romantic Incidents of History, from the Discovery of America to the Present Time* (1889), Elia Wilkinson Peattie recalls the Puritans' journey to America, lamenting that their "dear old pastor [John] Robinson, whom they looked forward with so much pleasure to meeting, died, like Moses, within sight of the promised land" (64). Hubert Howe Bancroft adopts a similar strategy in *History of the Pacific States of North America: Mexico* (1893), asserting that Hernán Cortés and his men, as they prepared to battle a large and well-equipped Indian army, were buoyed by the thought that a promised land and "trusty friends" lay just beyond the mountain range (498). Writers sustained the national Exodus narrative story line as they published stories of the nation's birth. In *Battles of America by Sea and Land: With Biographies of Naval and Military Commanders* (1878), Robert Tomes included a section devoted to the "Promised Land" in a series of vignettes that examined the Civil War. In his anthology *American Patriotism: Speeches, Letters, and Other Papers Which Illustrate the Foundation, the Development, the Preservation of the United States of America* (1880), Selim H. Peabody included John Quincy Adams' speech "Lafayette" (1834), in which Adams compares the French patriot to Moses, as neither of them entered his promised land: Lafayette did not live to see the fulfillment of his hope for the end of the French monarchy through the establishment of France as a republic (310). The Associated Veterans of the Mexican War continued this tradition of linking Exodus with nation building in its *History of the Celebration of the Fiftieth Anniversary of the Taking Possession of California and Raising of the American Flag at Monterey, Cal., by Commodore John Drake Sloat, U.S.N., July 7th, 1846*. It featured Eliza A. Pittsinger's poem "California's Golden Jubilee," which includes the lines, "'Tis here, 'Tis here, the Promised Land / 'Tis here in freedom's cause we stand" (31). American expansion demanded the development of businesses to foster economic growth. R. S. Russell's article "Importance of the Industry of Apiculture" (1892), published in the *American Bee Journal*, epitomizes how a new generation of writers embraced Exodus to sustain the national narrative. Russell asserts that God's promise to settle the Israelites in "a land flowing with milk and honey" reveals the two industries that are essential for any national economy. Americans had settled into their "promised land" and established creameries throughout the nation, but also needed to devote resources to the development of a honey industry. White writers also found the Exodus story to be an effective rhetorical tool for creating their literary history. In "Washington Irving's Literary Services" (1882), published in the *Ariel,* Edward C. Gale describes Washington Irving as America's first internationally acclaimed author, for "he was a national hunger, a prophet to whom the people looked to lead them to another promised land. At the summit of a literature, which if he did not create, he had at least the honor of ushering in, he did more perhaps to foster by example and precept the literary genius of America, but just then budding forth, than any other one" (83). Exodus remained central to the national narrative, a story that informed and influenced the continued development of American religion, politics, economics, and literature.

## Robert J. Harlan
## *Exodus, Migration, and the Rights of Citizenship*

The national Exodus narratives were virtually silent regarding the escalating violence, political setbacks, and economic distress affecting most African Americans in the late nineteenth century. Some black activists turned to episodes in the Exodus narrative to address their immediate desire for safety and freedom. Benjamin "Pap" Singleton, who described himself as the "father of the Black Exodus," soon became the most prominent Moses figure leading black migrants out of the South after President Rutherford B. Hayes withdrew federal troops, white Democrats resumed control of most state governments, and working and living conditions for African Americans deteriorated dramatically.[14] From the 1860s to the early 1900s, thousands of Southern blacks migrated to a midwestern promised land, a move several prominent black leaders, notably Frederick Douglass, opposed. Some black activists defended migration, however, sparking discussions reminiscent of those surrounding the integration versus emigration debates of the 1820s and 1850s. In 1879, when approximately six thousand African Americans migrated from the South to the Midwest, African American political activist Robert J. Harlan made his way to the National Conference of Colored Men of the United States in Nashville, Tennessee. Harlan, the son of Judge James Harlan and an enslaved African American woman, and the half-brother of US Supreme Court Justice John Marshall Harlan, who dissented in the *Plessy v. Ferguson* case, joined those who opposed Douglass' stance against the black exodus. In his speech "Migration Is the Only Remedy for Our Wrongs," delivered at the Conference on May 8, 1879, Harlan invokes Exodus to present migration as the chief weapon in his community's revolution against the oppression of black citizens.

Harlan presents migration as a choice provoked by the brutality of Southern leaders who breached their commitment to serve and protect the rights of all members of their communities. He explains, "If the leading

*Robert J. Harlan, state legislator and activist*

men of the South will make another Egypt of these bright and sunny valleys, then must the oppressed go forth into the promised land of liberty, into the Western States and Territories where the people are at peace and the soil is free, and where every man can secure a home for himself and family with none to molest him or make him afraid" (601–2). Unlike the Israelites, who experienced slavery after settling in the Promised Land but never returned to Egypt, African Americans repeatedly faced the danger of being forced into an Egypt-like existence because they remained in the land where their former oppressors regained political power. Harlan justifies migration as a response to the threat of the return of slavery in the South for African Americans. The escalation of violence, lack of job opportunities, and deterioration of social conditions created an untenable living environment for African American families. In expressing a desire for habitation in the western states, where "soil is free," Harlan alludes to the short-lived Free Soil Party, which opposed the extension of slavery into the western states, and posits the move as a political choice that could help shift the balance of power away from the South in national elections.

For Harlan, mobility and citizenship are inextricably linked, fundamental rights in a democratic society. He conflates the Exodus story with secular/republican discourse to affirm African Americans' right to migrate within their own country to escape oppression. He asserts,

> If we cannot [migrate], we are not free, no more than are the serfs of Russia, who, until lately, were a part of the estate and sold as such, but, if *we* are to be re-enslaved we may as well die on the road to liberty as at the feet of tyrants. We may as well expire

> contending for liberty, aye, and far better, than in base submission to degrading slavery. (602; emphasis in original)

While the United States had welcomed thousands of European immigrants seeking relief from political oppression and opportunities for economic advancement, it had encouraged the disenfranchisement and terrorization of African Americans. Harlan intimates that the United States cannot truly be a republic if it mimics feudal nations that enforce systems of serfdom. Instead of seeking a Moses figure to guide them out of their Southern Egypt, Harlan directs blacks to initiate a revolution against oppression by embracing Patrick Henry's motto, "Give me liberty or give me death," and leaving the South, a move that could cripple its economic system, which was dependent on the labor of African Americans. If they encounter violence, they will die honorably in the quest for freedom rather than in slavish submission to their oppressors.

### Frederick Douglass
### *Exodus, Violence, and the Responsibilities of Citizenship*

Although many black activists joined Harlan in supporting African Americans' 1879 Exodus to the Midwest, Frederick Douglass disassociated himself from the Exodusters movement. Douglass found a welcoming audience for his stance against migration among white middle-class Americans. In "The Negro Exodus from the Gulf States: Address before the Convention of the American Social Science Association, Saratoga Springs," delivered on September 12, 1879, nearly four months after Harlan's speech, Douglass appropriates the Exodus narrative to reconfigure the South as a contested promised land where collaboration between black workers and white employers is essential for the transformation of the South into an economic powerhouse in post-Reconstruction America. Although he opposes migration, Douglass invokes the Exodus story to hold the white "masterclass" responsible for the migration of African Americans from the South. Nevertheless, he argues that this "exodus" has convinced Southerners of their dependence on the "despised and hated negro" for prosperity and civilization. In the biblical narrative, Pharaoh emancipated enslaved Israelites but then pursued them, realizing his empire would stagnate without their labor. In effect, Douglass posits the South as an Egypt where former slaveholders are taskmasters who are aware of their need for cheap labor but unwilling to treat African American workers fairly. Yet unlike the Israelites, who left Egypt immediately after emancipation, former American slaves remained in their Egypt under highly qualified conditions of freedom. Hence, many decided to migrate and seek new opportunities in the promised land of their choice.

*Negro Emigrants on Their Way to Kansas*

Douglass attempts to dissuade African Americans from embracing western emigration by characterizing it as a protracted, expensive journey, stymied by formidable obstacles that block their entry into the midwestern promised land. He asserts, "[The freedman] lines the sunny banks of the Mississippi, fluttering in rags and wretchedness, mournfully imploring hardhearted steamboat captains to take him on board; while the friends of the emigration movement are diligently soliciting funds all over the North to help him away from his old home to the new Canaan of Kansas" (42). In the biblical narrative, the Israelites left Egypt with valuable goods they received from plague-weary oppressors who were eager for them to go. Conversely, Douglass posits black migrants as impoverished citizens stranded on the banks of the Mississippi, encountering Pharaoh-like white captains who refuse to facilitate their journey. Instead of bettering their condition, migration deepens African Americans' suffering. Although colonists, European immigrants, and even Douglass himself had experienced similar complications during their migration from oppressive societies, he refuses to acknowledge such difficulties as common challenges during the relocation process.

Because he believes democracy will ultimately prevail in the South, Douglass conflates the Exodus narrative with republican discourse to impel his audience to redirect their energies to resolving the issues that are initiating black migration. Although he believes African Americans increasingly view white oppressors as impediments to national progress, Douglass chastises migrants for exacerbating their problems by accusing the federal government of neglect, sabotaging their own success in the South, and impoverishing themselves by leaving their homes. In effect, Douglass suggests that black migrants who exercise human agency to solve their own problems are inhibiting their ability to obtain assistance from the government and sympathetic white citizens. Like Pilgrims who sailed to the New World to escape persecution, homesteaders who journeyed to the West to establish new communities, and Europeans who immigrated to the United States to escape unrest, black American citizens migrateed to the Midwest to find better employment and establish safe homes.

Although he opposes migration, Douglass acknowledges its value, while expressing a preference for integration as the best means for the restoration of the South and elevation of African Americans. Near the end of his speech he asserts, "Exodus is medicine, not food; it is for disease, not health—it is not to be taken from choice, but necessity. In anything like a normal condition of things, the South is the best place for the negro. . . . Let him stay there if he can, and save both the South and himself to civilization" (47–48). Douglass views Exodus as a remedy rather than a solution, something resorted to for healing rather than sustenance. Unlike Harlan, he argues that migration is not the choice of citizens but rather the remedy for the oppressed. He situates the future of the South in the presence of African Americans whose labor and talents will cultivate a society where both whites and blacks can thrive. Nevertheless, he conflates the Exodus narrative with secular discourse to remind whites of the violent consequences that can result from forcing blacks to stay in the South. He recalls African Americans who battled for freedom in the American Revolution, joined John Brown at Harpers Ferry, fought during the Civil War, or revolted against slavery in the spirit of Joseph Cinque, Toussaint L'Ouverture, Nathaniel Turner, Denmark Vesey, and Madison Washington (48). His focus on enslaved African Americans serves as a reminder of the slave-like conditions of the migrants and the violent acts against Americans that could originate from within the African American community. Nearly thirty years after Emancipation, African American citizens still lived in a nation where oppressive conditions demanded that they risk their lives for liberty.

## AME Bishop Daniel Payne and the Liberian Exodus Organizations
### *Exodus as Blueprint or Roadblock to Emigration*

Thousands of African Americans ignored Douglass' pleas and migrated to the Midwest, often lured by the promise of employment and safety in all-black towns. Others responded to the challenges of the Nadir by embracing colonization and seeking opportunities within African American expatriate communities in Africa, as had David Coker many years earlier. Rather than affiliate themselves with the American Colonization Society, African Americans developed their own means to reach Liberia with varied success. William M. Royal, an agent of the Liberian Company who was described as the "Black Moses of New Orleans" for his efforts to transport African Americans to the Republic of Liberia, was unable to persuade many to leave the United States.[15] However, African Americans in Charleston, South Carolina, formed the Liberian Exodus Association (LEA) to transport themselves to a West African Canaan on their own ship, the *Azor*. Despite a difficult transatlantic journey during which twenty-one emigrants died, the LEA considered the voyage a success and published *The Liberian Exodus. First Voyage of the Azor. Liberia a Delightful Country. Climate, Soil, and Productions. Character of the People in Liberia; and How They Live* (1878). In the pamphlet, white and black writers present competing Exodus stories that affirm Liberia both as a promised land for industrious African Americans and as a replica of the oppressive society blacks had hoped to escape.

Both white and black writers evoke Exodus to posit Africa as a land brimming with economic opportunities for enterprising African Americans. In a letter written for the *Charleston News and Courier* published in *The Liberian Exodus*, white reporter A. B. Williams, Esq., reports that "a magnificent country" awaits black emigrants—if they are willing to work in a land without government assistance (2). Like Coker in his letters to prospective emigrants in Baltimore, Williams instructs potential emigrants to bring tools and recruit family members to help clear land and plant crops. *The Liberian Exodus* also featured a report by Israel W. Moultrie, an African American emigrant who had settled in Liberia, that augments Williams' glowing reviews, informing potential emigrants that they can produce more crops with less land, eat foods available in the United States, spend American currency, and find better deals on staples such as sugar, meat, and clothing (7). Williams and Moultrie Americanize the emigrant experience as a homesteader's opportunity. Instead of migrating to a western American promised land like European immigrants and white Americans, however, African Americans would make a transatlantic journey to a home among their African brethren. Yet the two men offer disparate rationales for African

American settlement in Africa. Williams makes a sociological argument, lauding Liberia as a land where the African American is "capable of becoming much nearer a perfect man than he is in America," while simultaneously asserting that the "American negro" is beneath the "English Colony negro" and the "Liberian negro" (3). Although Williams acknowledges the progress African Americans have made in the United States after Emancipation, he presents them as best suited for Africa, a land where he ranks them below Africans, whom Europeans and white Americans viewed as inferior. Conversely, Moultrie doubles the Exodus narrative with republican rhetoric to emphasize economic opportunities that African Americans can create by simulating an "American" experience in Africa. He asserts,

> I will say without fear, this is the best country in the world;—a man can live happy here. . . . Charleston would be but a lighthouse to this place; and every person that can come, there is room sufficient for them, I my friends expect to die here, for every blow I strike is freedom. . . . [C]ome out here like we have, you will be done with serfdom, starvation and want. (7)

For potential black emigrants, Moultrie posits Charleston as a lighthouse to Liberia rather than a port city for America. Instead of languishing in underemployment or fending off perpetrators of racial violence, however, they could, like Moultrie, clear land, plant crops, and build homes, a lifestyle that reflected the fulfillment of the American dream in the West. Thus, Liberia would be appealing to African Americans who had experienced privation because of limited economic opportunities in the United States.

In a letter to the LEA published in *The Liberian Exodus*, Liberian residents J. T. Richardson, H. D. Brown, J. W. Hilson, C. L. Parsons, and T. G. Fuller affirm Moultrie's emphasis on American-styled land ownership and independence, noting that they welcomed emigrants on the *Azor* with assurances "that all men are endowed with certain inalienable rights, life, liberty and the acquirement of property" (6). They link the impetus for colonization to George Mason's Virginia Declaration of Rights, adopted by the Virginia Convention of Delegates in 1776:

> That all men are by nature equally free and independent, and have certain inherent rights, of which, when they enter into a state of society, they cannot, by any compact, deprive or divest their posterity; namely, the enjoyment of life and liberty, with the means of acquiring and possessing property, and pursuing and obtaining happiness and safety.[16]

Thus, Liberia is constituted as an extension of the United States where people of African descent can enjoy the rights and privileges associated with American citizenship. In seeking to assuage the concerns of the newcomers, the Liberian settlers reveal their imposition of Western ideologies on African cultures. Members of the welcoming party also report that they invite the newly arrived emigrants to "take part with us in the great work of civilizing and evangelizing a continent" (6). Like American colonists who claimed the New World as their promised land and attempted to Christianize Native Americans, African American emigrants associated with the LEA believed Christianity would elevate Africans, just as Absalom Jones, the ACS, and Alexander Crummell had advocated. Liberian settlers were encouraged to embrace Liberia's natural resources but rely on American values to transform the "homeland" into their promised land, the same principles that had led to their enslavement and oppression in the United States. Indeed, the American Colonization Society had introduced a three-tiered caste system that empowered white agents, favored light-skinned emigrants, and marginalized Africans.[17] By the time the LEA emigrants arrived, the colony had become a nation controlled by Africa American expatriates who had displaced the white agents but maintained the color caste system they had established.

Although the LEA enjoyed the support of AME Bishop Henry Turner, the prominent AME Bishop Daniel Payne vigorously opposed the organization. In 1878, when the LEA consecrated the *Azor*, Payne refused to dedicate the vessel.[18] That same year, Reverend C. H. Pearce, an influential leader of the AME Church in Florida who supported colonization, wrote a letter to Payne published in the *Christian Recorder* requesting that he clarify his position on African emigration. Payne responded in a seven-part letter in which he denounces the Liberian Exodus as an ill-advised venture that drew African Americans away from their native land.[19] He rejects Exodus as the primary narrative for the African American community because their experience deviates from the narrative account. Payne argues that the *Azor* venture "has been unfortunately called an 'Exodus.' I say unfortunately, because, if they mean what that historic name implies, then, they have given utterance to a great fallacy." He believes a Liberian exodus is implausible. "The 'Exodus' implies two things," Payne continues, "the perfect emancipation of an enslaved people, and the immediate destruction of their enslavers, and both accomplished by a miracle, in which the former, as a race, is forever separated from the latter as a race."[20] Unlike the Israelites, African Americans experienced multiple small-scale exoduses from the mid-eighteenth century until the end of the Civil War but were rarely permanently separated from their enslavers. When Congress outlawed slavery after the war, legislators did not punish former Confederates, and thus set the stage for the resurgence of Black Codes and racial violence against African

Americans. When Reconstruction failed, many African Americans migrated to all-black towns or segregated communities in the Midwest that often did not provide permanent relief from repressive conditions. Payne differentiates African Americans' fragmented, multiple experience of migration from the Israelites' singular Exodus, asserting, "These ideas [the emancipation of the Israelites and destruction of their enslavers] became facts in the case of Egyptian bondage—they can never be realized in the case of American slavery. The enlightenment and *salvation* of *humanity* was involved and needed in the former; no salvation of humanity is involved or needed in the latter" (emphasis in original). Although many enslaved African Americans and free blacks fought for the rights and privileges of citizenship in their native land, they had not been designated as God's "chosen people," miraculously emancipated, and given a special mission to evangelize the world. Like their predecessors who had selected specific portions of the Exodus narrative to address the needs of their communities at particular historical moments, supporters of Liberian emigration fashioned an Exodus story that represented the desires of their constituents but did not reflect the reality of their experiences.

In responding to the LEA's insistence on a program that addresses their brethren's needs, Payne employs the Exodus narrative to politicize the organization's motives. He argues that their misdirected plea for an "exodus" is the "offspring of disappointed political ambition. . . . Just as long as the leaders of this 'Exodus' held their seats in the Legislatures of Georgia and South Carolina, or played a successful part in the politics of these States, not a word was heard from their lips concerning African Emigration." African Americans had wielded considerable influence in state constitutional conventions that extended suffrage rights to all black males and developed a more equitable voter-districting system based on population rather than property. However, by the late 1870s Democrats regained control of Southern statehouses and systematically excluded African Americans from political office, restricted their rights, and limited their voting. While Liberian settlers emphasized land acquisition as the primary motivation for colonizing Africa, Payne contends that LEA officers would have opposed the Liberia exodus if they had been able to maintain their political positions in the United States. Even if African Americans were able to regain some political clout, Payne suggests that emigrationists had misread African realities as poorly as they had misapplied the Exodus narrative to African American migrations. He asserts,

> The hope of escaping from the oppression of the white man in America, and of finding an *asylum* from his power in Africa has doubtless influenced tens of thousands

> of the dupes of the "Exodus" movement. This hope is . . . vain . . . because, on their arrival . . . they will ascertain that . . . the white man has gone ahead and taken possession of the best portions of Africa.[21]

Like Daniel Coker, black emigrants would leave their native land, seeking both political and economic opportunities in a nation where they would not encounter racism and discriminatory practices. Europeans had preceded them, however, scrambling for the best land, expanding Christianity's reach, and wielding significant influence on nations' development within the continent. Even if African Americans segregated themselves in Liberia, they could not isolate themselves from the influence of white Americans and Europeans who controlled major economic markets and resources throughout the world.

Rather than rely on the Exodus story to justify emigration, Payne doubles the biblical narrative with the story of Noah to convey his global integrationist vision. African Americans' quest for an African promised land is imprudent in Payne's judgment, for "the races were never made for isolation, but for fraternity. . . . God has tested Ham by himself, Shem by himself, Japheth by himself." Here Payne invokes nineteenth-century biblical scholars' belief that humankind was descended from Noah's three sons, Ham, Shem, and Japheth. For centuries the races had lived separately. When they began to interact, however, Europeans emerged as dominant world powers. Payne assures readers that "He the Omnipotent God is now about to test these three brothers abreast of each other, for the benefit of each other and for the reconstruction of society, in order that He might develop in them a history, brighter, purer, more glorious than the past."[22] With the eradication of slavery, Payne envisions a reconstruction extending beyond the United States to a world in which humans live as equals. If African Americans segregate themselves in Liberia, they will never experience the blessings that come from developing integrated societies in which various peoples are devoted to fostering one another's well-being.

### Francis Grimké
### *Exodus and Radical African American Activism*

Instead of engaging in the western migration–versus–African emigration debates, other writers encouraged African Americans to seek integration in the United States. In early October 1902, the thirty-sixth annual Encampment of the Grand Army of the Republic (GAR) in Washington, D.C., encouraged African American Presbyterian minister and activist Francis Grimké to create a new Exodus-inspired racial uplift strategy to unify his

*The Reverend Francis Grimké, pastor of the Fifteenth Street Presbyterian Church, Washington, D.C., and activist*

fractured community. Grimké, the son of wealthy planter Henry Grimké and his enslaved mistress Nancy Weston, had moved to the North after laboring as a slave for the Confederacy during the Civil War and completed his education at Lincoln University and the Princeton Theological Seminary.

While attending Lincoln, Francis Grimké met his aunts, influential reformers Angelina Grimké Weld and Sarah Grimké, who helped pay for his education and supported him as he settled into a career. Francis Grimké became pastor of the Fifteenth Street Presbyterian Church in Washington, D.C., where he also engaged in civic activism. The GAR, a sociopolitical organization founded by white Union Army surgeon Benjamin F. Stephenson in 1866 for Civil War veterans, had established chapters in each state to meet the needs of veterans, influence local and national elections, sponsor a memorial day, and operate a Soldiers Home, which led to the development of the federal government's Veterans Administration. By 1890 more than four hundred thousand veterans had joined the organization. Each year the GAR held a multiday National Encampment that featured camping, dinners, parades, and memorials. Two days after the 1902 Encampment ended, Grimké preached a sermon, "A Resemblance and a Contrast between the American Negro and the Children of Israel, in Egypt, or the Duty of the Negro to Contend Earnestly for His Rights Guaranteed under the Constitution," to honor GAR members for fighting in the Civil War and including black veterans in their organization. In calling for African Americans to contend for their rights, however, he issues a direct challenge to Booker T. Washington's accommodationist methodology, which privileged manual labor over political gains. Grimké encourages African Americans to view their Exodus experiences as the impetus for the development of a new national organization that will initiate a radical push for the full restoration of their rights and privileges as American citizens.

Grimké begins with a comparative critical examination of African Americans' and the Israelites' experiences in slavery to determine if the Exodus story reflects their goals for racial uplift in the early twentieth century. In the biblical narrative, Jacob's family voluntarily traveled to Egypt for temporary lodging during a famine, but relocated there after Joseph secured good land and job opportunities for them. In contrast, Europeans had enslaved Africans and forced them to migrate to the Americas. Like the Israelites, Africans were few in number when they arrived in their land of bondage, but their population rapidly increased. Whereas Pharaoh attempted to curtail the slave population explosion by overworking the Israelites and killing their newborn baby boys, Americans created an oppressive domestic slavery system but did not mandate national population controls. On the contrary, Americans slavers became increasingly dependent on the natural increase of the slave population to support the institution after Congress outlawed the importation of enslaved Africans in 1807. There were major differences in the emancipation processes as well. The Israelites readily left Egypt when God sent Moses to emancipate them. Although the majority of the African American populace chafed under the adverse conditions of American slavery, most remained in the United States after the Civil War. Ultimately, there were more differences than similarities between African Americans' and the Israelites' experiences in slavery and freedom. African Americans overwhelmingly preferred integration in their American Canaan rather than migration to a foreign promised land. Because they lost many of their rights after Reconstruction ended, however, African Americans needed a new racial uplift model that would enable them to regain their citizenship status.

The dramatic changes in America's political system compelled Grimké to incorporate political discourse into his Exodus narrative to argue for a radical shift in African Americans' community uplift tactics. Describing the Republican Party, he asserts, "It used to be the Grand Old Party. It is no longer such. There isn't a single thing about it, either in what it is at the present doing, or in its purposes with reference to the future, to which the term 'grand' can be truthfully applied" (356–57). Republicans had initially supported antislavery initiatives, but gradually abandoned the causes of the African American community after the Civil War. With the support and encouragement of Andrew Johnson, Republicans reversed many of the gains African Americans made during Reconstruction, restricting voting rights and declaring the Civil Rights Act of 1875 unconstitutional. Like their predecessors, who had relied on white politicians, notably US senators Owen Lovejoy and Charles Sumner, to enact legislation that protected their freedom, African Americans needed the support of influential government officials in recovering their citizenship rights during the Nadir. With Republican President Theodore Roosevelt in the White House, Grimké may have hoped that the political climate was becoming more favorable for African Americans, for Roosevelt had appointed African Americans to federal posts and spoken out against lynching.

Rather than direct his audience to the Exodus story as the model for their new racial uplift strategy, however, Grimké instructs them to look to the GAR for inspiration. In so doing, Grimké shifts the thrust of early twentieth-century civil rights activism from physical movement to escape oppression to political organization to contest for change. He argues that the GAR deserves the title "Grand" because "the Army of the Republic . . . is the Army that put down the great Rebellion, and with it the accursed system of slavery, which was like a millstone about the neck of both races" (358). Here Grimké alludes to Jesus' admonition that it would be better to tie a millstone, a heavy grinding stone, around one's neck than offend Christians who exhibit a childlike trust in Him. He posits the Union Army as crushing a renegade political system that threatened the vitality of both white and black Americans. He is particularly pleased that African American veterans are members of the organization and participate in its annual Encampments, for they are a reminder that African Americans had fought in every major war since the founding of the nation. Just as Stevenson had created the GAR after the Civil War when the federal government failed to keep its promise to provide benefits for black and white veterans, African Americans, rather than lament the unfulfilled promises of Reconstruction, should establish their own national organization to remind the nation of their contributions, provide for the needs of their people, and demand the restoration of their rights. In effect, Grimké sees the need for an organization like the National Association for the Advancement of Colored People, which would be founded in 1909 by white reformers and African American activists "To Discuss Means for Securing Political and Civil Equality for the Negro."[23] He reconfigures mutual aid societies as organizations that galvanize African Americans to compel the nation to tend to the needs of their community.

As he reveals the structure of their new organization, Grimké conflates political discourse with the biblical story of John the Baptist to create a role model for leaders who will spearhead reform. He explains, "If we are to succeed; if we are to make the proper kind of a fight in this country for our rights, we have got to develop a class of men who cannot be won over by a few offices, or by being patted on the shoulder" (360). Grimké encourages his listeners to avoid the pitfalls of flattery offered by public office and politicians, a criticism that Payne also included in his critique of the Liberia Exodus Association. He argues that African Americans need

> men, who, like John the Baptist, are willing to be clothed in camel's hair, and to subsist on locusts and wild honey,—to wear the coarsest clothing, and be content with the plainest food, in order that they might be free to follow the dictates of their own conscience that they might be unhampered in the fight which they are making for their rights, and for the rights of their race. (360)

In the biblical narrative, John the Baptist lived an austere life as the herald of the Messiah, but thousands flocked to the desert to hear his message, which often included rebukes of the king and religious leaders. Unlike Frances E. W. Harper, who urged all African Americans to emulate the disunionist Moses in her essay "Our Greatest Want," Grimké directs them to model their political activism on John the Baptist by becoming principled men who will boldly challenge corrupt American politicians, businessmen, and clergy as well as critique the leadership establishment of their own race in instituting a new organization that will profoundly shift the focus of African Americans' approach to race relations from flight to fight. Such leaders would experience success only if they adopted a radical approach of eschewing any worldly entrapments that would hinder reform. Whereas John the Baptist had been divinely anointed from the womb, black activists, from Absalom Jones to Frederick Douglass, had appointed themselves or others to lead their brethren, but none had developed an effective national organization like the GAR to galvanize the race. Grimké differentiates African Americans' experience from that of the ancient Israelites by turning his congregation's attention to a successful integrated national organization. In time, spiritually driven activists would arise to develop the political power and economic resources that were essential for the success of racial uplift initiatives in early twentieth-century America.

## Conclusion

Grimké joined myriad African American writers who published Exodus narratives during the Nadir to address new setbacks in the struggle for civil rights. They encouraged African Americans to emulate Joseph and Moses, signaling the nation's regression into an Egypt for their people. Although these stories brought some relief, they did not solve the major problems blacks faced at this time. After losing their civil rights and being terrorized by racial violence in the South, some African American writers began searching for a new promised land. Numerous activists supported migration to a midwestern Canaan. Success was temporary, however, for African Americans soon learned that the racism they had hoped to escape in the South permeated the entire nation. Others recommended emigration to a Liberian promised land as the best means to find peace, freedom, and wealth, but life in the colony proved challenging and seldom reflected the optimistic reviews published in recruitment pamphlets. Most African Americans remained in the United States, refusing to give up hope of transforming the nation into a promised land. Life became so difficult, however, that some African American writers rejected the Exodus narrative because it did not reflect their community's experience, or reflected it only minimally, and urged their brethren to be far more cautious in drawing parallels between the Israelites' miraculous journey from slavery in Egypt to freedom in Canaan and oppressed African Americans' experience with slavery and qualified freedom in a segregated, discriminatory nation. As the final phase of the first era of the Afro-Atlantic Exodus narrative tradition drew to a close, the promise of freedom that had sustained a struggle for 126 years remained unfulfilled. Nevertheless, their hope for freedom and equality continually drew African Americans back into the biblical language-world to articulate their desire for settlement in American or foreign promised lands.

AFTERWORD

# The First Joshua Generation Stranded on the Border of Canaan (1895–1903)

*Now after the death of Moses the servant of the LORD it came to pass, that the LORD spake unto Joshua the son of Nun, Moses' minister, saying, Moses my servant is dead; now therefore arise, go over this Jordan, thou, and all this people, unto the land which I do give to them, even to the children of Israel.*

—Joshua 1:1-2

*The metropolitan press of the great city of New York, unanimously declared that Mr. Douglass was a fit example for all classes and conditions of people, be they black or white. Marvelous declaration! . . . As Israel, we mourn the loss of our Moses. God took him.*

—Tribute by Rev. William B. Derrick, D.D., of the A.M.E., of New York

*To me, [Booker T. Washington] seems one of the greatest of living men because his work is unique: the modern Moses, who leads his race and lifts it through education to even better and higher things than a land overflowing with milk and honey.*

—Andrew Carnegie, "To Tuskegee, $600,000: Mr. Carnegie's Gift," *New York Tribune*

*So far as Mr. Washington preaches Thrift, Patience, and Industrial Training for the masses, we must hold up his hands and strive with him, rejoicing in his honors and glorying in the strength of this Joshua called of God and of man to lead the headless host.*

—W.E.B. Du Bois, *The Souls of Black Folk*

Frederick Douglass' death in 1895 precipitated a leadership crisis in the African American community. Approximately one year earlier, on the fiftieth anniversary of the day he was sold as a slave in Talbot County, Maryland, Douglass had penned a letter to his friend the Reverend Grimké. Reflecting on the dramatic changes that had occurred over his lifetime, Douglass mused, "I cannot believe that the Almighty power that has brought us so near the promised land will now abandon us."[1] Although Douglass lived to see slavery ended, he still envisioned African Americans languishing in a wilderness experience after witnessing the failure of Reconstruction. Many writers and activists affirmed Douglass' view of race progress by eulogizing him as African Americans' Moses, thereby establishing the expectation that a Joshua figure would soon be anointed to facilitate their entry into and conquest of their American Canaan.[2] As African American authors began to advance their ideas regarding the type of leader they believed was essential for race advancement, three potential candidates emerged. In the months immediately following Douglass' death, W.E.B. Du Bois earned his Ph.D. in sociology from Harvard University, Booker T. Washington delivered what would become known as his "Atlanta Compromise Speech" at the Cotton States and International Exposition, and Ida B. Wells published *A Red Record: Tabulated Statistics and Alleged Causes of Lynchings in the United States, 1892–1894*. Their disparate methodologies for racial uplift—the Talented Tenth, industrial education, and public campaign, respectively—led to unresolvable conflicts in the twentieth century, creating rifts within the early Civil Rights Movement that would linger for decades.

The escalation in lynchings and proliferation of federal rulings that legalized racism affirmed African Americans' need for new leadership to unify the community in responding to challenges that continued to undermine their achievements. During the last decade of the nineteenth century, nearly one hundred African Americans were reported lynched each year. The US Supreme Court further exacerbated race relations through its affirmation of a "separate but equal" doctrine for public transportation in *Plessy v. Ferguson*, its linkage of literacy and jury selection to suffrage in *Williams v. Mississippi*, and its preservation of white Americans' right to operate segregated schools without providing educational opportunities for African American students in *Cumming v. Richmond County Board of Education*. The high court's disregard for African Americans' rights encouraged a "Judge Lynch" approach to justice, as race riots erupted in local communities such as Greenwood County, South Carolina, and Wilmington, North Carolina, in 1898 and New Orleans and New York City in 1900.

Despite these setbacks, African American activists and their constituents continued to seek innovative means to advance the cause of social justice. Black women took increasingly prominent roles in civic matters through the establishment of national organizations such as the National Association of Colored Women in 1896. African Americans also tended to the needs of specialized groups through institutions like the American Negro Academy, a membership-only think tank founded by black intellectuals in Washington, D.C., to examine racial problems and offer practical solutions. Although treated as second-class citizens, African Americans exhibited patriotism when the nation became embroiled in the Spanish-American War, making up twenty military units, including the Tenth Calvary, which fought with Theodore Roosevelt's Rough Riders. Some despaired of the continued denial of their rights and inability to pursue happiness in America, however, and embraced emigration to Liberia as a means to ameliorate their wrongs. But the majority stayed; 8.8 million African Americans resided in the United States in 1900. Although they made valiant attempts to diminish the influence of white supremacist ideologies on every facet of their lives, most African Americans agreed with Du Bois' assertion that the problem of the twentieth century would be the problem of the color line.

African American writers turned to the Exodus narrative for leadership models but disagreed about their progress along the road that stretched from Egypt toward the promised land. Some argued that Jim Crow laws signaled their stagnation in the wilderness, while others viewed themselves as dispossessed Israelites who should demand immediate, equal settlement in Canaan. African American writers and their supporters looked to the Moses and Joshua stories to express the community's desire for the immediate restoration of their civil rights and to encourage their brethren to intensify their involvement in reform. These competing Moses and Joshua stories reveal both the peril and promise of Exodus for African Americans. White civic leaders' embrace of the Moses story, notably Andrew Carnegie's, to delineate a race representative further complicated constructions of Afro-Atlantic Exodus narratives by shifting the trajectory of black America's journey back to Egypt. Even when one person emerged as a potential national leader, the biblical narrative did not enable the black community or the nation to develop a consensus regarding the type of Exodus experience African Americans needed to achieve their racial uplift goals, leaving them stranded on the border of their American Canaan.

### AME *Christian Recorder*
### *Joshua as Role Model for Church Leaders and the Laity*

In the late nineteenth century, African American writers increasingly looked beyond the Joseph and Moses narratives to the Joshua story for a new model of leadership that would enable them to implement more radical racial uplift initiatives. The *Christian Recorder* nurtured readers' identification with Joshua by featuring his narrative as a Sunday School lesson that instructed parishioners on how to apply its principles to their lives. In the final lesson of a twelve-part series on Old Testament history that the editors published in 1875, readers were asked to examine both spiritual and temporal concerns in the life of Joshua, including forgiveness for sinners, affirmation of the elderly, caution for lovers of wealth, and comfort for the fearful. In 1888, editors previewed another Sunday School series that culminated in the installation of Joshua as the Israelites' leader after the death of Moses. After narrating details from Joshua's courageous inauguration of the conquest of Canaan, readers were admonished to exhibit similar courage, strength, and faith in facing life's challenges.[3] In emphasizing the Joshua story, the *Christian Recorder* nurtured a Joshua generation, encouraging African Americans to steel themselves for the conflicts that would erupt from their attempts to integrate themselves into a racist society.

Indeed, African American writers' contributions to the *Christian Recorder* reflect their embrace of the Joshua narrative as a means of encouraging readers to focus their attention on building up their own homes, businesses, and churches into Canaan-like havens within an oppressive environment. In "A Help or Hindrance, Which?," AME Bishop Benjamin Tucker Tanner couples the narrative of Joshua's preparation for the conquest of Canaan with an exegesis of the biblical text from the influential *Pulpit Commentary* to advise readers how to infuse Christian principles into everyday choices regarding business pursuits, social relations, and personal habits. When Joshua encountered an armed stranger on the border of the Promised Land, he inquired, "Art Thou for us, or for our adversaries?"[4] Similarly, Tanner admonishes readers who prefer city life to rural living to interrogate their friends, question their business practices, and examine their own choices to eradicate any impediments on their path to the heavenly Canaan. Additionally, when the *Christian Recorder* faced financial challenges, the Reverend William J. Laws of Providence, Rhode Island, wrote a letter to the manager encouraging him to "hold on as with the iron grasp of a Samson, and the faith of a Joshua, until the victory shall have been proclaimed."[5] Both Israelite leaders overcame enormous odds in defeating formidable opponents who threatened their community's viability and spirituality. The writer expresses a need for strong, courageous editorial leadership to ensure the continued prosperity of the church. He explains, "We have taken such a high ground amidst the people of this land our fame is being felt among all. The RECORDER is regarded as a mighty power in the hands of the Almighty in diffusing light, knowledge, and wisdom among the people." The influential newspaper provided a potent, consistent counterattack against the debilitating effects of Jim Crow America.

AME pastors and administrators helped nurture the growth and impacted the perception of the church through leaders whom contributors affirmed as Joshuas. In his account of the church work in the Moberly, Missouri, District, the Reverend J. F. Taylor reports that Presiding Elder the Reverend B. F. Bates, an influential and popular pastor, had assumed his duties "like a Joshua or a Paul, [who] said under God he would succeed."[6] In so doing, Taylor projects an image of the denomination's continued development under the leadership of ministers who were equally effective as church administrators and community activists. The Reverend W. S. Kane adopts a similar approach in his description of the church's work in Canada, expressing a need for pastors who exhibit missionary enthusiasm: "Let us have such men who do not enter the ministry for dollars and cents, men who are like a Joshua in spirit, in walks as an Enoch, in zeal a St. Paul, then we shall soon capture the enemy's camps."[7] Like Taylor, he encourages readers to seek and support leaders who follow biblical models of successful spiritual guides. *Christian Recorder* contributors also looked to Exodus to construct a history for their church that presented it as an innovative, progressive spiritual center. In his letter to the editor of the *Christian Recorder*, the Reverend I. F. Aldridge of Friendship, North Carolina, evokes the Exodus story to characterize the AME church as Israelites who journeyed through the wilderness with Mosaic leaders and entered the Promised Land under the guidance of Joshuas. He explains, "the African M.E. Church and her leaders since 1816, and even back of that to the blacksmith shop, have been going forward and onward, leading the host on to victory. Some of them have crossed the great Jordan of death, and others are standing on the bank proclaiming—'On Jordan's stormy banks I stand, And cast a wistful eye To Canaan's fair and happy land, Where my possessions lie.'"[8] Other writers eulogized church administrators as Joshua figures, including Bishop Thomas Ward, who was lauded for his "labors, the daring, the battles and victories of this dauntless man of God."[9] This steady stream of Joshua stories valorized church leaders and enabled readers to place themselves on a trajectory of racial progress. Despite legal and political setbacks, the AME Church had continued to prosper. Its success served as a constant reminder of the potential for greater victories in African Americans' larger battle for civil rights.

Writers also relied on the Joshua story for guidance in nurturing church growth, drawing a parallel between the Israelites' successful conquest of Canaan and the AME Church's increasingly ambitious initiatives for local, national, and international development. The Reverend A. J. Kershaw focused on Joshua's instructions to the Israelites to prepare to cross the Jordan River into Canaan in advising a reluctant delegation to avoid the delay advised by Dr. W. H. Heard in affirming the union of the African Methodist Episcopal and African Methodist Episcopal Zion Churches.[10] When issuing reports about the church's annual conferences, attendees posited the delegates as Joshua figures. In 1881, the *Christian Recorder* editor participated in the Arkansas Conference in Forest City, Arkansas, presided over by Bishop Henry M. Turner, whom he describes as "the Napoleon of advanced thought and methods," who "imparted life and inspiration to every proceeding. . . . He is truly a Joshua; every where giving the command to 'go forward!' Forward in aspiration for a higher life, forward in the acquisition of knowledge, forward in obedience to God, loyalty to the Church and faithfulness to the sacred trust committed to our keeping."[11] The Reverend R. B. Brookins reported that delegates to the East Florida Annual Conference in 1890 arrived at the meeting "with a Joshua and Caleb-like resolution, saying in [their] actions and temperament, 'Let us go up at once and possess it, for we are fully able' "[12] before relating success in the Financial, Educational Missionary, and Sunday School departments. Each contributor applied the Exodus narrative to a situation that was completely within the AME Church's control. Despite the limitations of Exodus for advancing the civil rights agenda in their communities and nations, the story empowered *Christian Recorder* contributors and readers to nurture and develop Joshuas within their own religious institution who gained valuable experience in administrating local churches, regional districts, national organizations, and foreign missions that steeled them for the persistent challenges of racial uplift work.

## H. Rufus White
### *Booker T. Washington, a Joshua in African Americans' Camp*

The *Christian Recorder*'s success in nurturing Joshua leaders for the AME Church did not fulfill the need for national race leadership, however. Douglass' death in February of 1895, followed by Washington's speech at the Atlanta Cotton Exposition six months later, forced the African American community to grapple with the issue. Although Douglass' influence waned in his later years, particularly after his marriage to Helen Pitts and his controversial opposition to African American migration to the Midwest, none of the new activists, such as Francis Grimké, Ida B. Wells, Kelly Miller, Anna Julia Cooper, William Monroe Trotter, and Mary Church Terrell, galvanized the entire community. African American attorney H. Rufus White attempted to address the leadership void through the publication of his 1895 pamphlet titled *"A Joshua in the Camp," or, The Life of Booker T. Washington, of Tuskegee, Alabama* (1895)[13] in which he anoints Washington as African Americans' new leader. His selection of Washington as African Americans' Joshua exposes the limitations of the Joshua story as a model for national race leadership and as a unifying narrative for the fragmented African American community. White begins by invoking an episode from Exodus to characterize African Americans as a leaderless band of Israelites on the border of their American Canaan. He identifies Douglass as their dead Moses and describes them as wondering whether a Joshua is within their community. In so doing, he posits African Americans as an oppressed people who have not yet experienced the promised land of freedom and equality. Furthermore, by intimating that the African American community had unequivocally acknowledged Douglass as their Moses, he diminishes the contributions of Mosaic leaders like Martin Delany, Henry Highland Garnet, Mary Ann Shadd, and others who had developed racial uplift initiatives that sustained the community's quest for liberty and civil rights but often conflicted with Douglass' ideas.

In the biblical narrative, Joshua worked closely with Moses, and God selected him to lead because of his fidelity throughout the forty-year wilderness journey. White supports his choice of Washington as Joshua by detailing the Tuskegee Institute president's life story and professional accomplishments, and presenting accolades for Washington from newspaper editors and prominent Americans. By not including affirmations from any black activists or institutions, however, White authorizes himself to select a leader for the community based on his own criteria.

Many African Americans objected to individuals anointing a leader for their community. In "A Joshua in the Camp" (1896), the *AME Church Review* editors laud Washington as a capable leader but reject White's advocacy of a singular Joshua to lead African Americans.[14] The editors argue that "leaders are not made to order, they are born. They are not elected by the people to lead, they take their rightful place in spite of the people" (419). The editors suggest that God, not man, chooses leaders, just as he had anointed Joseph, Moses, and Joshua to guide the Israelites. Furthermore, they refuse to limit African Americans' options to the industrial training that Washington offered at Tuskegee Institute. In constructing their model of leadership, the editors turn to the teachings of Jesus, rather than the Exodus story, in asserting, "A house divided against itself cannot stand" (Matt 12:25) and "A city that is set on a hill cannot be hid" (Matt 5:14). The first passage references Jesus' rebuke of the Pharisees who accused him of casting out a demon by the power of devils. In the second, Jesus taught his followers that they are the light of the world, reflecting his love and goodness. The editors complicated their critique of White's methodology with an allusion to the Civil War, a time when a divided nation battled over states' rights and slavery. Andrew Johnson, the nation's compromising Joshua, had failed to reunite the country and protect the rights of all citizens. True leaders such as US senators Owen Lovejoy and Charles Sumner were easily identifiable, however. As black activists sought to reestablish their community after the failure of Reconstruction, the *AME Church Review* editors suggested that White's selection of Washington, the compromiser, would create rifts within the African American community since leaders who were forced upon a people divided rather than united. If Washington were to be their leader, he would assume that position without human intervention. The editors' comprehensive leadership plan requires a variety of activists to address the varied needs of the community. Skilled laborers, religious teachers, authors, secular educators, and inventors would provide "education of the head, the heart and the hands, and not any one to the neglect of the others" (421). As African American Christians, the editors advocated a holistic approach to becoming responsible citizens and building strong communities.

## W.E.B. Du Bois
### *Booker T. Washington as Potential Joshua*

In *The Souls of Black Folk* (1903), W.E.B. Du Bois further complicated conversations regarding Washington's fitness as a Joshua through his characterization of African Americans' journey from slavery to freedom as a sojourn to the promised land. Du Bois had acknowledged Washington as an important race leader, evidenced by the note of congratulations that he sent Washington after the Atlanta Cotton Exposition speech, but the men differed on the most effective means of facilitating African Americans' integration into American society and publicly challenged each other's ideas regarding racial uplift.[15] Although they agreed on some issues, for example, self-improvement, education, and business development, they disagreed on the best means to achieve these goals. By the early 1900s, Du Bois had become increasingly critical of Washington's methodology, particularly his refusal to publicly agitate for civil rights. In chapter 1 of *The Souls of Black*

*Dr. W.E.B. Du Bois, educator, civil rights activist, sociologist*

*Folk*, "Of Our Spiritual Strivings," Du Bois delineates the process by which the "headless host" of African Americans gained freedom, were empowered by suffrage, and discovered "book-learning" in their quest for equality (7). Nevertheless, he concludes, "The Nation has not yet found peace from its sins; the freedman has not yet found in freedom his promised land" (6). By depicting African Americans as a "headless host" struggling to reach Canaan, Du Bois suggests the need for a leader, which he explores in chapter 3, "Of Mr. Booker T. Washington and Others." He constructs a complex nexus of the pathos of a Negro spiritual, the inspiration of Lord Byron's verse, the radicalism of revolution, and the power of Exodus to construct a Joshua model of leadership that Washington must adapt in implementing a militant uplift strategy powerful enough to reconstruct the nation as a society in which African Americans can experience economic success and simultaneously secure their civil rights.

Du Bois frames his critique of Washington with a twofold epigraph that juxtaposes popular lines from Lord Byron's *Childe Harold's Pilgrimage* with a musical notation from the Negro spiritual "Great Camp Meeting in the Promised Land" to link early twentieth-century racial uplift efforts to the history of American reform, religion, and revolution. French rebels, American colonists, and antislavery advocates had invoked Byron's lines "Hereditary bondsmen! Know ye not / Who would be free themselves must strike the blow?" in advancing the cause of freedom. By using them, Du Bois draws a parallel between white Americans' and African Americans' embrace of revolution to acquire liberty. In *Souls*, Du Bois adds the line "From birth till death enslaved; in word, in deed, unmanned!," which stresses how slavery had stripped African Americans of their humanity both physically and intellectually. The second epigraph reveals the means through which African Americans conveyed and sought to fulfill their desire for spiritual and physical liberation on earth and in heaven. By linking the poem and song, Du Bois affirms the black man's struggle for equality as an American experience and asserts the need for a leader who will uncompromisingly demand the rights and privileges of citizenship for his people.

In creating his model of early twentieth-century African American leadership, Du Bois cites the methodologies of militant African American activists to justify the need for a radical approach. He describes Washington as a "successful man" who established Tuskegee Institute and won admirers in the North and South through "his program of industrial education, conciliation of the South, and submission and silence as to civil and political rights" (30). Du Bois tempers Washington's effective advocacy of working-class employment with a stinging critique of his methodology in acquiescing to white America's insistence on second-class citizenship for African Americans. He asserts that both envious and honest opponents had criticized Washington's leadership abilities. Du Bois positions his critique of his rival through the lens of history, highlighting prominent black leaders from the Maroons to Frederick Douglass to argue that Washington has become "a compromiser between the South, the North, and the Negro" whose commitment to manual labor would lead to "industrial slavery and civic death" (36, 40). In so doing, Du Bois suggests that Washington has initiated a reverse Exodus that will lead African Americans to Egypt rather than Canaan. African Americans now need a courageous new leader like Williams Wells Brown or David Walker to guide them into the promised land of America. Washington had disqualified himself by failing to honor the legacy of bold activists who preceded him.

Despite this harsh assessment, Du Bois recommends Washington as a *potential* Joshua for African Americans if he fulfills specific requirements for race leadership. He asserts, "So far as Mr. Washington preaches Thrift, Patience, and Industrial Training for the masses, we must hold up his hands and strive with him, rejoicing in his honors and glorying in the strength of this Joshua called of God and of man to lead the headless host" (59). In presenting Washington as a Joshua figure, Du Bois alludes to the story of Aaron and Hur holding up Moses' arms as Joshua led the Israelites' into a battle sparked by an unprovoked attack by the Amalekites (Exod 17).

Thus, he is suggesting that Washington become a Joshua-Mosiac race leader whose effectiveness is rooted in cooperation with religious leaders (as represented by Israel's high priest Aaron) and community activists (as represented by Moses and Aaron's assistant Hur) rather than the South or the nation. Du Bois' positioning of the Joshua-Mosaic figure supported by community leaders on the top of a mountain in the wilderness signals his belief that African Americans can triumph in their early twentieth-century battles against malicious violence so long as this leadership alliance is established and remains intact.

Du Bois expresses his concerns about Washington's suitability for Joshua-Mosaic leadership, however, by identifying characteristics that would signal the Wizard of Tuskegee's betrayal of the African American community. He warns, "But so far as Mr. Washington apologizes for injustice, North or South, does not rightly value the privilege and duty of voting, belittles the emasculating effects of caste distinctions, and opposes the higher training and ambition of our brighter minds,—so far as he, the South, or the Nation, does this,—we must unceasingly and firmly oppose them" (59). In singling out justice, suffrage, equality, and liberal arts education, Du Bois boldly identifies the key elements of his own racial uplift strategy that distinguish him from Washington and inform the "Credo" he would publish in 1904.[16] By linking Booker T. Washington with the South and the nation, Du Bois widens the breach between Washington and the African American community yet marks a clear path for Washington to reclaim his status as race leader.

## Andrew Carnegie
### *Booker T. Washington as the Modern Moses*

Andrew Carnegie's singling out of Washington as the "modern Moses" shifted the nation's attention away from Du Bois' identification of Washington as a potential Joshua in *The Souls of Black Folk*. The *Washington Bee* devoted attention to such speculations by publishing a letter to the editor from Charles R. Douglass, Frederick Douglass' son, on its front page. Charles Douglass distances himself from the debate, asserting that the problem is not in the quantity of leaders but in the dearth of followers. He explained, "My father was a friend of Booker T. Washington and also a friend of his work, and I am the same, but I do not indorse [*sic*] his Atlanta speech nor some of his subsequent utterances, and that is all there is in my opposition to him."[17] Charles Douglass' response reflected the sentiments of many black activists who initially supported Washington but tempered their enthusiasm as the effect of his "Compromise" on African Americans became more apparent.

Other African American newspapers in the North and Midwest valorized Washington as Douglass' successor, however, and urged their readers to accept him as their new Moses. In October of 1895, the *Omaha Daily Bee* praised Washington as the first model black citizen to emerge after Douglass' death and lauded his speech as the best delivered at the Cotton Exposition. The newspaper characterized him as "the wisest and truest leader of his race the country has ever known" and acknowledged him as "the Moses of the Black Belt," who offered education at Tuskegee Institute in "thrift and industry, self-respect and responsibility," which were essential for race progress.[18] In 1897 the *Appeal*, a black national newspaper published simultaneously in St. Paul, Minneapolis, Chicago, Louisville, St. Louis, and Dallas, affirmed Washington's position as national race leader and criticized African Americans who relied on the "press, pulpit, and would-be leadership" to mete out "harsh and unjust" criticisms and "obstacles of discouragement" rooted in "petty jealousy."[19] The newspaper writer supported Washington's philosophy regarding race relations, asserting, "The white people, North and South, believe in him and his work. He is doing much toward cementing the friendship between the educated and skilled Afro-Americans and the Southern white man." Ultimately, the writer contended that "[t]he race sooner or later must accept Booker T. Washington as its natural leader—'the Moses of his people,' as he is called down in the 'blackbelt' of Alabama. After all, who could fill the peculiar position occupied by this peculiar man, but the man himself?" In describing both Washington and his role as race leader as "peculiar," the writer inadvertently links the condition of African Americans and Washington to bondsmen and bondswomen who suffered within the "peculiar institution" of slavery, and hints at the debilitating effects of "peculiar" race-based initiatives on African Americans. Both writers represented the race issue as a Southern problem, however, further fragmenting the African American community and complicating the search for a national leader or the development of a national organization that could advance African Americans' civil rights efforts.

In the years following his Atlanta Cotton Exposition speech, Washington also encouraged the nation to view him as African Americans' Moses. During a lecture in Brooklyn in December of 1898, he opined that African Americans' "pillar of fire by night and pillar of cloud by day shall be property, skill, economy, education and Christian character. To us just now these the wheat, all else the chaff."[20] Here Washington emphasizes objectives that Americans link to respectability, while characterizing goals such as suffrage, equality, and civil rights as chaff, valueless articles that should be discarded. White newspapers, such as the Democratic-leaning *Richmond (Ky.) Climax*, published reports about the speech, lauding Washington as "the greatest man his race has produced, who promises to be the Moses of his people." The author of the article draws a distinction between those who followed the teachings of Douglass, who advocated voting rights for African Americans, and those who supported Washington's belief that enfranchising African Americans after the Civil War was a mistake. He urges African Americans to prize and protect suffrage but to direct their energies to the acquisition of education and property to "compel the respect of the Caucasian race by virtue and true worth."[21] The newspaper's commentary reflected the concerns of Washington's detractors. In America, citizens' votes affected the development of equitable public education and the enactment of property ownership laws. For African Americans, hard work did not guarantee equal access to education or property, particularly in the Southern agricultural system, which included a disproportionate percentage of African American sharecroppers, renters, and tenant farmers who found it increasingly difficult to earn a profit or cast a vote.

By the turn of the twentieth century, white newspapers throughout the nation regularly identified Washington as African Americans' Moses, securing his status as race leader and affirming his conservative racial uplift strategy as the solution to the problem of the color line. In 1900 the *Marietta (Ohio) Daily Leader* published a profile that declared, "Booker T. Washington is the Moses of the African people in the new world. He has been accepted by his race and the white people of the north and south as the man who shall lead a great branch of the human family out of the bondage of darkness and ignorance into usefulness and helpfulness, and he measures up to the requirements."[22] While the writer differentiates between the Northern and Southern white populace, acknowledging a measure of diversity of people and ideals, he identifies African Americans as a racial group that has embraced Washington, despite the contentious debates regarding his leadership that had emerged within the black activist community by this time. As African Americans' concerns regarding Washington's fitness for race leadership increased, white American newspaper editors continued to laud him as Moses, recasting his life story as an American myth to make it more palatable for a national white audience. In 1901 the Republican *Minneapolis Journal* published "The Slave Boy Becomes a Maker of Magistrates," which extols Washington's ascendancy to political influence through his pursuit of the path of humble race leadership. President Theodore Roosevelt had consulted Washington regarding Alabama's former governor Thomas Goode Jones' appointment as a federal judge. The writer claims that Washington's avoidance of politics in favor of the modest, prayerful betterment of his race brought him coveted influence. In the opening paragraph, the writer presents Washington's life narrative as a black Horatio Alger–like journey, describing him as an "uncared for pickaninny with not a friend or well-wisher in the world except his old black slave mother. . . . The years pass. The black boy, born in humility and poverty, becomes the Moses of his people, ordained to lead them out of the Egypt of their bondage by the road of industrial usefulness."[23] The selection of the term "ordained" suggests a belief in the divine nature of Washington's appointment, as well as a forceful confirmation of his calling by white Americans. In so doing, the writer positions African American citizens as slaves and locates their liberation in industrial employment. Indeed, the writer declares: "When the negro becomes a success, an indispensible factor in the industrial and commercial progress of the south, when he becomes a property-owner and a taxpayer, a hardworking thrifty citizen, he will not have to contend for political rights. He will have them."[24] Ironically, during the antebellum period enslaved African Americans had provided the labor that transformed the young nation into a formidable republic. During the Jim Crow era, property ownership became increasingly difficult, particularly in the South, where wages for industrial labor kept many African Americans hovering near the poverty line. Black home and land ownership rates still languished behind those for white Americans,[25] a by-product of the decimating effect of racism reflected most acutely in the rise of lynching, the enactment of federally sanctioned segregation, the passage of disenfranchisement legislation, and the limitation of employment options for African Americans.

Nevertheless, white Americans continued to view industrial training coordinated by Washington's Mosaic leadership as the best means for African Americans to earn their rights. In 1902, the *Minneapolis Journal* published "Tubs at Tuskegee: Part of the Regular Curriculum, Says Mrs. E. A. Russell," a report of Mrs. E. A. Russell's travels to the Southeast, including a visit to the Cotton Exposition in Charleston and Tuskegee Institute. Russell was most favorably impressed with the Tuskegee students' "earnestness" and "personal cleanliness," noting, "Booker T. Washington preaches the gospel of the bath tub and the tooth brush. Pupils at the school are required to take two baths a week and they are always neat and clean in their dress. . . . Washington is doing a great work and I believe he is inspired, just as was Moses to lead his children out of bondage."[26] She then provides a detailed account of the students' industriousness in both their work and studies. Such eyewitness reports by influential white social activists circulated images of African Americans that confirmed white Americans' views of their place and potential, affirmed Washington's status as race leader, and encouraged the nation to continue demanding that African Americans earn basic rights accorded to them by virtue of their citizenship nearly forty years after the Civil War had ended slavery.

Andrew Carnegie's pronouncement of Washington as the race's "modern Moses" permanently shifted the focus of early twentieth-century African American Exodus narratives regarding national race leadership away from the Joshua story. Newspapers throughout the country published Carnegie's letter announcing the bequest of $600,000 for the Tuskegee endowment and support of Washington and his wife, Margaret Murray Washington. Of Washington, Carnegie writes, "To me he seems like one of the greatest living men because his work is unique, the modern Moses, who leads his race and lifts it through education, to even better and higher things than a land flowing with milk and honey."[27] Carnegie characterizes Washington's work as "unique" despite the existence of institutions throughout the South such as Hampton Institute and the State Agricultural and Normal School for Negroes (renamed Alabama A&M University) that offered similar training for African Americans. He emphasizes education as being more important than civil rights, suggesting that African Americans are incapable of functioning as citizens without specialized training in a segregated institution

*Mr. and Mrs. Booker T. Washington, Andrew Carnegie (seated, front row), and Tuskegee Institute faculty and family*

supported by white philanthropy. In singling out African Americans for special support and providing sustenance for a race leader who meets white Americans' standards for greatness, Carnegie affirms the belief that African Americans can earn the respect of whites as well as their rights through hard work and helps shift attention away from the eradication of a white supremacist culture that would produce the *Birth of a Nation* within a decade.

The significance of Carnegie's endorsement is reflected in the intensification of criticisms that immediately erupted throughout the nation regarding the appropriateness of the designation and Washington's fitness for Mosaic leadership. In March of 1903, editors of the *Ardmore (Okla.) Daily Ardmoreite* featured a synopsis of an article published in the *Brown Book of Boston* that lauded leaders who arose from humble circumstances, namely George Washington, Abraham Lincoln, Booker T. Washington, and Jesus, as "the man who dares."[28] The editors of the *Daily Ardmoreite* affirmed George Washington's position at the head of the list but questioned the appropriateness of Booker T. Washington's placement beside Moses and before Jesus, describing it as "an open outrage on all decency and society and outside of Boston a matter of regreat [*sic*] to the readers of the publication allowing such stuff." Two months later, the white-owned, influential Republican *Wichita Daily Eagle* declared, "Andrew Carnegie calls Booker T. Washington the 'modern Moses,' but it is not recorded that any Andy gave the 'ancient Moses' any $600,000 to enable him to get his brethren out of the wilderness."[29] By the fall of 1903, the editorial board of the African American newspaper the *Broad Ax* had joined the chorus of criticism, accusing their "Moses" of "spending money like a drunken lord" while providing industrial education at Tuskegee.[30] Although criticisms from within and without the African American community, as well as the emergence of national civil rights organizations such as the National Association for the Advancement of Colored People, founded in 1909, prevented Washington from becoming African Americans' "modern Moses," the publicity surrounding his anointing encouraged the continued search for a Mosaic leader.

During the twentieth and early twenty-first centuries, African Americans continued to rely on the Exodus narrative to support their desire for equality, since the elimination of slavery did not guarantee equal rights for black citizens. As African Americans introduced their children to the biblical narrative and their Exodus stories, they assured the continued creation of narratives featuring an array of Exodus leaders, promised lands, and activist strategies to accomplish racial uplift goals. Martin Luther King Jr.'s invocation of Exodus in his famous 1968 "I've Been to the Mountaintop" speech in Memphis, Tennessee, is one of the most popular twentieth-century black Exodus narratives. Although many scholars have examined King's speech, none has provided a comprehensive analysis of the development of black Exodus narratives published after 1903, including visual representations by artists such as Jacob Lawrence and Romare Bearden and music by Bob Marley and Isaac Hayes.

Contemporary Exodus narratives enable us to understand why people of African descent have continued to claim the biblical story to support their civil rights initiatives for nearly two hundred and fifty years. On March 4, 2007, presidential candidate Senator Barack Obama delivered a speech at the Selma Voting Rights March Commemoration in which he presented a new type of black Exodus narrative that featured both Moses and Joshua generations who spearheaded civil rights initiatives for their people. Using language saturated with Exodus imagery, Obama declared,

> We're going to leave it to the Joshua generation to make sure it happens. There are still battles that need to be fought; some rivers that need to be crossed. . . . The previous generation, the Moses generation, pointed the way. They took us ninety percent of the way there. . . . So the question, I guess, that I have today is what's called of us in this Joshua generation? What do we do in order to fulfill that legacy; to fulfill the obligations and the debt that we owe to those who allowed us to be here today?[31]

Rather than identify one central Moses figure for the Civil Rights Movement, particularly Martin Luther King Jr., Obama acknowledges a "Moses generation" that also includes activists such as Ralph David Abernathy Sr., Ella Baker, Septima Clark, Marian Wright Edelman, Medgar Evers, James Farmer Jr., Jesse Jackson, Fannie Lou Hamer, John Lewis, the Little Rock Nine, Rosa Parks, Walter Francis White, and Malcolm X, as well as a host of unknown community leaders and citizens. He then suggests that the "Joshua generation" will ensure African Americans' passage into Canaan. In so doing, Obama places the African American community on the border of the promised land, the same position they occupied in 1903 when Du Bois characterized Booker T. Washington as a potential Joshua. Instead of anointing one Exodus leader, as did many of his predecessors, Obama calls for a Joshua generation to complete the work their Mosaic forebears had begun in waging numerous battles for multiple promised lands. Obama's Exodus narrative exemplifies the continued promise of the biblical story for the black community and compels scholars to analyze the multidimensional factors that contribute to the persistent presence of Exodus narratives in the Afro-Atlantic literary tradition.

# Notes

**Introduction**

1 All biblical citations are from the King James Version, unless otherwise noted.

2 Vincent Wimbush, *The Bible and African Americans: A Brief History* (Appleton, Wis.: Augsburg Fortress, 2002), 4.

3 In *The Negro in American Life and Thought: The Nadir, 1877–1901* (New York: Dial, 1954), historian Rayford Logan characterizes the Nadir as America's lowest point in race relations. Also see Logan's *The Betrayal of the Negro from Rutherford B. Hayes to Woodrow Wilson* (Cambridge, Mass.: Da Capo Press, 1997). See Frances Foster, "A Narrative of the Interesting Origins and (Somewhat) Surprising Developments of African American Print Culture," *American Literary History* (Winter 2005): 712-40, for discussion of the importance of the early black religious press.

4 Wimbush, *The Bible and African Americans*, 4. Emphasis added.

5 George Aichele et al., *The Postmodern Bible: The Bible and Culture Collective* (New Haven: Yale University Press, 1995), 286.

**Chapter 1**

1 Phillis Wheatley, "Letter to Rev. Samson Occum," *Connecticut Gazette*, March 11, 1774.

2 George Whitefield, "Religious Society," in *Selected Sermons of George Whitefield* (Philadelphia: Union Press, 1904), 14.

3 Albert J. Raboteau, "African Americans, Exodus, and the American Israel," in *Religion and American Culture: A Reader*, ed. David G. Hackett (New York: Routledge, 1995), 82.

4 Regina M. Schwartz, *The Curse of Cain: The Violent Legacy of Monotheism* (Chicago: University of Chicago Press, 1997), 58.

5 Priscilla Wald, *Constituting Americans: Cultural Anxiety and Narrative Form* (Durham, N.C.: Duke University Press, 1995), 2. Emphasis in original.

6 Michael Wigglesworth, "God's Controversy with New England" (1662), in *God's New Israel: Religious Interpretations of American Destiny*, ed. Conrad Cherry (Chapel Hill: University of North Carolina Press, 1998), 47.

7 See also Anthony Benezet, *Observations on the Inslaving, Importing and Purchasing of Negroes* (Germantown: Christopher Sower, 1760); Benjamin Lay, *All Slave-Keepers That Keep the Innocent in Bondage, Apostates* (Philadelphia: Author, 1737); *The Case of Our Fellow-Creatures, the Oppressed Africans, Respectfully Recommended to the Serious Consideration of the Legislature of Great-Britain, by the People Called Quakers* (London: James Phillips, 1784).

8 Stewart, a Boston customs official, had taken his slave James Somerset to England in 1769; Lord Mansfield prohibited Stewart from selling Somerset to a slave owner in Jamaica a few years later.

9 Mukhtar Ali Isani, "The Contemporaneous Reception of Phillis Wheatley: Newspaper and Magazine Notices during the Years of Fame, 1765–1774," *Journal of Negro History* 85, no. 4 (2000): 269.

10 Phillis Wheatley's biographer, Vincent Carretta, suggests that Wheatley's free status "may well have been a concession manipulated by Wheatley from Nathaniel Wheatley in exchange for her promise to return to Boston to care for his mother, her mistress: one promise for another." Carretta, Introduction to Wheatley, *Complete Writings*, ed. Vincent Carretta (New York: Penguin, 2001), xxvi–xxvii.

11 Isani, "Contemporaneous Reception."

12 Isani, "Contemporaneous Reception."

13 Although Dartmouth College was not established specifically for Native Americans, it offered limited educational opportunities for them. Fewer than 100 Native Americans attended Dartmouth between 1770–1965. In 1970 newly appointed president John G. Kemeny renewed the institution's commitment to education for Native Americans by aggressively recruiting Native American students and establishing the nation's first Native American Studies program. For further insights, see Colin G. Calloway, "Elezar Wheelock Meets Luther Standing Bear: Native American Studies at Dartmouth," in *Native American Studies in Higher Education: Models for Collaboration between Universities and Indigenous Nations*, ed. Duane Champagne and Jay Stauss (Walnut Creek, Ca.: AltaMira Press, 2002), 17–28; Cary Michael Carney, *Native American Higher Education in the United States* (New Brunswick, N.J.: Transaction Publishers, 1999).

14 "Petition for Freedom to Massachusetts Governor Thomas Gage, His Majesty's Council, and the House of Representatives, 25 May 1774," Jeremy Belknap Papers, Massachusetts Historical Society, 2012, accessed July 6, 2012, http://www.masshist.org/database/589use-onview-id.

15 Vincent Carretta, Introduction to Ottobah Cugoano, *Thoughts and Sentiments on the Evil and Wicked Traffic of the Slavery and Commerce of the Human Species* (1787), ed. Vincent Carretta (New York: Penguin, 2000), xiv.

16 When God introduced the Ten Commandments at Mount Sinai, he reminded the Israelites that he had delivered them out of the land of Egypt, "the house of bondage" (Exod 20:2).

17 In their introduction to *Black Atlantic Writers of the Eighteenth Century: Living the New Exodus in England and the America*s (New York: Palgrave Macmillan, 1995), Adam Potkay and Sandra Burr argue that Equiano constructs this correlation to present the

first stage of his "new Exodus" from slavery and thereby discredits two myths about Africans. They assert that "it runs contrary to the common (though fantastic) taunt that blacks are the cursed descendants of Ham who are ordained to serve God's chosen people—here, white Europeans—as slaves" and it "serves to correct his age's opposite and equally unreal view of Africa not as a damned but as an Edenic state" (11–12).

18 "And I will bring the blind by a way that they knew not; I will lead them in paths that they have not known: I will make darkness light before them, and crooked things straight. These things will I do unto them, and not forsake them" (Isa 42:16).

19 See Gen 41:42, 45.

20 Potkay and Burr contend, "The book of Acts to which Equiano appealed was of special importance to many blacks and their white abolitionist friends for its strong message of Christian universalism" (*Black Atlantic Writers*, 13). In "Moses and the Egyptian: Religious Authority in Olaudah Equiano's *Interesting Narrative*," Eileen Razzari Elrod further suggests that Equiano uses the frontispiece to engage his readers by declaring, "This life narrative . . . like other spiritual autobiographies produced in this period, will be religiously instructive as well as self-reflective in nature." Elrod, "Moses and the Egyptian: Religious Authority in Olaudah Equiano's *Interesting Narrative*," *African American Review* 35, no. 3 (2001): 413.

21 The name "Gustavus Vassa" had been popularized in England by Henry Brooke's play *Gustavus Vasa, the Deliverer of His Country*. Editions of the play between 1739 and 1797 helped keep the public engaged in discussions about political oppression. Ironically, the name that Equiano initially resisted, Gustavus Vassa, may have been more effective in advancing his antislavery cause than the name Jacob. After obtaining his freedom, Equiano preferred being called Gustavus Vassa. He may have hoped Britons would make the connection between the Dane's quest for freedom and his involvement in the antislavery movement. See Carretta in Olaudah Equiano, *The Interesting Narrative and Other Writings*, ed. Vincent Carretta (New York: Penguin, 2003), 252 n. 129.

22 See Exodus 2.

23 Adam Potkay argues that Equiano "knows he cannot be Moses, because the Christian dispensation has no room for the violent retaliation imagined by his younger self." Potkay, "Olaudah Equiano and the Art of Spiritual Autobiography," in "African-American Culture in the Eighteenth Century," special issue, *Eighteenth-Century Studies* 27, no. 4 (1994): 688.

24 See the discussion of Jamaica's Slave Laws of 1664 in Christopher L. Tomlins and Bruce H. Mann, eds., *The Many Legalities of Early America* (Chapel Hill: University of North Carolina Press, 2001).

25 Elrod argues that Equiano "provides readers with a familiar biblical story, an alternative context, to make his alien experience meaningful despite the inhering unfamiliarity that he argues for here. . . . The only way into his story here, he says to the reader, is to look beyond personal experiences to another textual one" ("Moses and the Egyptian," 417).

26 Mosaic law allowed mild forms of slavery in the Hebrew community. See Exod 21:20-21 and Lev 25:44-46.

27 Vincent Carretta argues that "Equiano's unquestioning willingness to participate in a project based on slave labor and to condone the slave trade as well as the pride he took in selecting slaves should not surprise us. . . . Equiano was convinced that his own experiences and observations as a slave enabled him to be a humane overseer

of slaves." Carretta also suggests that Equiano's experience as a slaver is essential to his transformation, for it enabled him to assert that like many English Christians, he needs a "second conversion" before he is convinced of the evils of the slave trade. Carretta, *Equiano the African: Biography of a Self-Made Man* (Athens: University of Georgia Press, 2005), 184–85.

28 For a discussion of Rowlandson's captivity experience, see Mary Rowlandson, *A Narrative of the Captivity, Sufferings and Removes of Mrs. Mary Rowlandson* (Boston: Thomas and John Fleet, 1791), and Kate Chedgzoy, *Women Writing in the British Atlantic World: Memory, Place, and History* (Cambridge: Cambridge University Press, 2007).

29 In *Black Atlantic Writers*, Potkay and Burns suggest that "like the biblical Joseph [Marrant] is reunited with a family that thought him dead" (11). Joanna Brooks also suggests that this episode in Marrant's life recalls the story of Joseph. She and other scholars have described Marrant as a type of Lazarus because of his repeated brushes with death and his conversion story; however, biblical Lazarus figures do not experience repeated cycles of death and resurrection, or conversion. See Joanna Brooks, *American Lazarus: Religion and the Rise of African-American and Native American Literature* (New York: Oxford University Press, 2003).

30 For the parable of the Prodigal Son, see Luke 15:11-32.

31 In *American Lazarus*, Joanna Brooks argues that Marrant can be viewed as Lazarus since his life is "a series of deaths and rebirths." Thus he becomes a Joseph-Lazarus figure who can address "slavery [as] an alienating and depersonalizing form of social death" (98–99). Karen A. Weyler also identifies a connection between Marrant's experience and the Lazarus story, but she asserts that Marrant is also alluding to the Parables of the Lost Sheep and the Prodigal Son. Weyler, "Race, Redemption, and Captivity," in *A Narrative of the Lord's Wonderful Dealings with John Marrant, a Black* (Charleston, S.C.: Nabu Press, 2011), and "Narrative of the Uncommon Sufferings and Surprizing Deliverance of Briton Hammon, a Negro man," in *Genius in Bondage: Literature of the Early Black Atlantic*, ed. Vincent Carretta and Philip Gould (Lexington: University Press of Kentucky, 2001), 49.

**Chapter 2**

1 John I. Carle, *A funeral sermon, preached at Rockaway, December 29, 1799, on the much lamented death of General George Washington* (Morristown, N.J.: Jacob Mann, 1800), 785.

2 Robert P. Hay, "George Washington: American Moses," *American Quarterly* 21 (1969): 788, 790.

3 Hay, "George Washington," 788, 790.

4 Brinch's homeland is described as "the kingdom of Bow-woo situate [*sic*] on the river Neboah or Niger in the interior of Africa" (3). Kari J. Winter suggests that textual evidence points to Mali as Brinch's homeland for the kingdom of Bow-woo has a similar phonetic structure as the "Bobo" people who lived near the Niger River. Additionally, the Bow-woo's cultural practices that Brinch describes in his narrative are very similar to those of the Dogon people who have long occupied this region. See Winter, Introduction to *The Blind African Slave, Or Memoirs of Boyrereau Brinch, Nicknamed Jeffrey Brace*, by Boyrereau Brinch (Madison: University of Wisconsin Press, 2004), 4–5.

5 Susan Willis, "Crushed Geraniums: Juan Francisco Manzano and the Language of Slavery," in *The Slave's Narrative*, ed. Charles T. Davis and Henry Louis Gates (New York: Oxford University Press, 1985), 202.

6 See Exodus 18.

7 Douglas R. Egerton, *Gabriel's Rebellion: The Virginia Slave Conspiracies of 1800 and 1802* (Chapel Hill: University of North Carolina Press, 1993), 51.

8 "Confessions of Ben Alias Ben Woolfork," Gabriel's Insurrection, September 16–30, 1800, James Monroe, Executive Papers, 1799–1802, Box 8, Folder 2, Library of Virginia, Richmond.

9 "Confessions of Ben Alias Ben Woolfork."

10 James Sidbury, *Ploughshares into Swords: Race, Rebellion, and Identity in Gabriel's Virginia, 1730–1810* (Cambridge: Cambridge University Press, 1997), 77; Gerald W. Mullin, *Flight and Rebellion: Slave Resistance in Eighteenth-Century Virginia* (New York: Oxford University Press, 1972), 154.

11 Sidbury, *Ploughshares into Swords*, 77.

12 Herbert Aptheker, *American Negro Slave Revolts*, 2nd ed. (New York: International, 1974), 219–26.

13 "And I am come down to deliver them out of the hand of the Egyptians, and to bring them up out of that land unto a good land and a large, unto a land flowing with milk and honey; unto the place of the Canaanites, and the Hittites, and the Amorites, and the Perizzites, and the Hivites, and the Jebusites" (Exod 3:8).

14 Absalom Jones, *A Thanksgiving sermon, preached January 1, 1808, in St. Thomas's, or the African Episcopal Church, Philadelphia on account of the abolition of the African slave trade, on that day, by the Congress of the United States* (Philadelphia: Fry & Kammerer, 1808).

15 "And the LORD said, I have surely seen the affliction of My people which are in Egypt, and have heard their cry by reason of their task-masters; for I know their sorrows; and I am come down to deliver them out of the hand of the Egyptians" (Exod 3:7-8).

16 See Lev 23:1-11; 1 Cor 15:20.

17 See Luke 2:8-14.

18 According to a Maryland law enacted in 1715, children born to white mothers and enslaved black fathers were subjected to servitude for thirty-one years. See Jeffrey R. Brackett, *The Negro in Maryland: A Study of the Institution of Slavery* (1889; Freeport, N.Y.: Books for Libraries Press, 1969), 32–34.

19 "Therefore shall ye lay up these my words in your heart and in your soul, and bind them for a sign upon your hand, that they may be as frontlets between your eyes. And ye shall teach them your children, speaking of them when thou sittest in thine house, and when thou walkest by the way, when thou liest down, and when thou risest up" (Deut 11:18-19).

20 "Only take heed to thyself, and keep thy soul diligently, lest thou forget the things which thine eyes have seen, and lest they depart from thy heart all the days of thy life: but teach them thy sons, and thy sons' sons" (Deut 4:9).

21 Floyd J. Miller, *Search for a Black Nationality: Black Emigration and Colonization, 1778–1863* (Urbana: University of Illinois Press, 1975), 56.

22 Jehudi Ashmun, *Memoir of the Life and Character of the Rev. Samuel Bacon, A.M.* (Washington City: J. Gideon, 1822), 249–50, Edward G. Howard Collection of Marylandia, Albin O. Kuhn Library and Gallery, University of Maryland, Baltimore County.

23 "The Negro's Prayer," *Genius of Universal Emancipation*, May 1833, 109.

24 Miller, *Search for a Black Nationality*, 56.

25 Josephus R. Coan, "Daniel Coker: Nineteenth Century Black Church Organizer, Educator and Missionary," *Journal of the Interdenominational Theological Center* 3, no. 1 (1975): 30.

26 See Elizabeth McHenry, *Forgotten Readers: Recovering the Lost History of African American Literary Societies* (Durham, N.C.: Duke University Press, 2002), 102.

27 Robert S. Levine, "Circulating the Nation: David Walker, the Missouri Compromise, and the Rise of the Black Press," in *The Black Press: New Literary and Historical Essays*, ed. Todd Vogel (New Brunswick, N.J.: Rutgers University Press, 2001), 29.

28 Jacqueline Royster, *Traces of a Stream: Literacy and Social Change among African American Women* (Pittsburgh: University of Pittsburgh Press, 2000), 164.

29 Mark A. Noll, *America's God from Jonathan Edwards to Abraham Lincoln* (New York: Oxford University Press, 2002), 387–89.

30 See John Ernest, *Resistance and Reformation in Nineteenth-Century African-American Literature* (Jackson: University of Mississippi Press, 1995), 33, 35.

31 During the nineteenth century, the three-volume *Holy Bible, Containing the Old and New Testaments According to the Authorised Version; with Explanatory Notes, Practical Observations, and Copious Marginal References* (New York: Samuel T. Armstrong, Crocker & Brewster, 1817) was viewed as the authoritative source for Bible study.

32 The author of the article quotes Thomas Scott's commentary on three scriptural passages regarding Mosaic laws that regulated slavery:

> "Exodus xxi:16, 'He that stealeth a man and selleth him, or if he be found in his hand, he shall surely be put to death.' . . . The text implies, that he who stole anyone of the human species, in order to make a slave of him, should be punished with death.
>
> "Deuteronomy xxiv:7, 'If a man be found stealing any of his brethren of Israel, and maketh merchandise of him, or selleth, then that thief shall die.' . . . Every man is now our brother, whatever may be his nation, complexion or creed. How then can the merchandising of men and women be carried on, or abetting those who do, without transgressing this commandment?
>
> "Deuteronomy xxiii:15-16, 'Thou shalt not deliver unto his master, the servant who has escaped from his master unto thee. I shall dwell with thee, in that place which he shall choose—though shalt not oppress him.' . . . To slaves who fled to the Israelites for protection, they were commanded to afford shelter and to show great kindness; to recommend their religion, and to give them an opportunity of learning it. The people of God must keep at a distance from cruelty and oppression, and ever be ready to patronise the cause of the oppressed" ("Biblical Exposition, by Thomas Scott," *Colored American*, June 8, 1839).

33 Noll, *America's God*, 391.

34 Reform societies include the American Board of Commissioners for Foreign Missions, founded in 1810; the American Bible Society, founded in 1816; the American Colonization Society, founded in 1817; and the Sunday and Adult School Union, later known as the American Sunday School Union, founded in 1817.

35 David S. Reynolds and Debra J. Rosenthal, eds., *The Serpent in the Cup: Temperance and American Literature* (Amherst: University of Massachusetts Press, 1977), 5, 13.

36 According to Reynolds and Rosenthal, some masters provided alcohol to enslaved blacks, hoping the intoxicating effect would make them forget their oppression. Additionally, many slaves harvested sugar used to distill liquor, and some slave traders bartered for slaves with rum (5).

37 "And Miriam, the prophetess, the sister of Aaron, took a timbrel in her hand; and all the women went out after her with timbrels and with dances. And Miriam answered them, Sing ye to the LORD, for he hath triumphed gloriously; the horse and his rider hath he thrown into the sea" (Exod 15:20-21).

38 The biblical narratives for the women cited are as follows: Deborah (Judges 4–5); Queen Esther (Esther 5, 7, and 9); Abigail (1 Samuel 25); and Huldah the prophetess (2 Chronicles 34).

39 "But speaking the truth in love, may grow up into him in all things, which is the head, even Christ" (Eph 4:15).

**Chapter 3**

1 Census of Population and Housing, 1840 Census, US Census Bureau, accessed March 1, 2012, http://www.census.gov/prod/www/abs/decennial/1840.html.

2 For an in-depth discussion of Exodus ideologies in the 1830s, see Eddie S. Glaude, *Exodus! Religion, Race, and Nation in Early Nineteenth-Century Black America* (Chicago: University of Chicago Press, 2000).

3 Jeffrey Ruggles, *The Unboxing of Henry Brown* (Richmond: Library of Virginia, 2003), 96–104.

4 Although many scholars have analyzed Brown's escape from slavery, none has examined Lee's characterization of Brown as a Moses figure. Cynthia Griffin Wolff characterizes Brown's escape in a box as a "reverse Middle Passage." Wolff, "Passing beyond the Middle Passage: Henry 'Box' Brown's Translation of Slavery," *Massachusetts Review* 37, no. 1 (1996): 23–44. Marcus Wood positions Brown as a Noah figure who prefigures Christ's resurrection. Wood, *Blind Memory: Visual Representations of Slavery in England and America, 1780–1865* (New York: Routledge, 2000), 110. Henry Louis Gates posits Brown as a Christ figure, escape artist, and inventor. Gates, Foreword to Henry Box Brown, *Narrative of the Life of Henry Box Brown* (New York: Oxford University Press, 2002), x.

5 Wood, *Blind Memory*, 106.

6 Ruggles, *The Unboxing of Henry Brown*, 167.

7 For additional analysis of Harper's appropriation of the Moses figure, see Melba Joyce Boyd, *Discarded Legacy: Politics and Poetics in the Life of Frances E. W. Harper, 1825–1911* (Detroit, Mich.: Wayne State University Press, 1994).

8 See William Lloyd Garrison, "Disunion," *Liberator*, June 15, 1855.

9 Robert Purvis, *Liberator*, June 13, 1856, University of Detroit Mercy, Black Abolitionist Archive, Doc. No. 17807, accessed March 1, 2012, http://research.udmercy.edu/find/special_collections/digital/baa/item.php?record_id=2199&collectionCode=baa.

10 A tide-waiter is a customs official.

11 "Political Intelligence: Politicians Should Never Meddle with Scripture," *National Era*, May 5, 1859.

12 "Sunday School Union. The Rev. Dr. Dyer. American Slavery," *Frederick Douglass' Paper*, June 10, 1852; "On Philemon and Onesimus. By a Citizen of Washington," *National Era*, October 26, 1848; "An Examination of the Mosaic Laws of Servitude. Slavery Defined," *National Era*, October 27, 1853 and November 3, 1853.

13 Harriet Beecher Stowe, *Uncle Tom's Cabin* (London: John Cassell, 1852), 173.

14 "All Rights for All!" *Frederick Douglass' Paper*, September 8, 1854.

15 P. Gabrielle Foreman and Reginald H. Pitts assert that the text "is prototypical of black antebellum writing in its tendency to blend and challenge the narrative forms

it incorporates, weaving together factual and fictional conventions. Indeed, *Our Nig*, functions as an autobiography characterized by its complex novelistic maneuvers just as surely as it is a brilliant novel that makes autobiographical claims." Introduction to Harriet Wilson, *Our Nig; or, Sketches from the Life of a Free Black (1859)*, ed. P. Gabrielle Foreman and Reginald Pitts (New York: Penguin, 2007), xxx.

16 Foreman and Pitts have suggested that Wilson's appropriation of Joseph's experience as an interpreter of dreams foreshadows her later involvement in spiritualism (*Our Nig*, xxxix, and 99 n. 13).

17 "Campbell and Stevens: History of Virginia and Georgia," *North American Review* (October 1848): 291–322.

18 Historians into the twentieth century continued associating Boone's exploration with the conquest of Canaan. Historian and cultural critic Archibald Henderson describes Daniel Boone as "having an irrepressible longing to reach that alluring promised land" of Kentucky territory. Henderson, "Daniel Boone in Kentucky," in *The Conquest of the Old Southwest: The Romantic Story of the Old Pioneers into Virginia, the Carolinas, Tennessee, and Kentucky, 1740–1790* (New York: Century, 1920), 144–59.

19 Benson J. Lossing, "Daniel Boone," *Harper's Monthly Magazine*, October 1859, 579.

20 Albert K. Weinberg argues that "[t]he magnitude and rich natural resources of the western American wilderness strengthened the conviction that Americans were chosen people. Surely this was land for the new children of Israel." Weinberg, *Manifest Destiny: A Study of Nationalist Expansionism in American History* (Chicago: Quadrangle, 1963), 113.

21 See Elizabeth McLagan, *A Peculiar Paradise: A History of Blacks in Oregon, 1778–1940* (Portland, Ore.: Georgian Press, 1980); and David Dary, *The Oregon Trail: An American Saga* (New York: Oxford University Press, 2005).

22 Thomas Bangs Thorpe, *The Master's House; or, Scenes Descriptive of Southern Life* (New York: T. L. McElrath, 1854), 208.

23 James Whitfield, *The Writings of James M. Whitfield: America and Other Writings by a Nineteenth-Century African American Poet*, ed. Robert S. Levine and Ivy G. Wilson (Chapel Hill: University of North Carolina Press, 2011), 127.

24 David M. Dean, *Defender of the Race: James Theodore Holly, Black Nationalist Bishop* (Boston: Lambeth, 1979), 1–27.

25 James Theodore Holly, *Facts about the Church's Mission in Haiti. A Concise Statement by Bishop Holly* (New York: Thomas Whittaker, 1897).

26 "The LORD is longsuffering, and of great mercy, forgiving iniquity and transgression, and by no means clearing the guilty, visiting the iniquity of the fathers upon the children unto the third and fourth generation" (Num 14:18).

27 See Deut 34:1-5.

28 See Luke 2 for the narrative of Anna's and Simeon's encounters with the baby Jesus during his dedication in the temple.

29 "Speak now in the ears of the people, and let every man borrow of his neighbour, and every woman of her neighbour, jewels of silver and jewels of gold" (Exod 11:2).

**Chapter 4**

1 Rabbi Dr. M. J. Raphall, *The Bible View of Slavery: A Discourse, Delivered at the Jewish Synagogue, B'nai Jeshurun, New York, on the Day of the National Fast, January 4, 1861* (New York: Rudd & Carleton, 1861); "The Pulpit and the Crisis," *New Englander and Yale Review* 19, no. 73 (1861): 140–60.

2 "Rabbi Raphall," *Liberator*, April 5, 1861; "Rabbi Raphall," *New York Tribune*, January 11, 15, and 22, 1861.

3 Goldwin Smith, *Does the Bible Sanction American Slavery?* (Oxford: John Henry & James Parker, 1863); F.D.M., "The Bible and American Slavery" *Living Age*, July 25, 1863, 163–65; "Goldwin Smith," *North American Review* (October 1864): 532–39; "The Bible and Slavery," *North American Review* (January 1864): 48–74; "Mr. Goldwin Smith on Jewish Slavery," *Living Age*, August 1, 1863, 204–5.

4 See Daniel 5 for the story of King Belshazzar and the handwriting on the wall; Isa 58:6, which describes the true fast as breaking yokes and setting the oppressed free; Matt 10:34 for Jesus' admonition that he came to bring a sword rather than peace; and Exod 3:8, which reveals God's assurance to Moses that he has come down to deliver the Israelites from slavery.

5 In this section, all Turner quotations are from Henry M. Turner, "The Plagues of This Country," *Christian Recorder*, July 12, 1862, n.p.

6 Turner is likely referencing Edward B. Elliot, author of *Horae Apocalypticae*, A commentary on the apocalypse, critical and historical (1844), and Joseph Cross, author of *Pisgah: Views of the Promised Inheritance. A Series of Dissertations on the Unaccomplished Prophecies* (1856).

7 "And afterward Moses and Aaron went in, and told Pharaoh, Thus saith the LORD God of Israel, Let my people go, that they may hold a feast unto me in the wilderness" (Exod 5:1). Emphasis in original.

8 See Exodus 7–11.

9 See Exodus 11.

10 "And the sixth angel sounded, and I heard a voice from the four horns of the golden altar which is before God, saying to the sixth angel which had the trumpet, Loose the four angels which are bound in the great river Euphrates. And the four angels were loosed, which were prepared for an hour, and a day, and a month, and a year, for to slay the third part of men" (Rev 9:13-15). "And I beheld when he had opened the sixth seal, and, lo, there was a great earthquake; and the sun became black as sackcloth of hair, and the moon became as blood; And the stars of heaven fell unto the earth, even as a fig tree casteth her untimely figs, when she is shaken of a mighty wind. And the heaven departed as a scroll when it is rolled together; and every mountain and island were moved out of their places" (Rev 16:12-14).

11 Holland, letter to the editor, *Messenger*, January 19, 1864.

12 Melissa Wilford, "One Flag, One Nation, One Destiny: African American Service in the Civil War," accessed March 1, 2012, http://www.factasy.com/civil_war/book/export/html/1313.

13 Harold Melvin Hyman, *Era of the Oath: Northern Loyalty Tests during the Civil War and Reconstruction* (New York: Octagon Books, 1978).

14 James McCune Smith, introduction to *A Memorial Discourse by Henry Highland Garnet, Delivered in the Hall of the House of Representatives, Washington City, D.C., on Sabbath, February 12, 1865* (Philadelphia: Joseph M. Wilson, 1865).

15 "And he that stealeth a man, and selleth him, or if he be found in his hand, he shall surely be put to death" (Exod 21:16).

16 "The Promised Land," *The Anderson Intelligencer* [Anderson, SC]. December 30, 1903: 6.

17 "And I saw thrones, and they sat upon them, and judgment was given unto them: and I saw the souls of them that were beheaded for the witness of Jesus, and for the

word of God, and which had not worshipped the beast, neither his image, neither had received his mark upon their foreheads, or in their hands; and they lived and reigned with Christ a thousand years" (Rev 20:4).

18 C. B. Crane, *Sermon on the Occasion of the Death of President Lincoln* (Hartford: Case, Lockwood, 1865), 28–29.

19 Henry Fowler, *Character and Death of Abraham Lincoln. A Discourse Preached at Auburn, N.Y., April 23, 1865* (Auburn, N.Y.: Wm. J. Moses Steam Press, 1865), 16.

20 Pliny H. White, *A Sermon Occasioned by the Assassination of Abraham Lincoln, President of the United States* (Brattleboro, Vt.: Vermont Record Office, 1865), 16.

21 Annie M. Smith, "Xenia Correspondence," *Christian Recorder*, May 20, 1865.

22 John Stevens Cabot Abbott and Russell Herman Conwell, "Andrew Johnson," in *Lives of the Presidents of the United States of America: From Washington to the Present Time* (Boston: B. B. Russell, 1870), 457.

23 Daniel Smith Lamb, ed., *Howard University Medical Department, Washington, D.C.: A Historical, Biographical and Statistical Souvenir* (Washington, D.C.: R. Beresford, 1900; repr., Freeport, N.Y.: Books for Libraries Press, 1971).

24 John F. N. Wilkinson, letter to the editor, *Christian Recorder*, April 30, 1864.

25 *Celebration by the Colored People's Educational Monument Association, in Memory of Abraham Lincoln: On the Fourth of July, 1865, in the presidential grounds, Washington, Part 3* (Washington, D.C.: McGill & Whiterow, 1865).

26 The extant copy of *Moses, a Story of the Nile* was published in 1869 as a second edition, but scholars believe the poem may have been published as early as 1865. Harper released revised editions of the poem in 1870 and 1889. See Boyd, *Discarded Legacy*; Frances E. W. Harper, *Minnie's Sacrifice, Sowing and Reaping, Trial and Triumph: Three Rediscovered Novels*, ed. Frances Smith Foster (New York: Beacon Press, 2000); Leslie W. Lewis, *Telling Narratives: Secrets in African American Literature* (Champaign: University of Illinois Press, 2007).

27 In 1662 colonial Virginia enacted legislation that stipulated: "Whereas some doubts have arisen whether children got by any Englishman upon a Negro woman should be slave or free, be it therefore enacted and declared by this present Grand Assembly, that all children born in this country shall be held bond or free only according to the condition of the mother; and that if any Christian shall commit fornication with a Negro man or woman, he or she so offending shall pay double the fines imposed by the former act." David Brion Davis and Steven Mintz, eds., *The Boisterous Sea of Liberty: A Documentary History of America from Discovery through the Civil War* (New York: Oxford University Press, 2000), 58.

28 AR, "How Does God Give Success in Battle?—Or a Plea for Prayer in Behalf of Our Country," *Christian Recorder*, August 30, 1862.

29 "'See That Ye Fall Not Out by the Way,'" *Christian Recorder*, September 24, 1870.

30 J.E.C., "Industry and Energy Are the Mighty Powers That Insure Success," *Christian Recorder*, January 15, 1870.

31 J. H. Cole, "XI. Punctuality," *Christian Recorder*, February 24, 1876.

32 The delegation, selected by members of black churches in Washington, D.C., during at meeting at Union Bethel AME Church, included Cornelius Clark, educator John F. Cook, John T. Costin, Asbury Methodist Church founder Benjamin McCoy, and black intellectual Edward Thomas, chairman. Abraham Lincoln, "Address on Colonization to a Deputation of Negroes," in *Collected Works of Abraham Lincoln*, vol. 5 (New Brunswick, N.J.: Rutgers University Press, 1955), 370–75; Kate Masur, "The

African American Delegation to Abraham Lincoln: A Reappraisal," *Civil War History* 56, no. 2 (2010): 117.

33 "The Barbados Expedition," *African Repository and Colonial Journal* 41 (1865): 157; "Benefits of Barbados Emigration," *African Repository and Colonial Journal* 41 (1865): 119–21; Burleigh Holder, "A History of Crozierville," *Liberia Studies Journal* 3, no. 1 (1970–1971): 21–30.

**Chapter 5**

1 Logan, *The Negro in American Life and Thought*, 11.

2 "A Record Sunday at Bethel A.M.E. Church, New York. Ordination of a Missionary to the Danish West Indies," *Christian Recorder*, March 22, 1900. See Eric Gardner, *Unexpected Places: Relocating Nineteenth-Century African American Literature* (Jackson: University Press of Mississippi, 2009) for discussion of the Christian Recorder's contributions to the African American literary tradition.

3 The first bishop was Richard Allen, the third bishop was Edward Waters, the sixteenth bishop was Wesley J. Gaines, the nineteenth bishop was Abraham Grant, and the twentieth-sixth bishop was Evans Tyree.

4 "A Record Sunday."

5 "And the LORD was with Joseph, and he was a prosperous man; and he was in the house of his master the Egyptian" (Gen 39:2).

6 See Charles Spencer Smith, *A History of the African Methodist Episcopal Church Being a Volume Supplemental to A History of the African Methodist Episcopal Church by Daniel Alexander Payne, D.D. LL.D, Late One of Its Bishops* (Philadelphia: Book Concern of the AME Church, 1922), 227, 414, 449.

7 See Adam Fairclough, *Better Day Coming: Blacks and Equality, 1890–2000* (New York: Penguin, 2002), 2–3.

8 Ida B. Wells, *The Red Record: Tabulated Statistics and Alleged Causes of Lynching in the United States* (1895), Project Gutenberg eBook, February 8, 2005, accessed March 1, 2012, http://www.gutenberg.org/files/14977/14977-h/14977-h.htm.

9 Letter to the editor, *Columbia (S.C.) Daily Phoenix*, September 17, 1872; and Speech of Hon. Robert Smalls, of South Carolina. In the House of Representatives, Friday, July 30, 1886. On the bill (H. R. 7167) for the relief of Mrs. Maria Hunter, Cong. Rec., Appendix, 49th Cong., 1st sess., A319–20.

10 D. H. Bowen, "Our Moses in North Eastern South Carolina," *Christian Recorder*, May 2, 1895, and May 9, 1895.

11 James Madison Bell, "The Progress of Liberty," in *The Poetical Works* (Lansing, Mich.: Wynkoop, Hallenbeck, Crawford, 1901).

12 Ethel M. Washington, *Union County's Black Soldiers and Soldiers of the Civil War* (Charleston, S.C.: History Press, 2011), 18.

13 See Nehemiah 1–2.

14 See Nell Irving Painter, *Exodusters: Black Migration to Kansas after Reconstruction* (New York: W. W. Norton, 1992).

15 "The Promised Land," *Anderson (S.C.) Intelligencer*, December 30, 1903, 6.

16 Roger L. Kemp, "Virginia Declaration of Rights," in *Documents of American Democracy: A Collection of Essential Works* (Jefferson, N.C.: McFarland, 2010), 53.

17 Frank Sherman, *Liberia: The Land, Its People, History, and Culture* (New York: New Africa Press, 2011), 29–30.

18 David W. Wills, "Exodus Piety: African American Religion in an Age of Immigration,"

in *Minority Faiths and the American Protestant Mainstream*, ed. Jonathan D. Sarna (Urbana: University of Illinois Press, 1998), 157.

19 Seven letters by Daniel Payne appeared under variations of the headline "African Emigration: Colored Americans and Africa—Colored Americans," *Christian Recorder*, August 8, 1878, August 22, 1878, September 12, 1878, September 26, 1878, and December 5, 1878. Two were published as "Evergreen Cottage, Near Wilberforce University, Xenia, O.," *Christian Recorder*, June 27, 1878, and August 1, 1878.

20 Payne, "Evergreen Cottage," June 27, 1878.

21 Payne, "Evergreen Cottage," August 1, 1878. Emphasis in original.

22 Payne, "Evergreen Cottage," August 1, 1878.

23 Charles M. Christian, *Black Saga: The African American Experience, a Chronology* (Washington, D.C.: Civitas Counterpoint, 1999), 272.

**Afterword**

1 Frederick Douglass, letter to Francis Grimké, April 24, 1886, Francis Grimké Papers, Moreland-Spingarn Library, Howard University, Washington, D.C.

2 "To the Unfading Memory of Hon. Frederick Douglass," *Washington Bee*, July 13, 1895; "His Body to Lie in State: Douglass's Remains for Five Hours at Metropolitan A.M.E.," *Washington Times*, February 25, 1895.

3 "Lessons Reviewed. Third Quarter of the International Series Closed," *Christian Recorder*, September 20, 1888; "Joshua's Commission. Lesson I, Fourth Quarter, International Series," *Christian Recorder*, September 27, 1888.

4 Benjamin Tucker Tanner, "A Help or Hindrance, Which?" *Christian Recorder*, November 7, 1895; commentary on Joshua, in *Pulpit Commentary*, vol. 3, ed. Henry D. M. Spence-Jones and Joseph Exell; and Joshua 5:13, American Standard Version

5 "Our Ministry," *Christian Recorder*, August 9, 1877.

6 J. F. Taylor, "Moberly (Mo.) District," *Christian Recorder*, August 7, 1890.

7 W. S. Kane, "Our Canada Letter," *Christian Recorder*, February 12, 1891.

8 I. F. Aldridge, "Servants of God," *Christian Recorder*, August 2, 1883.

9 C. R. Runyon, "A Tribute," *Christian Recorder*, June 28, 1894.

10 A. J. Kershaw, "Heardism Indicted," *Christian Recorder*, September 7, 1893. See also "Heardism Explained," *Christian Recorder*, May 4, 1893; and W. H. Heard, "Heardism Defended," *Christian Recorder*, May 25, 1893.

11 "Communications.—For the Christian Recorder. Our 'Log,'" *Christian Recorder*, December 22, 1881.

12 R. B. Brookins, "A Miscellaneous Letter," *Christian Recorder*, November 27, 1890.

13 H. Rufus White, *"A Joshua in the Camp," or, The Life of Booker T. Washington, of Tuskegee, Alabama* (Towson, Md., 1895).

14 "A Joshua in the Camp," review of White, *A Joshua in the Camp, AME Church Review* 12 (1896): 419.

15 W.E.B. Du Bois, "Du Bois Congratulates Washington on Atlanta Speech," *NAACP: A Century in the Fight for Freedom, 1909–2009*. Library of Congress, accessed July 11, 2012, http://myloc.gov/Exhibitions/naacp/prelude/ExhibitObjects/DuBois Congratulates.aspx.

16 W.E.B. Du Bois, "Credo," *Independent* 57 (October 6, 1904): 787.

17 Charles R. Douglass, "Not Disturbed in Mind. Dec. 21, 1895," *Washington Bee*, December 28, 1895.

18 "The Moses of the Black Belt: Leading His People out of the Bondage of Ignorance and Idleness," *Omaha Daily Bee*, October 7, 1895, 6.

19 "Booker T. Washington," *Minneapolis Appeal*, July 3, 1897.

20 "We Heartily Endorse the Work," *Richmond (Ky.) Climax*, December 21, 1898.

21 "We Heartily Endorse the Work."

22 "Booker T. Washington," *Marietta Daily Leader*, April 21, 1900

23 "The Slave Boy Becomes a Maker of Magistrates," *Minneapolis Journal*, October 8, 1901.

24 "The Slave Boy."

25 By 1900 approximately 50 percent of white Americans were homeowners, compared to 20 percent of African Americans. The disparity between farm owners was even larger. About 5 million white Americans operated farms, but only 750,000 African Americans were farmers at the turn of the twentieth century. In the South 116 black farmers worked an average of one thousand acres in 1910, a slight increase from 103 in 1900. Of those, 24 percent were African American–owned farms; the overwhelming majority of agricultural workers, 76 percent, were tenant farmed. Spencer D. Wood and Jess Gilbert, "Returning African Americans Farmers to the Land: Recent Trends and a Policy Rationale," accessed March 1, 2012, Land Loss Prevention Project, http://www.landloss.org/Wood%20--%20Returning.pdf; U.S. Commission on Civil Rights, *The Decline of Black Farming in America* (Washington, D.C.: U.S. GPO, 1982), 3; William J. Collins and Robert A. Margo, "Race and Home Ownership from the End of the Civil War to the Present," Department of Economics, Boston University, January 2011, accessed March 1, 2012, http://www.bu.edu/econ/files/2011/05/03_01-01-11_Race-Home-Ownership_Margo.pdf; U.S. Department of Commerce, Bureau of the Census, N*egro Population of the United States, 1790–1915* (1918; New York: Arno, 1968).

26 "Tubs at Tuskegee: Part of the Regular Curriculum, Reports Mrs. E. A. Russell. She Visited the Institute. The Intense Earnestness and Personal Cleanliness of the Pupils Impressed Her," *Minneapolis Journal*, April 12, 1902, 2.

27 Carnegie's gift to Tuskegee received national media attention. The following newspapers provide a sampling of this coverage: "Carnegie's Gift to Tuskegee," *Keowee (Walhalla, S.C.) Courier*, May 13, 1903; "Booker T. Washington Is Having What Seems Great, Good Luck," *Richmond (Va.) Times-Dispatch*, April 25, 1903; "To Tuskegee, $600,000: Mr. Carnegie's Gift," *New York Tribune*, April 24, 1903; "Andrew Carnegie Calls Booker T. Washington the 'Modern Moses,'" *Wichita Daily Eagle*, May 14, 1903, 4; "Carnegie Gives Financial Help. Contributes Six Hundred Thousand Dollars to Tuskegee. Requires Trustees to Make Provision for Booker T. Washington," *San Francisco Call*, April 24, 1903, 9. In his autobiography, Carnegie modified his characterization of Washington, describing the race leader as a "modern Moses and Joshua combined, leading his people both onward and upward." This change may have signaled a shift in Carnegie's understanding of Washington's work and African American citizenship. Andrew Carnegie, *Autobiography of Andrew Carnegie* (Boston: Houghton Mifflin, 1920), 277.

28 "In the March Number of the 'Brown Book of Boston,'" *Ardmore (Okla.) Daily Ardmoreite*, November 2, 1903.

29 "Andrew Carnegie Calls Booker T. Washington the 'Modern Moses.'"

30 "Booker T. Washington Is Spending Money Like a Drunken Lord in Order to Pose as the Infallible Leader of the Afro-American Race," *Chicago Broad Ax*, October 31, 1903.

31 Barack Obama, "Obama's Selma Speech. Text as Delivered," Lynn Sweet, The Scoop from Washington, blog, *Chicago Sun-Times*, March 7, 2007, accessed March 1, 2012, http://blogs.suntimes.com/sweet/2007/03/obamas_selma_speech_text_as_de.html.

# Bibliography


Abbott, John Stevens Cabot. "Andrew Johnson." In *Lives of the Presidents of the United States of America: From Washington to the Present Time*. Boston: B. B. Russell, 1870.

"African Colonization." *Liberator*, July 28, 1832, 2, 30.

Aichele, George, et al. *The Postmodern Bible: The Bible and Culture Collective*. New Haven: Yale University Press, 1995.

Aldridge, I. F. "Servants of God." *Christian Recorder*, August 2, 1833.

"All Rights for All!" *Frederick Douglass' Paper*, September 8, 1854.

"American Puritanism." *New Englander and Yale Review* 1, no. 3 (1843): 352–65.

"An Apology for Pharaoh." *Freedom's Journal*, June 29, 1827, and July 6, 1827.

Anderson, Osborne. *A Voice from Harper's Ferry: A Narrative of Events at Harper's Ferry; with Incidents Prior and Subsequent to Its Capture by Captain Brown and His Men*. Boston: Author, 1861.

"Andrew Carnegie Calls Booker T. Washington the 'Modern Moses.'" *Wichita Daily Eagle*, May 14, 1903, 4.

Aptheker, Herbert. *American Negro Slave Revolts*. 2nd ed. New York: International, 1974.

AR. "How Does God Give Success in Battle?—Or a Plea for Prayer in Behalf of Our Country." *Christian Recorder*, August 30, 1862.

Arnett, Benjamin W. *The Budget: Containing Biographical Sketches, Quadrennial and Annual Reports of the General Officers of the African Methodist Episcopal Church*. Dayton, Ohio: Christian Publishing House, 1884.

Ashmun, Jehudi. *Memoir of the Life and Character of the Rev. Samuel Bacon, A.M.* Washington City: J. Gideon, 1822. Edward G. Howard Collection of Marylandia, Albin O. Kuhn Library and Gallery, University of Maryland, Baltimore County.

The Associated Veterans of the Mexican War. *History of the Celebration of the Fiftieth Anniversary of the Taking Possession of California and Raising of the American flag at Monterey, Cal., by Commodore John Drake Sloat, U.S.N., July 7th, 1846.* Oakland, Calif.: Carruth & Carruth, 1896.

Bancroft, Hubert Howe. *History of the Pacific States of North America.* Vol. 4, *Mexico.* San Francisco: A. L. Bancroft, 1883.

"The Barbados Expedition." *African Repository and Colonial Journal* 41 (1865): 157.

"Benefits of Barbados Emigration." *African Repository and Colonial Journal* 41 (1865): 119–21.

Beecher, Henry Ward. *Patriotic Addresses in America and England from 1850 to 1885, on Slavery, the Civil War, and the Development of Civil Liberty in the United States.* Edited by John R. Howard. New York: Fords, Howard & Hulbert, 1891.

Bell, James Madison. "The Progress of Liberty." In *The Poetical Works.* Lansing, Mich.: Wynkoop, Hallenbeck, Crawford, 1901. Database of African American Poetry, 1760–1900. Alexandria, Va.: Chadwyck-Healy, 1995.

Benezet, Anthony. *Observations on the Inslaving, Importing and Purchasing of Negroes.* Germantown: Christopher Sower, 1760.

"The Bible and Slavery." *North American Review* (January 1864): 48–74.

"Biblical Exposition, by Thomas Scott." *Colored American,* June 8, 1839.

"A Bill to Prevent Negroes and Mulattoes from Coming to, or Residing in Oregon." *Oregon Exclusion Law (1849).* BlackPast.org. 2007–2011. Accessed February 3, 2012. http://www.blackpast.org/?q=primarywest/oregon-exclusion-law-1849.

"Bishop Hopkins on Slavery." *Christian Examiner* 63 (1857): 166–83.

"Booker T. Washington." *Marietta Daily Leader,* April 21, 1900.

"Booker T. Washington." *Minneapolis Appeal,* July 3, 1897.

"Booker T. Washington Is Having What Seems Great, Good Luck." *Richmond (Va.) Times-Dispatch,* April 25, 1903.

"Booker T. Washington Is Spending Money Like a Drunken Lord in Order to Pose as the Infallible Leader of the Afro-American Race." *Chicago Broad Ax,* October 31, 1903.

Bowen, D. H. "Our Moses in North Eastern South Carolina." *Christian Recorder,* May 2, 1895, and May 9, 1895.

Boulukos, George. *The Grateful Slave: The Emergence of Race in Eighteenth-Century British and American Culture.* Cambridge: Cambridge University Press, 2008.

Boyd, Andrew, ed. *A Memorial Lincoln Bibliography being an Account of Books, Eulogies, Sermons, Portraits, Engravings, Medals, etc., Published upon Abraham Lincoln, Sixteenth President of the United States, Assassinated Good Friday, April 14, 1865.* Albany, N.Y.: Andrew Boyd, 1870.

Boyd, Melba Joyce. *Discarded Legacy: Politics and Poetics in the Life of Frances E. W. Harper, 1825–1911.* Detroit, Mich.: Wayne State University Press, 1994.

Brackett, Jeffrey R. *The Negro in Maryland: A Study of the Institution of Slavery.* 1889. Freeport, N.Y.: Books for Libraries Press, 1969.

Bradford, William. "A Modell of Christian Charity." 1630. The Religious Freedom Page, University of Virginia Library. Accessed March 1, 2012. http://religiousfreedom.lib.virginia.edu/sacred/charity.html.

Brinch, Boyrereau. *The Blind African Slave, or, Memoirs of Boyrereau Brinch, Nicknamed Jeffrey Brace.* Edited by Benjamin F. Prentiss. St. Albans, Vt.: Harry Whitney, 1810.

Brookins, R. B. "A Miscellaneous Letter." *Christian Recorder*, November 27, 1890.

Brooks, Joanna. *American Lazarus: Religion and the Rise of African-American and Native American Literature.* New York: Oxford University Press, 2003.

———. "John Marrant's *Journal*: Providence and Prophecy in the Eighteenth-Century Black Atlantic." *North Star* 3 (1999). Accessed March 1, 2012. http://www.princeton.edu/~jweisenf/northstar/volume3/brooks.html.

Brown, Henry Box. *Narrative of the Life of Henry Box Brown, Written by Himself.* Introduction, by Thomas Gardiner Lee. Manchester, England: Lee & Glynn, 1851.

Burling, Elias. *A Call to Back-Sliding Israel and May Be as a Necessary Word of Caution and Admonition to the Inhabitants of East and West–Jersey, Pennsilvania, & as a Remembrancer to Them to Call to Mind Their Former State.* New York: William Bradford, 1694.

Callahan, Allen Dwight. *The Talking Book: African Americans and the Bible.* New Haven: Yale University Press, 2008.

Calloway, Colin G. "Elezar Wheelock Meets Luther Standing Bear: Native American Studies at Dartmouth." In *Native American Studies in Higher Education: Models for Collaboration between Universities and Indigenous Nations*, edited by Duane Champagne and Jay Stauss, 17–28. Walnut Creek, Calif.: AltaMira Press, 2002.

"Campbell and Stevens: History of Virginia and Georgia." *North American Review* (October 1848): 291–322. Making of America, Cornell University Library. Accessed March 1, 2012. http://cdl.library.cornell.edu/cgi-bin/moa/moa-cgi?notisid=ABQ7578-0067&byte=82707578.

Carey, Brycchan. *British Abolitionism and the Rhetoric of Sensibility: Writing, Sentiment, and Slavery, 1760–1807.* Basingstoke, U.K.: Palgrave Macmillan, 2005.

Carle, John I. *A funeral sermon, preached at Rockaway, December 29, 1799, on the much-lamented death of General George Washington.* Morristown, N.J.: Jacob Mann, 1800.

Carnegie, Andrew. *Autobiography of Andrew Carnegie.* Boston: Houghton Mifflin, 1920.

"Carnegie Gives Financial Help. Contributes Six Hundred Thousand Dollars to Tuskegee. Requires Trustees to Make Provision for Booker T. Washington." *San Francisco Call*, April 24, 1903, 9.

"Carnegie's Gift to Tuskegee." *Keowee (Walhalla, S.C.) Courier*, May 13, 1903.

Carney, Cary Michael. *Native American Higher Education in the United States*. New Brunswick, N.J.: Transaction Publishers, 1999.

Carretta, Vincent. *Equiano the African: Biography of a Self-Made Man*. Athens: University of Georgia Press, 2005.

*The Case of Our Fellow-Creatures, the Oppressed Africans, Respectfully Recommended to the Serious Consideration of the Legislature of Great-Britain, by the People Called Quakers.* London: James Phillips, 1784.

Cashin, Edward J. *Beloved Bethesda: A History of George Whitefield's Home for Boys, 1740–2000*. Macon, Ga.: Mercer University Press, 2001.

*Celebration by the Colored People's Educational Monument Association, in Memory of Abraham Lincoln: On the Fourth of July, 1865, in the presidential grounds, Washington, Part 3*. Washington, D.C.: McGill & Whiterow, 1865.

Census of Population and Housing, 1840 Census, US Census Bureau. Accessed March 1, 2012. http://www.census.gov/prod/www/abs/decennial/1840.html.

Chedgzoy, Kate. *Women Writing in the British Atlantic World: Memory, Place, and History*. Cambridge: Cambridge University Press, 2007.

Cherry, Conrad, ed. *God's New Israel: Religious Interpretations of American Destiny.* Chapel Hill: University of North Carolina Press, 1998.

Christian, Charles M. *Black Saga: The African American Experience, a Chronology*. Washington, D.C.: Civitas Counterpoint, 1999.

Church, Benjamin. *Liberty and Property Vindicated, and the St--pm-n Burnt*. Boston: Newest Printing Office, 1765. Accessed March 1, 2012. http://xtf.lib.virginia.edu/xtf/view?docId=chadwyck_ap/uvaGenText/tei/chap_AM0268.xml;brand=default.

Coan, Josephus R. "Daniel Coker: Nineteenth Century Black Church Organizer, Educator and Missionary." *Journal of the Interdenominational Theological Center* 3, no. 1 (1975): 17–31.

Cole, J. H. "XI. Punctuality." *Christian Recorder*, February 24, 1876.

Coleman, Elihu. *A Testimony against the Anti–Christian Practice of Making Slaves of Men Wherein It Is Shewed to Be Contrary to the Dispensation of the Law and Time of the Gospel, and Very Opposite Both to Grace and Nature.* New Bedford, Conn.: Reprinted for Abraham Shearman, 1733.

Collins, William J., and Robert A. Margo. "Race and Home Ownership from the End of the Civil War to the Present." Department of Economics, Boston University, January 2011. Accessed March 1, 2012. http://www.bu.edu/econ/files/2011/05/03_01-01-11_Race-Home-Ownership_Margo.pdf.

Commentary on Joshua. In *Pulpit Commentary*. Vol. 3. Edited by Henry D. M. Spence-Jones and Joseph Exell. New York: Funk & Wagnalls, n.d.

"Confessions of Ben Alias Ben Woolfork." Gabriel's Insurrection, September 16–30, 1800. James Monroe, Executive Papers, 1799–1802, Box 8, Folder 2. Library of Virginia, Richmond.

"Communications.—For the Christian Recorder. Our 'Log.'" *Christian Recorder*, December 22, 1881.

"Contrast between the Mosaic Servitude and American Slavery." *Colored American*, July 29, 1837.

Crane, C. B. *Sermon on the Occasion of the Death of President Lincoln*. Hartford: Case, Lockwood, 1865.

Crummell, Alexander. "A Sermon, Preached in Trinity Church, Monrovia, Liberia, West Africa, to the Barbadian Emigrants, May 14, 1865." *Christian Recorder*, November 11, 1856, and November 18, 1865.

Cugoano, Ottobah. *Thoughts and Sentiments on the on the Evil and Wicked Traffic of the Slavery and Commerce of the Human Species*. 1787. Edited by Vincent Carretta. New York: Penguin, 2000.

"Cyclopedia of American Literature." *Putnam's Monthly Magazine of American Literature, Science and Art* 7, no. 38 (1856): 170–74.

Dary, David. *The Oregon Trail: An American Saga*. New York: Oxford University Press, 2005.

Davis, David Brion, and Steven Mintz, eds. *The Boisterous Sea of Liberty: A Documentary History of America from Discovery through the Civil War*. New York: Oxford University Press, 2000.

Dean, David M. *Defender of the Race: James Theodore Holly, Black Nationalist Bishop*. Boston: Lambeth, 1979.

Delany, Martin R. *The Condition, Elevation, Emigration, and Destiny of the Colored People of the United States*. 1852. With an introduction by Toyin Falola. Amherst, N.Y.: Humanity Books, Prometheus Books, 2004.

Derrick, William B. "Tribute by the Rev. William B. Derrick, D.D., of the A.M.E. Church, of New York." In *Memoriam: Frederick Douglass*, edited by Helen Pitts Douglass, 41–43. Philadelphia: John C. Yorston, 1897.

"Dialogue Between Moses, Pharaoh and Others." *Colored American*, October 20, 1838.

Douglass, Charles R. "Not Disturbed in Mind. Dec. 21, 1895." *Washington Bee*, December 28, 1895.

Douglass, Frederick. "The Blood of the Slaves on the Shirts of the Northern People." *North Star*, November 17, 1848.

———. "The Claims of Our Race: An Interview with President Andrew Johnson in Washington, DC, on 7 February 1866." In *The Frederick Douglass' Papers*, 4:96–106.

———. *The Frederick Douglass' Papers: Series One, Speeches, Debates, and Interviews, 1864–80*. Edited by John W. Blassingame and John R. McKivigan. 5 vols. New Haven: Yale University Press, 1979–1992.

———. "Govern with Magnanimity and Courage: An Address Delivered in Philadelphia, Pennsylvania, on 6 September 1866." In *The Frederick Douglass' Papers*, 4:139–46.

———. "The Issues of the Day: An Address Delivered in Washington, DC, on 10 March 1866." In *The Frederick Douglass Papers*, 4:118–33.

———. Letter to Francis Grimké, April 24, 1886. Francis Grimké Papers, Moreland-Spingarn Library, Howard University, Washington, D.C.

———. *My Bondage and My Freedom.* 1855. In Douglass, *Autobiographies.* New York: Literary Classics of the United States, 1994.

———. *Narrative of the Life of Frederick Douglass, an American Slave, Written by Himself.* 1845. Edited by Houston Baker. New York: Penguin, 1982.

———. "The Negro Exodus from the Gulf States." *Frank Leslie's Popular Monthly* 9, no. 1 (1880): 39–48.

———. "The Negro Exodus from the Gulf States: Address before the Convention of the American Social Science Association, Saratoga Springs, September 12, 1879." In *The Life and Writings of Frederick Douglass*, edited by Philip S. Foner, 324–42. New York: International, 1955.

———. "What to the Slave Is the Fourth of July?" *Teaching American History.* 2006. "Frederick Douglass." April 25, 2007. Accessed March 1, 2012. http://teachingamericanhistory.org/library/index.asp?document=162.

Drayton, William. *The South Vindicated from the Treason and Fanaticism of Northern Abolitionists.* Philadelphia: H. Manly, 1836.

Du Bois, W.E.B. "Credo." *Independent* 57 (October 6, 1904): 787.

———. Letter from W.E.B. Dubois to Booker T. Washington congratulating Washington on his "Atlanta Exposition Speech," September 24, 1895. Booker T. Washington Papers, Manuscript Division, Library of Congress. "Du Bois Congratulates Washington on Atlanta Speech." *NAACP: A Century in the Fight for Freedom, 1909–2009.* Accessed January 29, 2012. http://myloc.gov/Exhibitions/naacp/prelude/ExhibitObjects/DuBoisCongratulates.aspx.

———. *The Souls of Black Folk: Essays and Sketches.* Chicago: A. C. McClurg, 1903.

Dunbar, Paul Laurence. "An Ante-bellum Sermon." In *The Complete Poems of Paul Laurence Dunbar*, 13–14. New York: Dodd, Mead, 1922.

Eddy, Richard. *The Martyr of Liberty: Three Sermons Preached in the First Universalist Church, Philadelphia, April 16, April 19, and June 1.* Philadelphia: H. W. Smith, 1865.

Egerton, Douglas R. *Gabriel's Rebellion: The Virginia Slave Conspiracies of 1800 and 1802.* Chapel Hill: University of North Carolina Press, 1993.

Elrod, Eileen Razzari. "Moses and the Egyptian: Religious Authority in Olaudah Equiano's *Interesting Narrative.*" *African American Review* 35, no. 3 (2001): 409–25.

Equiano, Olaudah. *The Interesting Narrative and Other Writings.* Edited by Vincent Carretta. New York: Penguin, 2003.

Ernest, John. *Resistance and Reformation in Nineteenth-Century African-American Literature.* Jackson: University of Mississippi Press, 1995.

"An Examination of the Mosaic Laws of Servitude. Slavery Defined." *National Era,* October 27, 1853, and November 3, 1853.

Fairclough, Adam. *Better Day Coming: Blacks and Equality, 1890–2000.* New York: Penguin, 2002.

F.D.M. "The Bible and American Slavery." *Living Age,* July 25, 1863, 163–65.

Foster, Frances Smith. "A Narrative of the Interesting Origins and (Somewhat)

Surprising Developments of African-American Print Culture." *American Literary History* (Winter 2005): 712–40.

Fowler, Henry. *Character and Death of Abraham Lincoln. A Discourse Preached at Auburn, N.Y., April 23, 1865*. Auburn, N.Y.: Wm. J. Moses Steam Press, 1865.

"The Free People's Hate of the People Enslaved." *Provincial Freeman*, October 13, 1855.

Gale, Edward C. "Washington Irving's Literary Services." *Ariel* 5, no. 6 (1882): 83.

Gardner, Eric. *Unexpected Places: Relocating Nineteen-Century African American Literature.* Jackson: University Press of Mississippi, 2009.

Garnet, Henry Highland, ed. *Walker's Appeal, with a Brief Sketch of his Life. By Henry Highland Garnet. And Also Garnet's Address to the Slaves of the United States of America.* 1848. New York: Arno and the *New York Times*, 1969.

———. "Let the Monster Perish." In *Lift Every Voice: African American Oratory, 1787–1900,* edited by Philip Sheldon Foner and Robert J. Branham, 432–42. Tuscaloosa: University of Alabama Press, 1998. Originally published in *A Memorial Discourse by Rev. Henry Highland Garnet, Delivered in the Hall of the House of Representatives, Washington City, D.C., on Sabbath, February 12, 1865.* Philadelphia: Joseph M. Wilson, 1865.

———. "Sketch of the Life and Character of David Walker." *North Star*, July 14, 1848.

Garrison, William Lloyd. "Disunion." *Liberator*, June 15, 1855.

Gates, Henry Louis. Foreword to Henry Box Brown, *Narrative of the Life of Henry Box Brown*, vii–x. New York: Oxford University Press, 2002.

Glaude, Eddie S. *Exodus! Religion, Race, and Nation in Early Nineteenth-Century Black America*. Chicago: University of Chicago Press, 2000.

Gliddon, George R., and J. C. Nott. *Types of Mankind: or, Ethnological Researches, Based upon the Ancient Monuments, Paintings, Sculptures, and Crania of Races, and upon the Natural, Geographical, Philological, and Biblical History: Illustrated by Selections from the Inedited Papers of Samu*. Philadelphia: Lippincott, Grambo, 1854.

"Goldwin Smith." *North American Review* (October 1864): 523–39.

"Great Speech of Hon. Charles Sumner, on Friday, 18th Inst." *Christian Recorder*, January 26, 1867.

Grimké, Angelina E. *Appeal to the Christian Women of the South*. New York: American Anti–Slavery Society, 1836. Accessed March 1, 2012. http://utc.iath.virginia.edu/abolitn/abesaegat.html.

Grimké, Francis. "A Resemblance and a Contrast between the American Negro and the Children of Israel, in Egypt, or the Duty of the Negro to Contend Earnestly for His Rights Guaranteed under the Constitution" (1902). In *The Works of Francis J. Grimké*. Vol. 1, edited by Carter G. Woodson, 347–64. Washington, D.C.: Associated Publishers, 1942.

Hale, Sarah J. *Liberia: or, Mr. Peyton's Experiments*. New York: Harper & Brothers, 1853.

Harlan, Robert J. "Migration Is the Only Remedy for Our Wrongs." In *Lift Every Voice: African-American Oratory, 1787–1900*, edited by Philip Sheldon Foner and Robert J. Branham, 599–602. Tuscaloosa: University of Alabama Press, 1998.

Harper, Frances E. W. "A Factor in Human Progress." *AME Church Review* 2 (1885): 14–18.

———. *Iola Leroy; or, Shadows Uplifted.* 1893. Edited by Frances Smith Foster. New York: Oxford University Press, 1988.

———. *Minnie's Sacrifice, Sowing and Reaping, Trial and Triumph: Three Rediscovered Novels.* Edited by Frances Smith Foster. New York: Beacon Press, 2000.

———. *Moses, a Story of the Nile.* Philadelphia: Merrihew & Son, 1869.

———. "Our Greatest Want." *Anglo-African Magazine* (1859): 160. Facsimile of first edition. New York: Arno and the *New York Times*, 1968.

———. "We Are All Bound up Together." In *A Brighter Coming Day: A Frances Ellen Watkins Harper Reader*, edited by Frances Smith Foster, 216–19. New York: Feminist Press, 1990.

Harris, J. William. *The Hanging of Thomas Jeremiah: A Free Black Man's Encounter with Liberty.* New Haven: Yale University Press, 2009.

Harris, Will. "Phillis Wheatley, Diaspora Subjectivity, and the African American Canon." In "Multicultural and Multilingual Aesthetics of Resistance." Special issue, *MELUS* 33, no. 3 (2008): 27–43.

Hay, Robert P. "George Washington: American Moses." *American Quarterly* 21 (1969): 780–91.

Hayden, Lewis. *Caste among Masons: Address before Prince Hall Grand Lodge of Free and Accepted Masons of the State of Massachusetts, at the Festival of St. John the Evangelist, December 27, 1865.* 2nd ed. Boston: Edward S. Coombs, 1866.

Heard, W. H. "Heardism Defended." *Christian Recorder*, May 25, 1893.

"Heardism Explained." *Christian Recorder*, May 4, 1893.

Henderson, Archibald. "Daniel Boone in Kentucky." In *The Conquest of the Old Southwest: The Romantic Story of the Old Pioneers into Virginia, the Carolinas, Tennessee, and Kentucky, 1740–1790*, 144–59. New York: Century, 1920.

"His Body to Lie in State: Douglass's Remains for Five Hours at Metropolitan A.M.E." *Washington Times*, February 25, 1895.

Holder, Burleigh. "A History of Crozierville." *Liberia Studies Journal* 3, no. 1 (1970–1971): 21–30.

Holland, Milton M. Letter to the editor. *Messenger*, January 19, 1864.

Holly, James Theodore. *Facts about the Church's Mission in Haiti. A Concise Statement by Bishop Holly.* New York: Thomas Whittaker, 1897.

———. "Thoughts on Hayti." *Anglo-African Magazine* 1 (1859): 185–87, 219–21, 241–43, 298–300, 327–29, 363–67. Facsimile of first edition. New York: Arno and the *New York Times*, 1968.

*The Holy Bible, Containing the Old and New Testaments According to the Authorised Version; with Explanatory Notes, Practical Observations, and Copious Marginal References.* New York: Samuel T. Armstrong, Crocker & Brewster, 1817.

Hyman, Harold Melvin. *Era of the Oath: Northern Loyalty Tests during the Civil War and Reconstruction*. New York: Octagon Books, 1978.

"In the March Number of the 'Brown Book of Boston.'" *Ardmore (Okla.) Daily Ardmoreite*, November 2, 1903.

Isani, Mukhtar Ali. "The Contemporaneous Reception of Phillis Wheatley: Newspaper and Magazine Notices during the Years of Fame, 1765–1774." *Journal of Negro History* 85, no. 4 (2000): 260–73.

———. "Wheatley's Departure for London and Her 'Farewell to America.'" *South Atlantic Bulletin* 42, no. 4 (1977): 123–29.

James, Ebenezer. Letter to the editor. *North Star*, March 16, 1849.

Jea, John. *The Life, History, and Unparalleled Sufferings of John Jea, the African Preacher, Compiled and Written by Himself*. Portsea, England: Author, 1815.

J.E.C. "Industry and Energy Are the Mighty Powers That Insure Success." *Christian Recorder*, January 15, 1870.

Jefferson, Thomas. "Second Inauguration Address, Monday, March 4, 1805." In *Inauguration Addresses of the Presidents of the United States: From George Washington to George W. Bush*. Washington, D.C.: U.S. GPO, 1989.

Jones, Absalom. *A Thanksgiving sermon, preached January 1, 1808, in St. Thomas's, or the African Episcopal Church, Philadelphia on account of the abolition of the African slave trade, on that day, by the Congress of the United States*. Philadelphia: Fry & Kammerer, 1808.

"A Joshua in the Camp." Review and editorial of White, *A Joshua in the Camp. AME Church Review* 12 (1896): 419–21.

"Joshua's Commission. Lesson I, Fourth Quarter, International Series." *Christian Recorder*, September 27, 1888.

*Journals of the Continental Congress, 1774–1789*. Vol. 5. Washington, D.C.: U.S. GPO, 1904–37.

Kane, W. S. "Our Canada Letter." *Christian Recorder*, February 12, 1891.

Kang, Nancy. "'As if I Had Entered a Paradise': Fugitive Slave Narratives and Cross-Border Literary History." *African American Review* 39, no. 3 (2005): 431–57.

Keckley, Elizabeth. *Behind the Scenes; or, Thirty Years a Slave and Four Years in the White House*. 1868. Edited by William L. Andrews. New York: Penguin, 2005.

Kemp, Roger L. "Virginia Declaration of Rights." In *Documents of American Democracy: A Collection of Essential Works*. Jefferson, N.C.: McFarland, 2010.

Kershaw, A. J. "Heardism Indicted." *Christian Recorder*, September 7, 1893.

Kidd, Colin. *The Forging of Races: Race and Scripture in the Protestant Atlantic World, 1600–2000*. Cambridge: Cambridge University Press, 2006.

Kling, David. *The Bible in History: How the Texts Have Shaped the Times*. New York: Oxford University Press, 2004.

Lamb, Daniel Smith, ed. *Howard University Medical Department, Washington, D.C.: A Historical, Biographical and Statistical Souvenir*. Washington, D.C.: R. Beresford, 1900. Repr., Freeport, N.Y.: Books for Libraries Press, 1971.

Lay, Benjamin. *All Slave-Keepers That Keep the Innocent in Bondage, Apostates*. Philadelphia: Author, 1737.

"Lessons Reviewed. Third Quarter of the International Series Closed." *Christian Recorder*, September 20, 1888.

Letter to the editor. *Columbia (S.C.) Daily Phoenix*, September 17, 1872.

Levine, Robert S. "Circulating the Nation: David Walker, the Missouri Compromise, and the Rise of the Black Press." In *The Black Press: New Literary and Historical Essays*, edited by Todd Vogel, 17–36. New Brunswick, N.J.: Rutgers University Press, 2001.

———. *Martin Delany, Frederick Douglass, and the Politics of Representative Identity*. Chapel Hill: University of North Carolina Press, 1997.

Lewis, Leslie W. *Telling Narratives: Secrets in African American Literature*. Champaign: University of Illinois Press, 2007.

*The Liberian Exodus. First Voyage of the Azor. Liberia a Delightful Country. Climate, Soil, and Productions. Character of the People in Liberia; and How They Live. Full Information of the Exodus Movement*. Charleston, S.C.: W. J. Oliver's Print, 1878.

Lincoln, Abraham. "Address on Colonization to a Deputation of Negroes." In *Collected Works of Abraham Lincoln*, vol. 5, 370–75. New Brunswick, N.J.: Rutgers University Press, 1955.

______. "Eulogy on Henry Clay at Springfield, Illinois." *Speeches and Writings,* vol. 1, 259–71. New York: Library of America, 1989

Logan, Rayford W. *The Betrayal of the Negro from Rutherford B. Hayes to Woodrow Wilson*. Cambridge, Mass.: Da Capo Press, 1997.

———. *The Negro in American Life and Thought: The Nadir, 1877–1901*. New York: Dial, 1954.

Lossing, Benson J. "Daniel Boone." *Harper's Monthly Magazine*, October 1859, 577–601.

Marrant, John. *Narrative of the Lord's Wonderful Dealings with John Marrant, a Black*. London: Gilbert & Plummer, 1785. Accessed December 19, 2011. http://www.archive.org/details/cihm_20674.

Masur, Kate. "The African American Delegation to Abraham Lincoln: A Reappraisal." *Civil War History* 56, no. 2 (2010): 117–44.

May, Cedrick. "John Marrant and Narrative Construction of an Early Black Methodist Evangelical." *African American Review* 38, no. 4 (2004): 553–70.

McHenry, Elizabeth. *Forgotten Readers: Recovering the Lost History of African American Literary Societies*. Durham, N.C.: Duke University Press, 2002.

McKinley, Carlyle. *An Appeal to Pharaoh: The Negro Problem, and Its Radical Solution*. New York: Fords, Howard & Hulbert, 1889.

McLagan, Elizabeth. *A Peculiar Paradise: A History of Blacks in Oregon, 1778–1940*. Portland, Ore.: Georgian Press, 1980.

"Memoirs of Generals Lee, Gates, Stephen and Darke." *Harper's New Monthly Magazine*, September 1858, 500–11. Accessed November 11, 2011. http://cdl.library.cornell.edu/cgi-bin/moa/moa-cgi?notisid=ABK4014-0017-72.

Miller, Floyd J. *The Search for a Black Nationality: Black Emigration and Colonization, 1778–1863*. Urbana: University of Illinois Press, 1975.

"The Moses of the Black Belt: Leading His People out of the Bondage of Ignorance and Idleness." *Omaha Daily Bee*, October 7, 1895, 6.

"Mr. Goldwin Smith on Jewish Slavery." *Living Age*, August 1, 1863, 204–5.

Mullin, Gerald W. *Flight and Rebellion: Slave Resistance in Eighteenth-Century Virginia.* New York: Oxford University Press, 1972.

Nast, Thomas. "Andrew Johnson's Reconstruction, and How It Works." *Harper's Weekly*, August 12, 1866, 530.

"The Negro's Prayer." *Genius of Universal Emancipation*, May 1833, 109.

Noll, Mark A. *America's God from Jonathan Edwards to Abraham Lincoln*. New York: Oxford University Press, 2002.

Obama, Barack. "Obama's Selma Speech. Text as Delivered." Lynn Sweet, The Scoop from Washington. Blog, *Chicago Sun-Times*, March 7, 2007. Accessed March 1, 2012. http://blogs.suntimes.com/sweet/2007/03/obamas_selma_speech_text_as_de.html.

"On Philemon and Onesimus. By a Citizen of Washington." *National Era*, October 26, 1848.

"The Oregon Question." *North American Review* (January 1846): 214–53. Accessed March 1, 2012. http://cdl.library.cornell.edu/cgi-bin/moa/moa-cgi?WWnotisid=ABQ7578-0062-11.

Otis, James. *The Rights of the British Colonists Asserted and Proved.* Boston, 1764.

"Our Ministry." *Christian Recorder*, August 9, 1877.

Painter, Nell Irving. *Exodusters: Black Migration to Kansas after Reconstruction.* New York: W. W. Norton, 1992.

Paine, Thomas. *Common Sense, Addressed to the Inhabitants of America*. Philadelphia: W. & T. Bradford, 1776.

Payne, Daniel. "African Emigration: Colored Americans and Africa—Colored Americans." *Christian Recorder*, August 8, 1878, August 22, 1878, September 12, 1878, September 26, 1878, and December 5, 1878.

———. "Evergreen Cottage, Near Wilberforce University, Xenia, O." *Christian Recorder*, June 27, 1878, and August 1, 1878.

Peabody, Selim H. *American Patriotism: Speeches, Letters, and Other Papers Which Illustrate the Foundation, the Development, the Preservation of the United States of America.* New York: American Book Exchange, 1880.

Peattie, Elia Wilkinson. *The Story of America: Containing the Romantic Incidents of History, from the Discovery of America to the Present Time*. San Francisco: R. S. King, 1889.

Perry, Mark. *Lift Up Thy Voice: The Grimké Family's Journey from Slaveholders to Civil Rights Leaders*. New York: Penguin, 2002.

"Petition for Freedom to Massachusetts Governor Thomas Gage, His Majesty's Council, and the House of Representatives, 25 May 1774." Jeremy Belknap Papers, Massachusetts Historical Society, 2012. Accessed July, 6, 2012. http://www.masshist.org/database/589use-onview-id.

"Political Intelligence: Politicians Should Never Meddle with Scripture." *National Era,* May 5, 1859.

Potkay, Adam. "History, Oratory, and God in Equiano's *Interesting Narrative*." *Eighteenth-Century Studies* 34, no. 4 (2001): 601–14.

———. "Olaudah Equiano and the Art of Spiritual Autobiography." In "African-American Culture in the Eighteenth Century." Special issue, *Eighteenth-Century Studies* 27, no. 4 (1994): 677–92.

Potkay, Adam, and Sandra Burr, eds. *Black Atlantic Writers of the Eighteenth Century: Living the New Exodus in England and Americas*. New York: Palgrave Macmillan, 1995.

Prince, Mary. *The History of Mary Prince, a West Indian Slave, Related by Herself.* 1831. Rev. ed. Edited with an introduction by Moira Ferguson. Ann Arbor: University of Michigan Press, 1998.

"The Promised Land." *Anderson (S.C.) Intelligencer*, December 30, 1903, 6. Historic American Newspapers—Chronicling America. Library of Congress.

"The Pulpit and the Crisis." *New Englander and Yale Review* 19, no. 73 (1861): 140–61.

Purvis, Robert. *Liberator*, June 13, 1856, University of Detroit Mercy, Black Abolitionist Archive, Doc. No. 17807. Accessed March 1, 2012. http://research.udmercy.edu/find/special_collections/digital/baa/item.php?record_id=2199&collectionCode=baa.

Raboteau, Albert J. "African Americans, Exodus, and the American Israel." In *Religion and American Culture: A Reader*, edited by David G. Hackett, 73–88. New York: Routledge, 1995.

"Rabbi Raphall." *Liberator*, April 5, 1861.

"Rabbi Raphall." *New-York Tribune*, January 11, 15, and 22, 1861.

Raphall, Rabbi Dr. M. J. *The Bible View of Slavery: A Discourse, Delivered at the Jewish Synagogue, B'nai Jeshurun, New York, on the Day of the National Fast, January 4, 1861*. New York: Rudd & Carleton, 1861.

"A Record Sunday at Bethel A.M.E. Church, New York. Ordination of a Missionary to the Danish West Indies." *Christian Recorder*, March 22, 1900.

Reynolds, David. *America, Empire of Liberty: A New History of the United States.* New York: Basic Books, 2009. WW

Reynolds, David, and Debra J. Rosenthal, eds. *The Serpent in the Cup: Temperance and American Literature*. Amherst: University of Massachusetts Press, 1977.

Rhodes, Jacob. *The Nation's Loss: A Poem on the Life and Death of the Hon. Abraham Lincoln, Late President of the United States, Who Departed This Life, in Washington, D.C., April 15, 1865.* Newark, N.J.: F. Starruck, 1866. Literature Online. 1996–2012. ProQuest LLC. Alexandria, Va.: Chadwyck-Healey, 1994.

"Right of Petition." *Colored American*, July 28, 1838.

Rock, John S. "What if the Slaves Are Emancipated?" In *Lift Every Voice: African American Oratory, 1787–1900*, edited by Philip Sheldon Foner and Robert James Branham, 359–68. Tuscaloosa: University of Alabama Press, 1997.

Rowlandson, Mary. *A Narrative of the Captivity, Sufferings and Removes of Mrs. Mary Rowlandson*. Boston: Thomas & John Fleet, 1791.

Royster, Jacqueline. *Traces of a Stream: Literacy and Social Change among African American Women*. Pittsburgh: University of Pittsburgh Press, 2000.

Ruggles, Jeffrey. *The Unboxing of Henry Brown*. Richmond: Library of Virginia, 2003.

Runyon, C. R. "A Tribute." *Christian Recorder*, June 28, 1894.

Russell, R. S. "Importance of the Industry of Apiculture." *American Bee Journal* 29 (1892): 516–18.

Saillant, John. "'Wipe away All Tears from Their Eyes': John Marrant's Theology in the Black Atlantic, 1785–1808." *Journal of Millennial Studies* 1, no. 2 (1999). Accessed December 11, 2011. http://www.bu.edu/mille/publications/winter98/saillant.PDF.

Schama, Simon. *Rough Crossings: Britain, the Slaves, and the American Revolution*. New York: HarperCollins, 2007.

Schwartz, Regina M. *The Curse of Cain: The Violent Legacy of Monotheism*. Chicago: University of Chicago Press, 1997.

Scott, Thomas. "Biblical Exposition, by Thomas Scott." *Colored American*, June 8, 1839.

"'See That Ye Fall Not Out by the Way.'" *Christian Recorder*, September 24, 1870.

Sewall, Samuel. *The Selling of Joseph: A Memorial*. 1700. Edited by Sydney Kaplan. Amherst: University of Massachusetts Press, 1969.

Shadd, Mary Ann. *A Plea for Emigration; or, Notes of Canada West*. 1852. Edited by Richard Almonte. Oklahoma City: Mercury Press, 1998.

Sherman, Frank. *Liberia: The Land, Its People, History, and Culture*. New York: New Africa Press, 2011.

Sidbury, James. *Becoming African in America: Race and Nation in the Early Black Atlantic*. New York: Oxford University Press, 2007.

———. *Ploughshares into Swords: Race, Rebellion, and Identity in Gabriel's Virginia, 1730–1810*. Cambridge: Cambridge University Press, 1997.

Simms, William Gilmore. "Progress in America: Or, a Speech in Sonnets, on Great Britain and the United States; Not Delivered Either in Parliament or Congress." *United States Democratic Review* (February 1846): 91–95. Accessed March 1, 2012. http://digital.library.cornell.edu/cgi/t/text/text-idx?c=usde;idno=usde0018-2.

"The Slave Boy Becomes a Maker of Magistrates." *Minneapolis Journal*, October 8, 1901.

Smalls, Robert. Speech of Hon. Robert Smalls, of South Carolina. In the House of Representatives, Friday, July 30, 1886. On the bill (H. R. 7167) for the relief of Mrs. Maria Hunter. Cong. Rec., Appendix, 49th Cong., 1st sess., A319–20.

Smith, Annie M. "Xenia Correspondence." *Christian Recorder*, May 20, 1865.

Smith, Charles Spencer. *A History of the African Methodist Episcopal Church Being a Volume Supplemental to A History of the African Methodist Episcopal Church by Daniel Alexander Payne, D.D. LL.D, Late One of Its Bishops*. Philadelphia: Book Concern of the AME Church, 1922.

Smith, Goldwin. *Does the Bible Sanction American Slavery?* Oxford: John Henry & James Parker, 1863.

Smith, James McCune. Introduction to *A Memorial Discourse by Henry Highland Garnet, Delivered in the Hall of the House of Representatives, Washington City, D.C., on Sabbath, February 12, 1865*. Philadelphia: Joseph M. Wilson, 1865.

Stevens, William Bacon. *A History of Georgia, from Its First Discovery by Europeans to the Adoption of the Present Constitution* (1848).

Stewart, Maria W. "An Address Delivered at the African Masonic Hall." In *Spiritual Narratives*. Introduction by Sue E. Houchins. New York: Oxford University Press, 1988.

———. "Mrs. Stewart's Farewell Address to Her Friends in the City of Boston." 1833. In *Spiritual Narratives*. Introduction by Sue E. Houchins. New York: Oxford University Press, 1988.

———. *Religion and the Pure Principles of Morality, the Sure Foundation on Which We Must Build*. 1831. In *Spiritual Narratives*. Introduction by Sue E. Houchins. New York: Oxford University Press, 1988.

Stowe, Harriet Beecher. *Uncle Tom's Cabin*. London: John Cassell, 1852.

Street, Nicholas. *The American states acting over the part of the children of Israel in the wilderness, and thereby impeding their entrance into Canaan's rest: or, The human heart discovering itself under trials*. New Haven, Conn.: Thomas & Samuel Green, 1777.

Stringfellow, Thornton. "The Bible Argument; or, Slavery in the Light of Divine Revelation." In *Cotton Is King, and Pro-slavery Arguments*, edited by E. N. Elliot. Augusta, Ga.: Pritchard, Abbott & Loomis, 1860.

Stroyer, Jacob. *Sketches of My Life in the South, Part I*. Salem, Mass.: Salem Press, 1879.

"Sunday School. First Quarter. Twelve Lessons in Old Testament History. Lesson XII. Sunday, March 28. Lesson Service Josh. 24. 1–13. God's Mercies to Israel." *Christian Recorder*, March 18, 1875.

"Sunday School Union. The Rev. Dr. Dyer. American Slavery." *Frederick Douglass' Paper*, June 10, 1852.

Swaminathan, Srividhya. *Debating the Slave Trade: Rhetoric of British National Identity, 1759–1815*. Burlington, Vt.: Ashgate, 2009.

Tanner, Benjamin Tucker. "A Help or Hindrance, Which?" *Christian Recorder*, November 7, 1895.

Taylor, J. F. "Moberly (Mo.) District." *Christian Recorder*, August 7, 1890.

"Temperance Celebration." *Colored American*, July 29, 1837.

Thorpe, Thomas Bangs. *The Master's House; or, Scenes Descriptive of Southern Life*. New York: T. L. McElrath, 1854.

Tomes, Robert. *Battles of America by Sea and Land: With Biographies of Naval and Military Commanders*. Vol. 1. New York: Patterson & Neilson, 1878.

Tomlins, Christopher L., and Bruce H. Mann, eds. *The Many Legalities of Early America*. Chapel Hill: University of North Carolina Press, 2001.

"To Tuskegee, $600,000: Mr. Carnegie's Gift." *New York Tribune*, April 24, 1903.

"To the Unfading Memory of Hon. Frederick Douglass." *Washington Bee*, July 13, 1895.

"Tubs at Tuskegee: Part of the Regular Curriculum, Reports Mrs. E. A. Russell. She Visited the Institute. The Intense Earnestness and Personal Cleanliness of the Pupils Impressed Her." *Minneapolis Journal*, April 12, 1902, 2.

Turner, Henry M. "The Plagues of This Country." *Christian Recorder*, July 12, 1862.

U.S. Commission on Civil Rights. *The Decline of Black Farming in America*. Washington, D.C.: U.S. GPO, 1982.

U.S. Department of Commerce, Bureau of the Census. *Negro Population of the United States, 1790–1915*. 1918; New York: Arno, 1968.

Wald, Priscilla. *Constituting Americans: Cultural Anxiety and Narrative Form*. Durham, N.C.: Duke University Press, 1995.

Washington, Ethel M. *Union County's Black Soldiers and Soldiers of the Civil War*. Charleston, S.C.: History Press, 2011.

"We Heartily Endorse the Work." *Richmond (Kentucky) Climax*, December 21, 1898.

Wedderburn, John. *The Axe Laid to the Root; or, A Fatal Blow to Oppressors, Being an Address to the Planters and Negroes of the Island of Jamaica*. Numbers 1–6. 1817. In *"The Horrors of Slavery" and Others Writings by Robert Wedderburn*, edited by Iain McCalman, 65–77. Cambridge: Cambridge University Press, 1991.

Weinberg, Albert K. *Manifest Destiny: A Study of Nationalist Expansionism in American History*. Chicago: Quadrangle, 1963.

Wells, Ida B. *The Red Record: Tabulated Statistics and Alleged Causes of Lynching in the United States*. 1895. Project Gutenberg eBook, February 8, 2005. Accessed March 1, 2012. http://www.gutenberg.org/files/14977/14977-h/14977-h.htm.

Weyler, Karen A. "Race, Redemption, and Captivity." In *A Narrative of the Lord's Wonderful Dealings with John Marrant, a Black*. Charleston, S.C.: Nabu Press, 2011.

———. "Narrative of the Uncommon Sufferings and Surprizing Deliverance of Briton Hammon, a Negro Man." In *Genius in Bondage: Literature of the Early Black Atlantic*, edited by Vincent Carretta and Philip Gould, 39–53. Lexington: University Press of Kentucky, 2001.

Wheatley, Phillis. *Complete Writings*. Edited by Vincent Carretta. New York: Penguin, 2001.

———. "Letter to Rev. Samson Occum." *Connecticut Gazette*, March 11, 1774.

Wheeler, Roxann. "'Betrayed by Some of My Own Complexion': Cugoano, Abolition, and the Contemporary Language of Racialism." In *Genius in Bondage: Literature of the Early Black Atlantic*, edited by Vincent Carretta, 17–38. Lexington: University Press of Kentucky, 2001.

Wheelock, J. A. "The New Northwest." *Harper's New Monthly Magazine* (1898).

White, H. Rufus. *"A Joshua in the Camp," or, The Life of Booker T. Washington, of Tuskegee, Alabama.* Towson, Md., 1895. HathiTrust Digital Library. Accessed July 9, 2012. http://babel.hathitrust.org/cgi/pt?id=loc.ark%3A%2F13960%2Ft3mw2h62s;page=root;view=image;size=100;seq=9.

White, Pliny H. *A Sermon Occasioned by the Assassination of Abraham Lincoln, President of the United States.* Brattleboro, Vt.: Vermont Record Office, 1865.

Whitefield, George. "Religious Society." In *Selected Sermons of George Whitefield.* Philadelphia: Union Press, 1904.

Whitfield, James M. *The Writings of James M. Whitfield: America and Other Writings by a Nineteenth-Century African American Poet.* Edited by Robert S. Levine and Ivy G. Wilson. Chapel Hill: University of North Carolina Press, 2011.

Whitney, Adeline T. "Exodus." *Atlantic Monthly* 54, no. 9 (1862): 492–93.

Wigglesworth, Michael. "God's Controversy with New England" (1662). In *God's New Israel: Religious Interpretations of American Destiny*, edited by Conrad Cherry, 41–53. Chapel Hill: University of North Carolina Press, 1998.

Wilford, Melissa. "One Flag, One Nation, One Destiny: African American Service in the Civil War." Accessed March 1, 2012. http://www.factasy.com/civil_war/book/export/html/1313.

Wilkinson, John F. N. Letter to the editor. *Christian Recorder*, April 30, 1864.

Willis, Susan. "Crushed Geraniums: Juan Francisco Manzano and the Language of Slavery." In *The Slave's Narrative*, edited by Charles T. Davis and Henry Louis Gates. New York: Oxford University Press, 1985.

Wills, David W. "Exodus Piety: African American Religion in an Age of Immigration." In *Minority Faiths and the American Protestant Mainstream*, edited by Jonathan D. Sarna, 136–90. Urbana: University of Illinois Press, 1998.

Wilson, Harriet. *Our Nig; or, Sketches from the Life of a Free Black.* 1859. Edited by P. Gabrielle Foreman and Reginald Pitts. New York: Penguin, 2007.

Wimbush, Vincent. *The Bible and African Americans: A Brief History.* Appleton, Wis.: Augsburg Fortress, 2002.

Winter, Kari J. Introduction to *The Blind African Slave, Or Memoirs of Boyrereau Brinch, Nicknamed Jeffrey Brace*, by Boyrereau Brinch, 3–84. Madison: University of Wisconsin Press, 2004.

Winthrop, John. "A Modell of Christian Charity" (1630). In *God's New Israel: Religious Interpretations of American Destiny*, edited by Conrad Cherry, 37–41. Chapel Hill: University of North Carolina Press, 1998.

"Wisdom and Her Children." *Provincial Freeman*, December 22, 1855.

Wolff, Cynthia Griffin. "Passing beyond the Middle Passage: Henry 'Box' Brown's Translation of Slavery." *Massachusetts Review* 37, no. 1 (1996): 23–44.

Wood, Marcus. *Blind Memory: Visual Representations of Slavery in England and America, 1780–1865.* New York: Routledge, 2000.

Wood, Spencer D. and Jess Gilbert. "Returning African Americans Farmers to the Land: Recent Trends and a Policy Rationale." Accessed March 1, 2012. Land Loss Prevention Project. http://www.landloss.org/Wood%20--%20Returning.pdf.

# Credits

The Photographs and Prints Division of the Schomburg Center for Research in Black Culture, The New York Public Library, Astor, Lenox and Tilden Foundations provided the image of Rector Absalom Jones. Used by permission.

The Manuscripts, Archives and Rare Books Division of the Schomburg Center provided the images of Daniel Coker and Henry Box Brown. Used by permission.

The General Research & Reference Division of the Schomburg Center provided the images of Bishop Henry M. Turner, Rev. Alexander Crummell, Robert Harlan, and Negro Immigrants on Their Way to Kansas. Used by permission.

The Print Collection, Miriam and Ira D. Wallach Division of Art, Prints and Photographs, The New York Public Library, Astor, Lenox and Tilden Foundations provided the images of James Theodore Holly and John S. Rock. Used by permission.

The Library of Congress, Prints and Photographs Division, Washington, D.C., provided the images of Sergeant-Major Milton M. Holland, Booker T. Washington, W.E.B. DuBois, and "Andrew Johnson's Reconstruction, And How It Works" by Thomas Nast in *Harper's Weekly* 10.505 (September 1, 1866): 552–53. Used by permission.

The General Collection, State Library and Archives of Florida, Tallahassee, Florida provided the image of Bishop Abraham Grant. Used by permission.

Daniel Wallace Culp, *Twentieth-Century Negro Literature: or A Cyclopedia of Thought on the Vital Topics Relating to the American Negro.* Naperville, Ill.: J. L. Nicolas, Co., 1902 provided the image of Rev. Francis Grimké.

# Scripture Index

# General Index